The Missing Girls and Women of China, Hong Kong and Taiwan

D1596636

The Missing Girls and Women of China, Hong Kong and Taiwan

A Sociological Study of Infanticide, Forced Prostitution, Political Imprisonment, "Ghost Brides," Runaways and Thrownaways, 1900–2000s

Hua-Lun Huang

McFarland & Company, Inc., Publishers
Jefferson, North Carolina, and London

Excerpts in Chapters 1 and 2 from the author's article "Where Are Our Daughters, Mothers, Sisters, and Wives? A Typological Analysis of Missing Women and Girls in Greater China, 1900–2000s" originally appeared in the *Asian Journal of Criminology* 4:2 (2009): 85–106.

LIBRARY OF CONGRESS CATALOGUING-IN-PUBLICATION DATA

Huang, Hua-Lun, 1962–
    The missing girls and women of China, Hong Kong and Taiwan : a sociological study of infanticide, forced prostitution, political imprisonment, "ghost brides," runaways and thrownaways, 1900–2000s / Hua-Lun Huang.
        p.   cm.
    Includes bibliographical references and index.

    ISBN 978-0-7864-4029-0
    softcover : acid free paper ∞

    1. Missing persons — East Asia.   2. Missing children — East Asia.
3. Sex of children, Parental preferences for — East Asia.   4. Female infanticide — East Asia.   5. Women — East Asia — Social conditions — 20th century.   6. Prostitutes — East Asia — Social conditions — 20th century.   7. Women's rights — East Asia.   I. Title.
HV6762.A77H83 2012
362.83 — dc23
                                                    2011052679

BRITISH LIBRARY CATALOGUING DATA ARE AVAILABLE

Front cover images © 2012 Shutterstock

Manufactured in the United States of America

McFarland & Company, Inc., Publishers
    Box 611, Jefferson, North Carolina 28640
    www.mcfarlandpub.com

To my parents

Contents

List of Tables

Preface

This book is about missing females of Greater China.

As an "X file" of East Asian history and sociology (especially demography and women's studies), this topic, at least in the past twenty years, did not attract much attention from sociologists and historians of East Asia. Partially for this reason, it is not easy for social scientists to find a book that contains information on this subject. On the other hand, even when researchers do mention missing women/girls in their publications, they usually focus on a macro- or micro-level issue, instead of lost females per se. Not surprisingly, this prevents sociology and history students from creating a conceptual framework to distinguish among the circumstances that could lead to lost persons, including females.

My main purpose in writing this book is to help solve these problems: by using the region of Greater China as an example, I hope to provide social scientists with research on missing women and girls, including their socioeconomic categories and the social causes of female disappearance. While most cases and categories examined in this book are from the East, I think they must have many counterparts in the West. I hope that this book will bring to light the social problem of lost children and women, and I hope, this problem will gain attention in the future. I also believe that this book can serve as a reference point for those scholars who want to engage in a similar study.

In this book, I suggest dividing missing females into eight categories (see Chapter 1 beginning on page 15). These categories are not econometric or regressional models used by economists and sociologists to forecast or to interpret economic or social trends. Instead, they are simply conceptual tools which can assist writers on gender issues in investigating those social circumstances under which females disappear. The eight typologies of missing women/girls proposed in this book are not all-inclusive; they are merely representative instances.

In the course of working on this book, I benefited a lot from the Institute of Sociology (IOS) at the Academia Sinica in Taiwan. Without the help of IOS, it would have been impossible for me to collect the out-of-print and key literature used in this book. With this in mind, I would like to sincerely thank Dr. Michael H.H. Hsiao, Dr. Yang-Chih Fu, and Dr. Chin-Fen Chang for giving me the opportunities to do research at the IOS. I also want to thank my sociology colleagues at the University of Louisiana and my friends and relatives in China, Hong Kong, Japan, and Taiwan. Without their assistance, it would have been impossible for me to complete a big project like this.

Introduction

In the past two decades, the reasons why females are victimized by violent behavior have been studied by numerous criminologists, human rights activists, and sociologists. In these studies, some scholars focus on how wars turned women into sex slaves (Barstow, 2000; Stiglmayer, 1994; Zuckerman, 2003). Some explore how women and children were trafficked and sold as prostitutes (Altink, 1995; Altman, 2001; Brown, 2000; Davidson, 2005; Farr, 2005; Gaon & Forbord, 2005; King, 2004; Malarek, 2004; Skrobanek et al., 1997). Some report how certain Chinese, Filipino, Indonesian, Korean, Malaysian and Taiwanese women were driven to become the so-called comfort women before and during World War II (Hicks, 1995; Kim-Gibson, 1999; Yoshimi, 2000). Some examine how the dowry culture promotes cultural murder/female infanticide (Oldenburg, 2002; Sen, 2002). Some analyze the possible linkage between abnormal mentalities and "lust murder" (Purcell & Arrigo, 2006).

Numerous articles and books have been published about the relationship between women/young girls and human trafficking, massacre, the sex industry (specifically prostitution, pornography, and sex tourism), slave labor, and other forms of violence/gender discrimination. Yet few writers systematically address the typology of missing women and young girls. Put more precisely, most sociologists and criminologists specializing in gender issues tend to focus on the subject of female victimology. Partially because of this concentration, most gender specialists endeavor to identify, differentiate, and elaborate the factors that may turn physical abuse, sexual harassment, and other patterns of violence against females into institutionalized practices. On the other hand, missing women/young girls are generally defined as dependent variables because, in theory, they are victims of institutionalized violence (that is, the emergence of these populations is, in one way or another, caused by unjust gender arrangements, such as

3

the one-child policy and dowry custom). Given the mainstream research approach, it is not surprising that a nomenclature for missing females is still not fully formed in existing demographic and sociological literature.

The goals of this book are to identify the missing women/young girls in Greater China (that is, China, Hong Kong, and Taiwan) and to develop a typology for such populations. By using missing women/young girls in this district as examples, I argue that missing females comprise different actors and life experiences. These diverse actors and experiences, if conceptualized individually, will provide gender experts with an alternative (see Chapter 1) with which to study gender inequality. The conceptualization of these distinct elements will also pave the way for gender specialists and law enforcement authorities in the West to distinguish between the various types of missing women/young girls in the future.

Missing Females: An Underdeveloped Area in Gender Study

In gender study, one of the underlying hypotheses shared by scholars and investigative reporters is that males and females do not enjoy equal socioeconomic status (especially in Confucian societies, Islamic countries, and patriarchal states). Accordingly, males enjoy more opportunities to accumulate wealth, obtain power, and gain prestigious jobs. Based on this assumption, almost all gender specialists try to itemize or theorize unfair institutionalized arrangements (such as androcracy, arranged marriage, and foot-binding) or cultural factors (such as androcentrism, misogyny, and the tradition of son preference). In countless situations, these let females become victims of employment discrimination, family violence, forced prostitution, kidnapping, sexual assault, or even murder. In this regard, current research on female victimology from criminologists, sociologists and women's rights advocates seem to concentrate on the following four aspects.

The first group of researchers can be exemplified by those feminist writers who explore the female body (Hesse-Biber, 2007; Weitz, 2003). These "FBIs" (female body investigators) argue that, from the 1960s onwards, the female body seems to have become a "commodity" in industrialized countries, especially in open societies. Accordingly, in places like (licensed) brothels, topless clubs, and escort services, the female body, just like commercial products, can be bought and sold. Working from the presupposition that the female body has been objectified in modern America and many other countries, some researchers, by examining the functions of various parts of female body (arms, back, breasts, cheeks, ears, eyes, hair, hands, hips, legs, lips, mouth, neck, nose, shoulders, waist, and so forth), attempt to explain why these parts, to a varying extent, have erotic implications for men. Such gender researchers declare that the female body contains delicate and ambiguous sex "signals" (Morris, 2005; Yalom, 1997). These subtle and vague signals are overtly and deliberately transformed by adult magazines and websites, the media in general, into erotic signs (such as the provocative gestures of Marilyn Monroe). Since these signs have become freely accessible, many males appear to view the female body as something that can be arbitrarily obtained and discarded. Such a belief naturally will distance men from empathy with females or even encourage some to attack, physically or sexually, females ranging from family members, friends, and sex workers to strangers.

From the perspective of sociological theory, the research paradigm adopted by FBIs is symbolic interactionism. This paradigm, in a broader sense, is applied by some experts in human sexual behavior to the implications of sexuality. According to these scholars, sexuality is a trait that has no universally accepted definition in human societies (whether ancient or modern). Because of definitional divergence, the meanings, qualities, and patterns of sexuality can be artificially, subjectively, or even uniquely constructed in most social and cultural settings. In this regard, Godbeer (2002) describes, from a historical viewpoint, how sexuality-related thoughts, customs, and regulations developed in North America in the seventeenth and eighteenth centuries. Hawkes (2004) and Versluis (2008) analyze the roles played by sexual behavior in Western culture, specifically in Christian societies. Holland (2006) examines why human history, for the most part, is his (instead of her) history. Nagel (2003) compares the diverse meanings of sexuality in the contexts of colonialism, globalization, military conquest, race, nationalism, tourism, and war. From the evolutionary angle, Miller (2000) and Shlain (2003) report in great detail the different dimensions involving sexuality and the functions that sexuality contributes to human societies. All of these publications, together with others, reveal that sexuality is an attribute that can be culturally, legally, and socially created and transformed. This situation inevitably put females in a position susceptible to prejudice, exploitation, and manipulation.

In addition to showing how different parts of the female body can provide erotic qualities and meanings and how such qualities and meanings, in different context, will condition males' perceptions of females, some researchers of female victimology focus attention on the sex industry. For such researchers, inter-gender relationships in sex industries are directed essentially by pecuniary exchanges. As a result of this, females who provide "services" will, more often than not, experience verbal or physical violence (varying from simple harassment to intimidation to torture and sometimes even homicide). On the other hand, given that workers in sex industries are stigmatized persons, analyzing the socio-demographic characteristics of these industries will show how and why females are forced to play inferior roles in order to acquire financial rewards from men. This approach can be exemplified by Albert's (2001) examination of the Mustang Range brothel in Nevada; Allison's (1994) ethnographic accounts of a hostess club in Tokyo, Japan; the surveys by Bishop and Robinson (1998), Brazil (1998), and Seabrook (2001) on sex tourism in Singapore, Thailand, and other Southeast Asian countries; Chapkis (1996), Frank (2002), Jordan (2004), and Langley's (1997) descriptions of exotic dancers in strip clubs; and numerous studies on pornography (Jenkins, 2001; Kipnis, 1999; Tang, 1999), prostitution in general (Barry, 1995; Elias et al., 1998; Hodgson, 1997; Outshoorn, 2004), and military prostitution in particular (Moon, 1997; Sturdevant & Stoltzfus, 1993).

Unlike researchers of the female body, sexuality, and the sex industry who try to identify the contextual factors (both micro and macro) that account for female victimology, some criminologists and sociologists seek to elucidate the core features of violence against women (especially sexual assault and domestic abuse). These experts maintain that the social characteristics of sex crime and family violence can be profiled (Barnett et al., 2005; Buzawa & Buzawa, 2002; Hines & Malley-Morrison, 2005; Holmes & Holmes, 2009a: 147–169; Hazelwood & Michaud, 2001; Michaud & Hazelwood, 1999). Hence, if the cultural, demographic, and socioeconomic forces that can lead to violence against women and girls are singled out and analyzed thoroughly, then not only can females take better measures to avoid being victimized by males, the steps taken by law enforcement authorities to prevent rape and spouse abuse/child mistreatment can also become more effective and practicable. Working from the assumption that female victimology is caused by a few predictable factors, some writers address the patterns and dynamics of sexual violence (Cling, 2004; Hodgson & Kelley, 2004); some portray the central features of sex crimes (Holmes & Holmes, 2002, 2009b); some detail the typologies and processes of forcible rape (Amir, 1971; Scully, 1990); some focus on the motivations and geographic locations of sexual homicide (Geberth, 2003; Ressler et al. 1988; Schlesinger, 2003); and some report the patterns and dynamics of domestic violence (Barnett et al., 2005; Buzawa & Buzawa,

2002; Hines & Malley-Morrison, 2005; Kurst-Swanger & Petcosky, 2003; Malley-Morrison & Hines, 2004).

After reviewing the mainstream paradigms (that is, sociology of the female body, sexuality, the sex industry, and violence against women) adopted by criminologists and sociologists to explore gender issues (especially issues related to gender discrimination and female victimology), it should become obvious that the subject of missing women/girls is a minor field in gender studies.[1] Due to this "unorthodox" or "atypical" status in sociology and criminology, lost females are generally defined as subordinate problems or phenomena of androcentric beliefs (which can lead to the objectification of the female body) and patriarchal practices (specifically the sex industry and sexual violence). Such a cause-effect model can be suitably exemplified by Malarek's (2004) field study of human trafficking and forced prostitution in Europe.

Logically, it is undeniable that some females have become lost populations because of certain androcentric ideas and patriarchal arrangements advantageous to the development of sex industries and the occurrence of some sexually violent behaviors (for instance, abduction rape). However, people who follow the conventional paradigms in examining the demographic characteristics and other relevant qualities of missing females may come across some methodological problems. One of the most noteworthy is that the traditional paradigms appear to have become "habitual domains" of thinking, if not stereotypes. As a result, these paradigms may underestimate or oversimplify the diversity of lost women/girls. This limitation can be illustrated by the fact that certain missing females (such as murdered baby girls, segregated female lepers, ghost brides, and misplaced women who have Alzheimer's disease) are rarely probed by scholars (in both the West and the East) as such females vanish from the world mainly because of sociocultural reasons, rather than the expansion of sex industries or the escalation of sexually violent behaviors.

In addition to the problem of underestimating and oversimplifying the variety of lost females, the dominant paradigms of gender research seem to presume that missing women/girls will, more often than not, be found/rescued, as Flowers' (2001) account of runaway teens reveals, or face continual threat of death, as Cheng's (1987) memoir shows. These two prospects, of course, are foreseeable outcomes for numerous missing females. However, the traditional paradigms do not theorize about the relationship between fluctuations of circumstances and the fortunes of missing women/girls. Therefore, the following two questions usually cannot be answered satisfactorily:

- Why are certain lost females more likely to be found/saved (or slain) than others (for example, why were the comfort women, regardless of what country or region they came from, who were sent to Southeast Asia in the 1940s more likely to lose their life than their counterparts stationed in Hong Kong and Taiwan)?
- How should deserted women who were neither slaughtered nor able to return to their native soils be categorized (such as those Chinese and Korean comfort women who could not return to their hometown because they were abandoned by Japanese troops in places like Southeast Asian jungles in 1944–45)?

To help gender researchers as well as demographers look at the variety and variation of missing females, a nomenclature for such populations is developed in the next chapter. This taxonomy could pave the way for gender writers to scrutinize a subject matter that has been overlooked by sociologists and criminologists for decades.

Methodology

As mentioned earlier, most researchers in the field of women's studies tend to concentrate their attention on the factors (individual or structural) that may lead to female victimology. Because of this trend, female victimology seems, to an extent, to have become a synonym for women's studies or gender inequality research. Compared to female victimology, few categories regarding missing women or young girls have been systematically proposed. This situation inevitably will hinder gender researchers from comparing the disappearing females of different societies.

I do not deny that missing wives and daughters can be a problem related to female victimology. However, I also believe that a taxonomy of missing females is currently underdeveloped in criminology and sociology. Before proposing a possible taxonomy, I will summarize the core features of lost females. These features will serve as the methodological basis of this book.

The first characteristic of missing women/young girls is that they are often part of hidden populations. Therefore, for analysts, measuring the configuration of these populations is, more often than not, problematic.[2] Since records about missing women/young girls are frequently unavailable, incomplete, or even unreliable, it seems more meaningful as well as more feasible to study the qualitative aspects of these populations rather than to create quantitative models (for instance, regression models) to describe them.

Besides the problems associated with the measurement of missing women/young girls, lost females should not be analyzed in the context of fatality. This is because lost females in various circumstances may be lucky enough to survive and reappear. With this possibility in mind, using theories or concepts related to death/mortality rate to scrutinize missing women/young girls is a highly dubious approach from a methodological point of view.

Just as lost females should not be explored in the context of casualty, neither is fleeing from home a suitable context for researchers to examine lost females. This is due to the fact that numerous missing women/young girls are kidnapped persons. Simply viewing these people as runaways will oversimplify the problem and mislead the general public.

Finally, many people (including possibly some gender specialists) tend to suppose that lost females will eventually be sold to places like brothels, topless clubs, or escort companies. Therefore, disappearing females can, to a considerable extent, be found in sex industries (especially in the prostitution business). This perspective is perhaps too optimistic about the destiny of lost females because in addition to those missing women/young girls who are located in the sex industry, an unknown number of women are incarcerated in institutions, such as reeducation camps and mental hospitals in modern China. Overstating the role of the sex industry may prevent writers on gender issues from noticing those missing females who are clandestinely arrested, imprisoned, or even executed by authoritarian/totalitarian governments.

Based on the above statements, it should become clear that missing women/young girls (if they remain alive) are "invisible," (clandestinely) incarcerated, inaccessible, and/or illegitimate populations. At the present time, these qualities have not been addressed and conceptualized comprehensively. Given that the theme of missing females is still a new area of sociology, criminology, (Asian) history and other relevant disciplines, I employ the following research methods to enrich this young field.

First, a systematic collection of published literature: I have gathered a large amount of information (written in English, Chinese, and Japanese) about Chinese missing girls/women. Such information, which is scattered widely among various sources like academic journals, books, internets, investigative reports, local registers, magazines, monographs, newspapers, and official gazettes, will be introduced in appropriate chapter.

Second, research trips: I went to China, Hong Kong, and Taiwan twice. These trips allowed me to collect "eye-washing" material like pictures (which can provide gender researchers with visual evidence regarding missing women and girls), to engage in participant observations, and to conduct some interviews. In addition to field study, as a Visiting Scholar I did sociological and historical research at the Academia Sinica of Taiwan. These studies allowed me to use both sociological and historical approaches to examine the subject matter of this book.

In the next chapter, a classification system for disappearing women/ young girls will be proposed. Then several possible categories of missing women/young girls in Greater China will be analyzed. Lost females who have few chances to return to mainstream society (such as female political prisoners, drowned/aborted baby girls, ghost brides, and segregated/ostracized female lepers) will be examined in Part I, while those who have certain opportunities to come back (such as comfort women, female smugglers, abducted women, runaway girls/escaped wives, and misplaced women with Alzheimer's disease) will be discussed in Part II. After these different categories of missing females are scrutinized, some implications about the study of missing women/girls will be summarized in the final chapter. These implications may help gender specialists formulate hypotheses about misplaced and drifting populations in general and lost females in particular.

Defining the Concept of Missing Females

Before inspecting the socioeconomic characteristics of missing women/ girls in Greater China, the notion of *missing females* will be defined. This definition will serve as the selection criterion for target populations in this book. It should be noted that defining the idea of *missing females* is challenging. First, from a purely semantic angle, the term *missing females* seems to be self-evident. This is because it denotes those women/girls whose whereabouts and fates are unknown to their families as well as to social control agencies (especially authorities in charge of population census), like American troops who were classified as MIA (missing in action) during and after the Korean War and Vietnam War. With such an apparent rhetoric implication, official definitions for the term *missing females* are virtually nonexistent in the laws (both civil and criminal) and statistical books of Greater China.

Hardly any sociologists/demographers who have examined the topic of missing women/girls have provided definitions for the concept. For these scholars, the phenomenon of missing females is strongly related to imbalanced sex ratios. So if someone tries to explain this phenomenon, s/he must first investigate those acts (such as gender-selective abortion and female infanticide) that are triggered by gender prejudice/discrimination and patriarchal culture (specifically the culture of son preference). The population proportions between males and females in any country (or region) will then be compared via statistical/time series analysis. Finally, a possible figure for lost females from a known area during a certain period can be reported. Since identifying the factors that may lead to a distorted population structure and estimating the number of missing women/girls seem to have become the chief concern among researchers of missing women/girls (including Banister, 2004; Coale, 1991; Coale & Banister, 1994; Croll, 2000; Das Gupta, 2005; Hudson & den Boer, 2004; Jiang et al., 2005; Johansson & Nygren, 1991; Klasen, 1994; Klasen & Wink, 2002; Li, et al., 2004; Sen, 1990; Tuljapurkar et al., 1995), it is not surprising that these population experts did not make an attempt to define the term *missing females.*

Given that legal and sociological definitions for the term *missing females* are extremely difficult, if not impossible, to obtain, the concept is defined in this book as follows:

> Missing females represent diverse populations. Such populations are exceptionally susceptible to physical and/or sexual violence because of their stigmatized identities (from the perspectives of both formal and informal social control agencies), atomized statuses (i.e., conditions deviating from the social security networks set up by social control or social welfare agencies), and (permanent/temporary) ostracized positions.

Based on this definition, the three C (category, context, and cause) problem of missing females will be analyzed and explicated in this book. The quantity of such females will be mentioned only if data are available.

PART I

The Study of Missing Females

CHAPTER 1

Conceptualization of Missing Females: A Classification System

In comparative-historical sociology, one of the most noteworthy approaches to explaining social movements and revolutions is structuralism — more specifically, Max Weber's structuralism. According to this approach, no social movements or revolutions take shape overnight or in a vacuum. On the contrary, all social movements and revolutions are actions caused by the interaction of two sets of variables. The first set is composed of structural factors (such as the economic system, government pattern, population density, religious institution, social class, and technological level). These factors, according to the theory of structuration suggested by Giddens (1986), constitute the stable dimension of a society. They can be characterized as temporal continuity (Little, 1991: 103) or societal totality (Giddens, 1986: 2) because they last for years or even centuries and serve as boundaries constraining the actions of society's members.

The second set of variables consists of actors/agents who can establish various relationships (Roth & Wittich, 1978: 38–46). These actors form the dynamic aspect of a society because their actions can bring either stability or turmoil to a society. Such actions are temporally predictable because, to a varying extent, they are constrained by social norms, legal stipulations, rules imposed by economic/political organizations, and other structural factors that can maintain administrative and regulative order (Roth & Wittich, 1978: 51).

Based on the two notions of *structure* and *agency*, some sociologists (including della Porta & Diani, 1998; McDaniel, 1991; Skocpol, 1979, 1994; Wickham-Crowley, 1991) try to show that social movements as well

15

as revolutions stem from clashes between ingrained institutions (specifically organizational arrangements) and groups of individuals who intend to change long-established interpersonal relationships. For these researchers of social revolutions, almost no social movements or revolutions will come into being if unequal or unjust practices and establishments experienced by disadvantaged people are not socially constructed (Klandermans, 1992)[1] and if underprivileged persons are not mobilized to take actions (Ferree, 1992; Tarrow, 1994).

A Classification System for Missing Females Based on the Connection Between Agency and Structure

Inspired by the two concepts of *agency* and *structure*, a categorization system for lost females is proposed in this book. The construction of this conceptual system includes the following three steps.

First, given that *agency* and *structure* may converge in a certain social setting, the three overarching notions of *agency*, *structure*, and *setting* will serve as the skeleton or root factors of the classification system recommended in this book.

Second, based on this three-component casual [configuration] (Stinchcombe, [1968] 1987: 59), *personal choice, possibility of participating in mainstream job market*, and *sociological locus*[2] are chosen to be the operational variables for *agency*, *structure*, and *setting* (see Table 1-1). These variables are defined as follows:

TABLE 1-1. OPERATIONAL VARIABLES OF THE THREE CONCEPTS AGENCY, STRUCTURE, AND SETTING

Overarching Concepts		Operational Variables
Agency	→	Personal Choice
Structure	→	Possibility of Participating in Mainstream Job Market
Setting	→	Sociological Locus

The first variable, *personal choice*, is an *agency* factor. It refers to whether agents (that is, missing females) have taken actions to leave their home or parents.

The second variable, *possibility of participating in mainstream job market*, is a *structure* factor. It refers to whether missing females have experienced structuralized or institutionalized violence — that is, whether missing females have been "controlled through violence or its threat, paid nothing [or paid meagerly for dangerous/dirty jobs], and economically exploited" (Bales, 2005: 4).

The third variable, *sociological locus*, refers to any location in which structuralized/institutionalized violence and agents come together. Since some loci allow certain lost females to be reunited with family members and some do not, this variable will show the outcomes brought about by the interaction between missing women/lost girls and structuralized violence.

Each of these three variables can be divided into two different levels (see Table 1-2). First, the variable *personal choice* is split into *forced* or *voluntary* migration. The former includes those missing females who are compelled to leave their homes/parents. The latter consists of those women/teen girls who choose to run away from home and go to new or unfamiliar places for individual reasons.

Second, the variable *possibility of participating in mainstream job market* is separated into *involvement* or *noninvolvement* of labor directed by institutionalized violence. The former suggests that certain missing females (whether their migration is forced or voluntary) will lose personal freedom and become slave workers. The latter implies that some lost women and young girls (including drowned or aborted infant girls) are luckier because they are not turned into slave laborers.

TABLE 1-2. TRANSFORMATION OF OPERATIONAL VARIABLES (*PERSONAL CHOICE, POSSIBILITY OF PARTICIPATING IN CONVENTIONAL JOB MARKET, AND SOCIOLOGICAL LOCUS*) INTO RANKED VARIABLES

Operationalized Variables		Ranked Variables
Personal Choice	→	Forced migration
		or
	→	Voluntary migration
Possibility of Participating in Mainstream Job Market	→	Involvement of highly exploitative labor
		or
	→	Noninvolvement of highly exploitative labor
Sociological Locus	→	Unlikely reunification with family
		or
	→	Likely reunification with family

Finally, the variable *sociological locus* is divided into *unlikely* or *likely* reunification with family. The former denotes that some missing females have few chances to survive or to leave the status of marginalized/isolated populations. The latter indicates that certain lost wives/daughters have better chances to be reunified with their family or to return to their hometown.

Based on different combinations of these ranked variables, a classification system for missing females in Greater China is constructed (see Table 1-3). This system contains eight typologies. Each of the typologies can be exemplified by a certain type of missing women/young girls in China, Hong Kong, and/or Taiwan, as the following chapters demonstrate.

TABLE 1-3. A CLASSIFICATION SYSTEM FOR MISSING FEMALES
AND LOST GIRLS IN GREATER CHINA

Typologies		Composition Components
FIU Type	=	*Forced* migration + *Involvement* of slave labor + *Unlikely* reunification with family
FNU Type	=	*Forced* migration + *Noninvolvement* of slave labor + *Unlikely* reunification with family
FIL Type	=	*Forced* migration + *Involvement* of slave labor + *Likely* reunification with family
FNL Type	=	*Forced* migration + *Noninvolvement* of slave labor + *Likely* reunification with family
VIU Type	=	*Voluntary* migration + *Involvement* of slave labor + *Unlikely* reunification with family
VNU Type	=	*Voluntary* migration + *Noninvolvement* of slave labor + *Unlikely* reunification with family
VIL Type	=	*Voluntary* migration + *Involvement* of slave labor + *Likely* reunification with family
VNL Type	=	*Voluntary* migration + *Noninvolvement* of slave labor + *Likely* reunification with family

PART II

Missing Females
Dead or at High Risk

CHAPTER 2

Female Political Prisoners

In Taiwan under martial law, political imprisonment (PI) is dubbed *jin hei lao* (literally "entering a black jail") or *zuo hei jian* (literally "sitting in a black prison"). Both expressions refer to the dreadful experience of being sent to a secret jail that is unregulated and unsupervised by the law. In the late 1980s and 1990s, when Taiwan became a democratized region, they were two of the most loathed (as well as most frequently mentioned) terms on that island because they reminded people of the catastrophes (regardless of individual ordeals or social problems caused by family disorganization) brought about by the government (particularly law enforcement agencies and national security units).

Although PI or political policing (see Huggins, 1998; Turk, 1981), as a method of social control seems harsh and is opposed by numerous civil rights advocates, it appears much more humane, merciful, and desirable than many bloody practices of state terror. In the first place, unlike political murder and racial annihilation, the purpose of political policing is to "define the parameters of political debate [as well as political activities]" (Theoharis, 1996: 207), instead of depriving certain categories of people of life. Given that political policing attempts to detect, watch, and, if necessary, arrest those "dangerous individuals" (Theoharis, 1996: 202) who might organize or join subversive movements, so political imprisonment, at least in theory, will let a society remain integrated and prevent the political power of ruling elites from being challenged or even replaced.

Second, given that the goal of political incarceration is to put radical elements under close check, imprisoned conspirators, defectors, or militants who have "truly repented" may be set free after a (long) period of confinement. This allows political prisoners to resume their normal lives and enables government to remind people of the outcome of betraying the interests of the state or challenging the authority of government.

Third, even though political prisoners are set free, they still bear a conspicuous stigma. That identity suggests that some people still pose a threat to social stability and the system of political imprisonment is an adequate practice for government agents to safeguard social order. Put differently, political imprisonment can be turned into a lawful measure by state managers. It can offer national security units legitimate excuses to suppress treacherous movements and/or to make political liberals keep silent.

Finally, political imprisonment can assist state managers in establishing a national data bank of "suspect" people. With such a data bank, not only can the demographic characteristics of disloyal and belligerent political activists be kept permanently, but law enforcement, the military, and national security authorities can deter radical social movements from taking shape and can gain the upper hand in cracking down on the activities of existing insurgent movements. All of these attributes make political policing a popular social control technique.[1]

Political Imprisonment During the Final Years of the Qing Dynasty, 1900–1911

From the perspective of military history, China was undoubtedly a militarily and politically underdeveloped country in the nineteenth century. During this period, not only had the Manchurian government gone through a fiasco in the Opium War (Fay, 1997), but it experienced a series of military defeats, diplomatic crises, and large-scale rebellious movements. Since imperial China was ineffectual in suppressing insurrectionary movements (for instance, the Taiping and the Nien movements of the 1850s and 1860s, which were repressed not by government troops but by private forces and foreign mercenaries) as well as incompetent in coping with military challenges from the West and Japan, it gave Western powers and Japan opportunities to sign unequal treaties, with various demands, with the Chinese government during the second half of the nineteenth century (especially in the 1850s, 1860s, and 1890s).

Under the circumstance of substandard military power and second-rate international status, some reform-minded intellectuals and bureaucrats strongly urged the Qing emperor to carry out modernization programs (especially those which could upgrade China's military technologies) so as to get rid of Western barbarians and recover the lost territories. After more than two decades of disputes among liberal (pro–Westernization) and traditionalist (pro–Confucianism) scholar-officials, this appeal was finally accepted by the emperor in the 1870s. As a result, the Qing authorities during the 1870s and 1880s sponsored several self-strengthening programs in hopes of turning China into a militarily powerful country.

Despite the fact that a number of self-strengthening programs were carried out, the Sino-Japanese War of 1894 proved that the reforms (including the renewal of military facilities and weapons) engaged in by the Manchurian Court were a total failure: the Chinese navy was wiped out completely by its Japanese counterpart. Since this national shame indicated clearly that the military power of China was still too frail to vie for the West and Japan, a few people (including overseas Chinese) began to support financially (or even participate directly in) the Republican movement organized by Sun Yat-sen in the early 1890s (Ma, 1990). Unlike moderate political reformers who believed that the modernization of China should not involve transformation of an entire agricultural society (let alone abolition of the imperial political system), these pro-revolution persons (among those whose identities were known, very few were females) considered that only when the Manchurian rulership was replaced by a new government could China avoid being colonized by the West or Japan.

Simply speaking, starting from the 1890s (particularly after the Sino-Japanese War), the Manchurian authorities experienced more and more terrorist attacks allegedly initiated by revolutionaries. In an effort to purge all anti–Manchurian movements, the Qing officials hired numerous people (among them waiters/waitresses in tea houses, shop owners, street peddlers, manual workers, and even beggars) as informants to identify and search for antigovernment networks, organizations and core members. Under the operation of this massive network of surveillance, an unknown number of political terrorists were caught. As long as these desperados were detained, the Qing officials, almost without exception, used extremely cruel methods to force confessions. After interrogation, such criminals would normally be executed within days (or even hours). Since the great majority of these treason cases were handled efficiently and professionally by the Qing authorities, it seems reasonable to conclude that during the final years of the Qing dynasty (approximately from 1900 to 1911), political prisoners experienced two things: first, during incarceration they would have to endure a variety of excruciating punishments (which will always lead to permanent injuries); then, whether these tough guys pleaded guilty or not, they would be beheaded in public places (usually in bazaars) as examples for the public. The main function of these examples was to warn people of the horrible outcomes of involving in antigovernment activities.

Executing political radicals, however, was not the ultimate purpose of cleansing political dissidents for the Qing authorities. What was far more important was the eradication of all potentially seditious elements. With this in mind, innumerable people who had a biological or common-law relationship with the apprehended revolutionaries would also be held as prisoners by security agents (because such suspects were deemed by the Manchurian regime as probable insurrectionists). After being taken into custody, these innocent people (including young girls and aged women) would customarily be sent/sold to wild wild western and southern provinces, such as Xinjiang, Qinghai, Gansu, Guizhou, and Yunnan, or to Manchuria to serve as maidservants or slaves for prominent provincial people (businessmen, gentry, indigenous rulers, officials, and so on). No one knows how many females went missing (because of disease, extreme weather, natural disaster, animal attack, and the like) during this process of compulsory population migration. Neither can anyone ascertain how many of these exiled females forced to be slaves were mistreated to death by their masters.

Political Imprisonment During the Warlord Era, 1912–1927

When the last emperor of the Qing dynasty announced his abdication in 1911, China, at least in theory, should have become a democratic country governed by law. But in reality, China became a fragmented and unruly state because many leaders of local militias and private forces (who, since 1850s, had helped the Qing Court to suppress rebellious movements, see above) took advantage of the status of a political vacuum brought about by the collapse of the central government to expand and secure personal power. This phenomenon made warlordism the most prominent feature of Chinese politics in the 1910s and 1920s (McCord, 1993; Sutton, 1980).

For researchers and political sociologists, warlordism is inseparable from multi-regime politics: on the one hand, warlords, especially leading ones, will search for all possible means (ranging from military attack to nonmilitary actions like bribery) to obtain exclusive hold over a region. (This domination, of course, will let a warlord enjoy absolute authority in his fiefdom.) On the other hand, competing warlords, in one way or another, could create contingent legal or even political systems to collect taxes and to recruit (young) males into the army. These systems, before they collapsed (perhaps wiped out by armed struggle), allowed warlords to secure financial benefits and to supply manpower for their armies. All of these resources in turn gave warlords a good chance to weaken or even annihilate their opponents.

At any rate, warlord regimes will always bring destructive events to a country or society. Since these events as a rule will lead to social disorganization (or even anarchy), it is not surprising that warlords must rely on assassination, terror imposed by death squads, or other violent means to reinforce their power and to accumulate personal wealth.

If violent measures are utilized frequently by warlords (especially powerful ones) to subdue their competitors, then military campaign was clearly the most efficient and effectual channel. In this regard, political imprisonment is undoubtedly a waste of time for warlords because it would cost them several years to achieve the desired political goals (for instance, having political prisoners repent and change their political stance). Furthermore, political imprisonment was costly, for it required warlords to spend money (which otherwise could be used to purchase weapons) on maintaining political prisons. For these reasons, political confinement, in comparison with military conquest, massive execution, and other time/cost-saving methods, was not preferred by the Chinese warlords.

Based on the statements above, it should not be difficult to understand why cases of political confinement during the years of warlord politics were rare (if not nonexistent). This feature did not change significantly after 1927 as China was unified (at least nominally) by the Northern Expedition Army led by Chiang Kai-shek.

In the following section, I discuss how and why the Kuomintang (the Nationalist Party, or KMT) government created a system of political imprisonment during the Nanking Decade, the interval of the Sino-Japanese War, the final years of the Nationalist-Communist armed struggle, and the era of the refugee regime. Thanks to the emergence of this system, an unknown number of females (whether political dissidents, liberal intellectuals, communist supporters, or even secret agents) were arrested and disappeared mysteriously in prison.

The Kuomintang (Nationalist Party) State and Political Imprisonment, 1927–1987

The warlord age of Republican China ended (at least technically) in 1927 after the Northern Expedition Army led by Chiang Kai-shek defeated or reorganized a number of warlord troops. Although these victories paved the way for the Nationalists to establish a nationwide regime, this regime, to use the words of the Bible, was made out of clay (Daniel 2:45) because it was merely an amalgam of highly heterogeneous and seemingly incompatible elements, namely, Nationalist loyalists, former warlords who had been incorporated into the Nationalist camp, and communists (see Eastman, et al., 1991). Given that the Nationalist government was composed of players with conflicting goals and diverse ideologies, the Chiang Kaishek regime, before it withdrew entirely to Taiwan in 1950, had to depend on radical (or scandalous) governing techniques (such as physical assault, assassination, manslaughter, and intimidation) to unify the contending factions, to safeguard the ruling power of the Kuomintang elites, and to suppress dissident movements. Of these techniques, political imprisonment was without a doubt the most noteworthy institution in producing missing populations/females. One factor directly related to this social problem was that the agencies in charge of political policing were hardly regulated by the law. That made KMT's political prisons function like abysses, too deep and dark for people to find their relatives. This matter can be demonstrated by the next four phases of Nationalist politics.

I. The Nanking Decade (1927/1937)

The Kuomintang government was an impotent and vulnerable regime in the late 1920s. Not only did the communists refuse to accept fully the legitimacy of the governing status of the Nationalists, but former warlords, no matter whether they held a pro–Chiang stance or not, sought ways to preserve their vested interests and financial privileges. These political, military, and financial divisions are illustrated in the map on page 27.

The KMT government was obviously in a predicament before 1937 because its ruling status was either challenged explicitly or boycotted implicitly. These troubles and obstacles, to an extent, left political heads and military commanders of the Nationalist state few choices but to employ extraordinary and irregular means (especially violent ones) to expand the authority of the central government and to achieve the goal of unifying post-warlord China. Such a dilemma is summarized vividly in the following paragraph:

> The Kuomintang ruled largely by naked force. Unable to win popular support, it compelled submission. Incapable of developing — much less utilizing — democratic institutions, it simply imprisoned ... its opponents and its critics [Isaacs, 1961: 295].

So before 1987 as martial law was lifted in Taiwan, the Nationalist regime, through the development and institutionalization of a sweeping secret police system (see below), depended heavily on extrajudicial methods to solve political disagreements. These methods, to a varying extent, helped Chiang Kai-shek and his right-hand men to carry out the supreme will of the Kuomintang state.[2]

The first act taken by the Chiang regime to achieve the goal of sending secret agents to every corner of China was to enlarge the size of the *zhong guo guo min dang dang wu diao cha ke* (the Investigation Section of Party Affairs of the Kuomintang, ISPAKMT) in 1929. Before its organizational level was upgraded, the ISPAKMT, or what Wakeman (2003: 37) called *mi cha zu* (the Secret Investigation Group), was a seemingly negligible administrative division within the Ministry of Organization. Not only was the number of agents working for the ISPAKMT small (no more than twenty when the Nationalist government was installed in Nanking in 1927 [Zhang, 1988: 6]), but the ISPAKMT did not have sufficient financial resources to install a nationwide secret agent system to monitor and, if possible, counterattack the mobilization efforts of the communists in rural areas. All of these limiting factors, however, did not deter the ISPAKMT from performing its special missions, such as gathering intelligence about the illegal activities of the farmers; watching the movements of those former warlords who had participated in anti–Chiang Kai-shek activities; and censoring various treasonous publications. (One possible reason that the ISPAKMT could carry out these missions was that the ISPAKMT had the authority to command the KMT armies to arrest Chinese Bolsheviks and any persons considered to be communists or communist followers.) So despite its ostensibly inconsequential size, the ISPAKMT were clearly very critical for the Nationalists to safeguard their power bastion or ruling stronghold (Jiangsu and Zhejiang provinces). This significant position led Chiang Kai-shek to appoint the Chen brothers[3] (Chen Guo-fu and Chen Li-fu, who later became the leaders of the so-called CC faction within the Nationalist Party) to oversee the professionalization and institutionalization of the ISPAKMT in 1928 (Zhao, 1994: 60–61).[4]

As soon as they were chosen by Chiang to direct the ISPAKMT and to develop the secret service system of the Kuomintang state in 1928, the Chen brothers took action to continue the practice of White Terror, beginning in April 1927 when the Kuomintang forces (including the Northern Expedition Army, the local troops of Jiangsu and Zhejiang, and the Green Gang-turned-armed-pickets) orchestrated a series of massacres in Shanghai, Nanchang, and other cities to exterminate the communists and left-wing workers (see Martin, 1996; Wakeman, 1995). One of the terrorist acts ordered by the Chens was to launch a comprehensive incarceration program to put in jail as many Chinese communists and left-wing Nationalists sympathetic with communist doctrines as possible.[5] Chen (1988: 249) reports that, during the three years (1928, 1929, and 1930) of large-scale arrests, at least 15,000 high- and middle-level communist cadres, ordinary members of the Chinese Communist Party, and communist supporters were sent to military prisons or to the so-called *fan xing yuan* (introspection institutes) or *gan hua yuan* (reformatory institutes) to undergo re-education and brainwashing courses.[6]

In 1929, the party affairs investigation section of the Kuomintang was expanded into the investigation department of party affairs of the Kuomintang (IDPAKMT), or *zhong guo guo min dang dang wu diao cha chu*.[7] With more personnel and other organizational resources allocated by the Nanking government to the IDPAKMT, Chen Guo-fu and Chen Li-fu recruited many of their confidants into the IDPAKMT. That act, within a short period of time, enabled the Chens to form the CC clique within the Nationalist regime. Moreover, since many high-ranking or senior secret agents of the CC branch were assigned to other high-level civil service positions, the Chens, before 1949, became two of the most powerful figures in Nationalist China.

Although the Chens and their confidants in the IDPAKMT enjoyed an extraordinarily influential status in the secret service community of Republican China, their political power and position soon encountered competition from the other newly established secret service agency — the Blue Shirt Society (Chang, 1985). Compared with the IDPAKMT, the Blue Shirt Society (BSS) apparently received more interest from Chinese and Western historians.[8] This academic discriminatory treatment was probably a result of the fact that the expansion of the Blue Shirt Society was much faster than that of the IDPAKMT. That made the BSS look like an agency superior to the IDPAKMT in leadership, administrative efficiency, and contribution to the Nationalist state. In addition, the BSS as well as its successor organizations tended to become involved in state-endorsed crimes more frequently than those associated with the IDPAKMT. These included assassinating highly influential political liberals and dissidents in the 1930s–40s and murdering certain suspect Nationalist military commanders who might change their side during the final stage of the Civil War in the late 1940s (see the following pages). These extralegal acts may have resulted in more accounts about the Blue Shirt Society than about the IDPAKMT.

No matter how the Blue Shirt Society is analyzed, this organization, according to historians and the memoirs of some former members of the BSS, resulted chiefly from several significant historical events taking place in 1931.

In the first place, Chiang Kai-shek launched civil wars in 1928, 1929, and 1930 to conquer de facto independent warlords and to centralize his political authority. Since Chiang, besides resorting to military force, also used nonmilitary tactics (such as bribery), Chiang's armies luckily defeated a number of the best-trained and well-equipped warlord forces. These triumphs inspired Chiang to take necessary means to deal with senior Nationalist figures who did not support him. In February 28, 1931, Chiang gave order to put Hu Han-min, who was a liberal thinker and then the head of the Li Fa Yuan (the legislative branch of the Kuomintang government), into custody to warn adherents of anti–Chiang movements not to continue their activities. The detention of Hu, however, did not achieve the goal expected by Chiang, namely, to unify the power of the Nanking regime. On the contrary, a group of high-ranking Nationalist officials and military commanders left Nanking and installed a separatist KMT government in Guangzhou to challenge the political authority of Chiang. This resistant act, needless to say, put great pressure on Chiang because Chiang could not be sure whether he could again depend on his troops to suppress the oppositional movement led by his comrades (anyhow, these very important persons controlled armies too). In the end, Chiang was forced to convene a series of peace conferences to solve the political crisis provoked by the Hu case (Chen, 1989: 607–646).

Before the Hu Han-min case was worked out completely, the Kwantung army of Japan waged, without issuing any warning beforehand, a sweeping attack on Manchuria in September 1931 to eliminate Zhang Xueliang, the so-called *dong bei wang* (the king of Manchuria), from that region. This attack, dubbed the 918 Incident, not only forced hundreds of thousands of Manchurians to seek asylum in the Nationalist areas, but allowed the Japanese military to establish a puppet regime (the Manchukuo, headed by the last emperor of the Qing dynasty, Puyi) in Manchuria to divide the sovereignty of the Nationalist state.

For the people living in the Nationalist districts, the 918 Incident was undoubtedly a national crisis. Accordingly many people, particularly students, took part in demonstrations and rallies to express their anti–Japan position.[9] Numerous people also requested that the Chiang regime alter its non-resistance policy and take a tougher stance toward Japan to reclaim Manchuria.[10] All of these anti–Japanese public protests, together with the highly provocative Hu case, brought enormous pressures on Chiang Kai-shek and his administration.

In December 1931, Chiang proclaimed his retirement to alleviate the political predicaments he faced. This stigma in Chiang's political career provided the Blue Shirts with the necessary patronage to take shape along the following principles[11]:

> Chiang Kai-shek should be the permanent highest leader; graduates of the Whampoa [Huang Pu] Academy should serve as the leading cadre, with future expansion to form around that nucleus; and the Three People's Principles should be implemented, using "communist organizational methods" and adding the spirit of ... bushido or ... fascism [Eastman, 1990: 36].

In March 1932, the organization of Blue Shirts was set up officially in Nanking.[12] The core adherents of the Blue Shirts, all of whom were highly faithful to Chiang, then elected Chiang Kai-shek as president of that society and divided themselves into six groups: secretariat, organization, training, propaganda, military affairs, and secret service (Chang, 1985: 5). Each of these departments, through different channels, cautiously recruited patriotic students, loyal servicemen, and other pro–KMT social groups into the Blue Shirts.[13] Thanks to these recruiting activities, the membership of the Blue Shirts increased considerably before the eve of the Sino-Japanese War.[14]

Of the six departments of the Blue Shirts, the *te wu chu* (the secret service department, or SSD) was especially noteworthy. Not only was the SSD suspected of innumerable assassinations (whether successful or abortive) and political imprisonment, it had become the chief competitor of the KMT's party affairs investigation department.[15] The power struggle between the SSD and the IDPAKMT had already begun as early as the summer of 1932. During that summer, agents of the SSD were sent to the police academy and the Special School of Local Autonomy (SSLA) in Zhejiang province to rid those two schools of the IDPAKMT (Zhang, 1992: 285).[16] Such fighting over the educational resources of military colleges and party-run schools soon extended into other areas. For example, in 1932, 1933, and 1934, when the fourth and the fifth anticommunist campaigns were still underway, agents of the SSD and the IDPAKMT sought ways to dominate the *you jian jian cha suo* (the mail censorship offices) and the *dian bao jian cha suo* (the telegram censorship offices) located in the Nationalist regions (Liu & Wu, 1994: 87; Zhao, 1988: 217).[17] Chiefs and directors of the IDPAKMT and the SSD also competed with each other to control the checkpoints at airports and harbors; the police bureaus, anti-smuggling departments, and military police corps in large cities; and the investigation departments of garrison commands in provinces substantially governed by the Kuomintang (Liu & Wu, 1994: 88). All of these contentions often made the relationship between the IDPAKMT and the SSD antagonistic and tense (these rivalries tended to be overwhelming in provinces partially or merely nominally governed by the Chiang administration). Mutual hostility between the IDPAKMT and the SSD, in turn, led an unknown number of disloyal, disobedient, or undisciplined secret agents (including female ones) to be sent to the previously mentioned *fan xing yuan* and *gan hua yuan* to repent. Some agents were even treated like felons and incarcerated in maximum-security military prisons.[18]

The continual competition and enmity between the IDPAKMT and the SSD naturally caused Chiang Kai-shek to fear that the secret service of the Nanking regime would become useless. To end this impasse, the Military Commission's Bureau of Investigation and Statistics (MCBIS), under the directive of Chiang Kai-shek, was established in Nanking in the spring of 1934. Both the investigation department of party affairs of the Kuomintang and the secret service department of the Blue Shirt Society were ordered to merge into the MCBIS; the IDPAKMT became the first division of the MCBIS while the SSD became the second division.

Putting the IDPAKMT and the SSD under the same roof, however, did not solve the problem of internal friction because rival secret service agents still could not cooperate with one another. On the contrary, the competition between the IDPAKMT and the SSD became even more acute.[19] The mutual antagonism between the first division of the MCBIS, directed by Xu En-zeng, and the second division of the MCBIS, led by Dai Li, increased after 1934. There were uncountable corrupt, malicious, and/or untrustworthy agents (including, again, female ones) who became victims of the power struggle among Xu, Dai, and other high-level officials (Zhang, 1988: 31).

Although the oppositional relationship between the first division of the MCBIS (transformed from the IDPAKMT) and the second division of the MCBIS (converted from the SSD) persisted into the period of the Sino-Japanese War (see the next section), secret agents of the Nationalist state, no matter what and which branches they were assigned, were "suspected of being everywhere" (Eastman, 1990: 75) after the mid–1930s. Since Chiang's ears and eyes (or "loyal dogs," as claimed by Dai Li [Wang & Li, 1995: 277]) grew swiftly in number, the Nanking government was able to monitor and suppress all movements which challenged the authority of Nationalist government.[20] Even some rebellions taking place in districts not firmly governed by the Chiang administration were put down by secret agents of the Nanking regime.[21]

In brief, considering the depictions above, it should be clear that in the late 1920s/early 1930s when a secret service system began to take shape in Nationalist China, tens of thousands of red elements (that is, civil rights activists, high school and university students who participated in anti-fascism demonstrations, and liberal intellectuals who criticized the Chiang government) were arrested and detained by secret police. Since these communist associates (both males and females) were regarded by managers of the Nationalist state as perilous components or public enemies, such persons always had to overcome many barriers before they could regain freedom. In other words, a substantial portion of them might have been kept everlastingly behind closed doors or even executed clandestinely. On the other hand, during the processes of massive apprehension (which involved lots of political schemes and dirty games), numerous female secret agents were convicted wrongly as communists. These ill-fated females likewise were sent to jail where, unless they were lucky, they would have to stay in segregated cells for years. Unfortunately, it is essentially impossible for modern researchers to examine the details of these political cases.

II. The Period of the Sino-Japanese War (July 1937–August 1945)

For Chiang Kai-shek, the Japanese invasion of China's territories was not the first priority. He believed that Japan would never have enough human resources to conquer the enormous land, the massive population, and the diverse customs of China, so the military actions of the Japanese forces in China before 1937 were largely tolerated, if not downplayed. In contrast, the communist movement caused far more concern among ruling elites of the Nationalist state (despite the fact that the equipment and power of the Red Army was much inferior to and far less threatening than the Japanese). By treating the communists as the chief competitor for state power, the military leaders of Kuomintang in general and Chiang Kai-shek in particular employed both inconspicuous methods (such as abduction) and purely violent means (such as massacre) to eradicate the communist plague. Under this zero-tolerance policy, almost all law enforcement and secret service resources of the Nanking government were spent on the investigation and annihilation of communism-related elements (Eastman, 1984). That gave underground communists an extremely restricted space to expand their organizations and to recruit followers.

Before the Chiang Kai-shek government could initiate a fatal strike on the communist forces in late 1936/early 1937, the Sian Incident[22] and the entire control of North China by Japanese troops in the first half of 1937 forced the Kuomintang authorities to suspend the sixth communist suppression war (which would otherwise destroy totally the Chinese Red Army). These unexpected events, along with the condition that the anticommunist wars carried out by the Nationalists had become extremely unpopular because social elites (via the media or propaganda) urged strongly that all Chinese must unite together to resist the invasion of Japan, gave the communists critical opportunities to survive.[23] Facing the enormous public demands that the Nationalists and the Communists must cooperate with each other to repel the encroachment of the Japanese, Chiang Kai-shek (no matter how unwilling he was) at last allowed the Red Army to join the Nationalist forces in August 1937 to deal with the crises brought on by the Japanese.[24]

The Nationalists' acceptance of the red ingredients, however, did not last very long.[25] As soon as the Japanese military ceased to wage large-scale military acts in south and central China (which enabled the Nationalists to establish a refugee regime in Chungking in late 1938), anticommunist activities resumed.

The first step taken by the Chiang regime to eliminate the communists was to reorganize the Military Commission's Bureau of Investigation and Statistics, in 1938. As mentioned previously, the secret service agencies of the Kuomintang government during the Nanking Decade can be categorized into two major branches: the investigation section/department of party affairs of the Kuomintang headed by Xu En-zeng, and the Secret Service Department of the Blue Shirts commanded by Dai Li. These two systems were ordered to incorporate into the MCBIS in 1934 because agents of different working background/department affiliation clashed with one another frequently. Having these contending agents work for the same organization was considered essential in reducing mutual hostility.

After the MCBIS became a unit, it worked out several troublesome political problems (by means of intimidation, kidnapping, or even murder) for the Chiang regime during the last two and a half years of the Nanking Decade. However, despite the fact that the MCBIS had become a powerful (as well as notorious) institute in the mid–1930s, the occupation of Shanghai (in September-October 1937) and Nanking (in December 1937) by the Japanese troops seriously undermined the internal organization and the routine operation of the MCBIS. This disaster can be characterized by the fact that the great majority of command centers and investigation stations of the MCBIS in Shanghai and Nanking were identified and destroyed by the Japanese. That made numerous secret agents of the MCBIS unable to receive instructions from their superiors. Under this highly dangerous and stressful condition, a certain number of the unemployed MCBIS secret agents (males and females) surrendered to the Japanese or the Japan-backed puppet governments in North and Central China in order to survive in the Japanese-held territories.[26]

The collapse of the secret service agencies was, needless to say, a catastrophe to Chiang Kai-shek and his regime because the Chungking government, after losing its ears and eyes, had almost become deaf and blind during the first year of the Sino-Japanese War. For the sake of retrieving the hearing power and vision for the Nationalist state, restructuring the MCBIS so that it could restore the ability to keep track of the communists and to collect information about Japanese troops/puppet regimes became a priority for Chiang.

The reorganization of the MCBIS began in August 1938. The proceeding of this project basically followed two independent lines: on the one hand, the first division of the MCBIS was upgraded, expanded, and renamed the Central Executive Committee's Bureau of Investigation and Statistics (*zhong yang zhi xing wei yuan hui diao cha tong ji ju*, or Zhong Tong, ZT). Xu En-zeng still remained as the director of Zhong Tong, the Chinese FBI (Wakeman, 2003: 302). On the other hand, the second division of the MCBIS was also enlarged in staff and promoted hierarchically. In the end, it inherited the title of the Military Commission's Bureau of Investigation and Statistics of the Nationalist government (*jun shi wei yuan hui diao cha tong ji ju*, or Jun Tong, JT) and became the nucleus of the MCBIS. Dai Li continued to serve as the head of Jun Tong, the Chinese CIA. With this organizational adjustment, the Chungking regime regained, step by step, the ability to watch and hear.[27] The treacherous activities of the communists and anti–Chiang Kai-shek figures were again put under close surveillance after 1938 when the Sino-Japanese War had entered a stalemate.

Once the Chungking government reacquired the capacity to learn about the radical acts of the left-wing elements in 1939, the next step taken by the Chungking authorities to suppress the communist and other anti-KMT movements was to create new military prisons and reestablish the infamous introspection and reformatory institutes in Sichuan and contiguous provinces. As noted previously, before the Chiang Kai-shek administration became a refugee regime in November/December 1937, the Kuomintang government had set up a number of *fan xing yuan* and *gan hua yuan* in Nanking, the capital, and provinces firmly dominated by the Nationalists. Although these buildings and campuses might give outsiders an impression that they were simply political training schools reserved for seditious persons (especially communist suspects and activists from political reform movements) to change their poisonous thoughts, these structures for former prisoners were by no means educational or didactic facilities. On the contrary, they were nothing but quasi concentration camps. People who were locked in these reeducation agencies always had to seek alternatives to survive in the extraordinarily poor living environment:

> The cages of the *fan xing yuan* ... usually were very small. The walls and floor of these cages were often wet. Prisoners inside the cages usually could not ever get sufficient light and fresh air because it was common for five persons to be locked up in a small cage no larger than 48 square feet in size. Overcrowding, in turn, made the cages as hot as a steamer in the summer.... As to food, each of the prisoners, according to the official rules, was supposed to get food costing 1.5 (Chinese) dimes each day. But in fact, because the prison authorities withheld most of the money, the daily food acquired by each of the prisoners usually cost less than 1 (Chinese) dime. Such a circumstance was harsh enough to deprive someone of life. But even worse was that all the prisoners had to put on heavy fetters.... That made many people unable to walk because of paralysis. [In any event], *fan xing yuan* was a somber place, like hell. Some people became blind because of living in the dark cages [for a long time]. Some people got severe intestinal and stomach diseases [because of the low quality of the food]. Some people became disabled because of suffering cruel tortures. All of these, in a gradual manner, aimed to put the prisoners to death. For those people who were persevering enough to finish their sentences and were lucky enough to be released from the death-dominated *fan xing yuan*, almost all had to suffer permanent injuries on their body [Lin, 1991: 131–32; original texts were written in Chinese].

Despite the inhumane nature of *fan xing yuan* and *gan hua yuan*,[28] the Nationalists, as soon as they installed an emergent government in Chungking in late 1938, took actions to build similar agencies in provinces of northwestern China (especially in Shaanxi, where Yanan, the capital of the communist state, was located).[29] On the other hand, since the Nationalists and the Communists were allied partners in fighting against Japan (at least technically), it was politically and militarily inappropriate for the Kuomintang to preserve the old title of *fan xing yuan* or *gan hua yuan*. To solve this problem, the Chungking regime, while maintaining the original managerial, organizational, and training styles of *fan xing yuan* or *gan hua yuan*, set up various instructional regiments, construction brigades, and training camps (such as the youth camps, the labor corps, and the peaceful national salvation corps) to sustain the practice of incarcerating the communists and other left-wing elements (Zhang, 1988: 33).[30] Regardless of the continual protest from the communists, it was estimated that more than 100,000 communist suspects, political campaigners (mainly human rights advocates), anti–Kuomintang students, traitors,[31] undisciplined secret agents,[32] and senior prisoners who had been detained in *fan xing yuan, gan hua yuan,* or military prisons before the Sino-Japanese War[33] were locked up in these socially and geographically isolated regiments, brigades, and corps between 1938 and 1949.

In addition to restoring the penal system of *fan xing yuan/gan hua yuan* and resuming the practice of using military prisons to hold unruly civilians, the Chungking regime created a few concentration camps in Southwest China (above all in Yunnan and Guizhou) to make sure that no communist movement would take shape during wartime.[34] These concentration camps, in terms of function, had two characteristics that distinguished them from military prisons and *fan xing yuan/gan hua yuan.* The first one was that, compared to introspection or reformatory institutes which would keep criminals and communist suspects from all social strata and occupational groups in custody, concentration camps in Southwest China seemed to be accommodations for hard-core communists (for instance, captured communist guerrilla fighters) and would-be communists (for instance, former warlord-turned-Kuomintang politicians/military commanders) only. In other words, the prison population composition of concentration camps tended to be more homogeneous than that of *fan xing yuan* and *gan hua yuan* because only communist adherents, devotees, and fanatics were eligible to be sent to those camps. Second, since prisoners of concentration camps were regarded as the greatest threat and the most malicious enemies to the Nationalist state, the prison authorities employed two methods to get rid of these seeds of disaster. The first means, as Sa's (1985: 186) memoir indicates, was that almost all the political prisoners sent to the concentration camps would suffer some kind of cruel torture and mistreatment.[35] These mistreatments and tortures, almost without exception, would cause serious and permanent injuries to the body of victims. Only the fortunate and strong ones could survive.[36]

If the prisoners were tough enough to get over the miscellaneous tortures, then the next test awaiting them would be the horrible prison milieu. Meng's (1996) description of one of the concentration camps in Guizhou provides an example:

> In this concentration camp, all rooms except the prisoner cells had illumi-nating equipment. At night, the lamps of those "offices" of secret agents and guards and the main routes of the camp were always turned on. [By contrast], the insides of all cells were always dark and gloomy. Only a flick-

ering small bulb, which looked like a ghost fire from hell, was hanging in the doorway of each cell.... Even during the daytime, the insides of the cells were quite dark. This shivering circumstance was caused by some factors. [First], the window of each cell was only as big as a bowl. No sunlight could ever enter the cell except through this window.... [Second], secret agents usually covered tightly the window by a black cloth. That made the prisoners unable to see the light and to know the alteration of day and night. Even so, this small window was the only channel for the prisoners to breathe outside air. It was also the passage for the prisoners to get prison food, although the food was so crude that even animals might not want to eat it. In addition to these poor living conditions, each of the small cells was jammed frequently with people. It was not unusual for more than 40 persons to live in a cell no larger than 72 square feet. [Living in such a tiny space], it was impossible for people to turn their body when they slept. The prisoners also could not stretch their hands and feet when they stood. The strong odors of sweat, excrements, and urine led almost every prisoner to be suffocated.... Even people with iron-like bodies would get illnesses like stomachache, edema, night blindness, rheumatism, and paralysis if they were locked in the concentration camps [for a period of time]. This situation would be even worse for those people who had suffered tortures, because besides illnesses, they would have to endure various injuries in their bodies [Meng, 1996: 123–24; original texts were written in Chinese].

Briefly speaking, the Nationalist state-installed concentration camps were similar to death camps established by Nazi Germany. Few, if any, people who entered these camps and survived could leave without eternal wounds because the environment was so poor that it would seem that only animals should be housed there.

Although the Chiang regime in Chungking had set up concentration camps in Southwest China during the first three years of the Sino-Japanese War, the quantity and size of these camps appeared small. This condition did not change remarkably until the U.S. Navy helped the Nationalist government to expand the magnitude of concentration camps in 1942 and 1943. As mentioned in the previous section (see note 8 of this chapter), before the U.S. Pacific Fleet in Hawaii was hit badly by Japan in December 1941, the Military Commission's Bureau of Investigation and Statistics led by Dai Li had already decoded the message that the Japanese navy would launch an air raid on Pearl Harbor. By ordering Xiao Bo, the assistant military attaché of the Republic of China embassy in Washington and the liaison officer of the MCBIS in the United States, to pass this intelligence to the authorities of the U.S. Navy, Dai Li and his MCBIS hoped that the Roosevelt administration would take a tougher policy toward Japan so that the blockade raised by Japanese troops on South China could be lifted. Despite the MCBIS's continual warnings, the U.S. Secretary of the Navy and other navy commanders did not take the MCBIS's intelligence seriously. Therefore, there was no reason to believe that Japan would carry out a raid against the American naval base (Meng, 1996: 7; Shen, 1994: 207–208). More than 2,000 unsuspecting American sailors were killed in the several hours following the Pearl Harbor attack.

The Pearl Harbor incident, of course, led the U.S. to declare war on Japan. On the other hand, since the American military needed to collect data about the oceanic current, meteorology, and geographic characteristics of the East and South China seacoast so that the U.S. Marines could land in coastal China to fight against the Japanese troops (this plan was never carried out), it was necessary for the U.S. to find a Chinese partner to obtain the records. The MCBIS, given that it had demonstrated extraordinary ability in gathering intelligence, naturally became the ideal candidate for that partnership. Dai Li also wanted to develop a cooperative relationship with the U.S. because the MCBIS desperately needed weapons, ammunition, and other military materials. Only the Americans could offer sufficient military supplies. Under this reciprocal and complementary situation, the MCBIS and the U.S. Navy began to carry out several unofficial exchange programs in the spring of 1942. This teamwork caused the U.S. military to transport bullets, jeeps, machine guns, pistols, and communication equipment to the MCBIS. As a trade, the MCBIS helped the U.S. Navy to detect the activities of Japanese troops in East and South China and to assemble the meteorological data about the West Pacific coast.

The cooperative relationship between the MCBIS and the U.S. Navy became formalized after the Sino-American Special Technical Cooperative Organization (SACO) was established in Chungking in 1943 (Yu, 1996). Following the foundation of the SACO, American advisors (including weapon experts and special agents) began to work closely with the intelligence service forces and guerrillas of the MCBIS stationed in the villages and underdeveloped suburbs surrounding Chungking. As a result, the technical and supportive personnel of the SACO became known as the "rice-paddy navy" (Wakeman, 2003: 305). The MCBIS kept acquiring handsome military supplies and various technical supports from its American partners. These military resources were exceptionally critical for Dai Li because, in terms of eliminating the communist elements, they gave the MCBIS the required power to do the necessary jobs. These jobs can be epitomized by the creation of a new town on Gele (literally "song of joyfulness") Mountain, Sichuan:

> During the course of the war Dai Li's men, with help of American supplies and funds, transformed the terraced farmlands [of Gele mountain] into a

sprawling network of eight hundred buildings. The complex included barracks, a parade ground and armory, rifle and pistol ranges, classrooms, police dog kennels, pigeon cotes, radio communications shacks, a prison, and interrogation facilities [Wakeman, 2003: 302].

In those interrogation facilities, detainees (particularly uncooperative and defiant ones) were put in a torture chamber. Then some or even all of the following trials would be imposed on them (Wakeman, 2003: 306):

• Searing breasts with flaming irons
• Piercing each finger with sharp bamboo splinters
• Flooding nostrils with icy water
• Wracking body with electric currents

If detainees still refused to confess or give in after suffering these tortures, then the first possible outcome was that they might be thrown into a hydrochloric acid pool (Wakeman, 2003: 305). Almost no historian has mentioned the function and open hours of that pool. However, certain people (including females) might have lost their life in that pool because it was after all a part of the torture chamber.

Compared to tossing prisoners alive into a hydrochloric acid pool, locking captives in concentration camps seemed to be a far more common punishment. One of these camps constructed by Dai Li's men was called *Bai Gong Guan* (i.e., Bai mansion; the original site of this prison was believed to be the home of Bai Ju-yi, a famous poet of the Tang dynasty). This camp "was described by one of its ... surviving inmates as a Hades where ... prisoners 'underwent seven of the forty-eight tortures' of hell." (Wakeman, 2003: 305).

Simply speaking, starting from 1943, the MCBIS, under the patronage of the SACO, became increasingly resourceful. Accordingly, more and more death camps were installed in Guangdong (Qujiang), Guangxi (Guilin), Shaanxi (Xian), Hunan (Hengyang), Sichuan (Qijiang and Chengdu), Yunnan (Kunming), and many other locations (Lin, 1991: 126–28). These hellish establishments eventually could be seen in all the provinces of Southwest China after 1945 (which made political imprisonment a conspicuous and inescapable part of the Nationalist state). Given that concentration camps were ubiquitous, innumerable females (whether they were true communists or not) were transferred to these horrible places and denied contact with the outside world. No official archives, however, can be found in regard to the whereabouts of these females confined in Dai Li's dungeons.[37]

III. The Years of Civil War (1945–1949)

For the Nationalist government in Chungking, the Sino-Japanese War would have been an endless war of attrition if the U.S. had not dropped atomic bombs on Hiroshima and Nagasaki in August 1945: with more than one million Japanese forces firmly dominating Manchuria, North China, and a large part of Central and South China, it seemed very unlikely that the Nationalists could do anything truly effective to change the military and political situation. The political and military impasse was broken, however, when Japan, after several years of governing the richest parts of China, surrendered to the Allies in August 1945. One immediate consequence of this huge and dramatic transformation, unexpected by many Chinese and Japanese, was the breakdown of the political equilibrium established by competing political players during wartime.

During the first two years of the Sino-Japanese War, the Japanese military installed puppet governments in North, Central, and South China to suppress anti–Japan movements and to perpetuate Japan's interests/privileges. While (Chinese) managers of these puppet regimes (including those of Manchuria) were deemed by the Chinese masses loyal to the Chiang Kai-shek government as defectors and traitors, these collaborationists at least restored and maintained a social order in Japanese-occupied areas. That contribution, to a certain extent, allowed authority figures of those puppet states to enjoy legitimate political power comparable to that of the Chungking government. In addition to diverse ruling bodies staffed and buttressed by pro–Japan Chinese elites and the Japanese military, the communists set up several guerrilla bases in northwestern China after the Long March. This proletarian regime, after 1940, became progressively more resourceful and powerful (Taylor, 2009: 171). Therefore, it functioned as another self-sufficient state (of course, the economic and political systems of this state, such as abolishing currencies, were totally unacceptable to the Chungking authorities). Finally, some former-warlord-turned-Kuomintang-politicians tried to restore their home turf in West, Southwest, and South China after the Chiang Kai-shek government had become a refugee regime in 1938 (most of these frontier regions were unoccupied by Japan during wartime). To achieve this goal, these ambitious former warlords recruited young males "at a much faster pace than [that of] the Central Army [commanded by Chiang Kai-shek]":

> These warlords continued the old system of each unit recruiting in its own favorite hunting ground, relying on the enticements of money and freedom from drudgery, as well as appeals to regional or national patriotism to sign up young men [Taylor, 2009: 162].

All of these recruiting efforts, unsurprisingly, gave ex-warlords the power to contend with the puppet regimes and the Reds for the sovereignty of the Nationalist state.

The conditions that permitted a divided political situation to exist during the war years largely disappeared after World War II. (Chinese collaborationists had lost their Japanese patrons while former warlords could no longer compete with the American-equipped Chiang Kai-shek army.) The only exception was Mao Tse-tung and his communist forces. This advantageous environment precipitated Chiang Kai-shek and his military commanders to resort to the simplest and most convenient method, military repression, to solve the communist problem. Chiang and his counselors may have believed that the task of eliminating the communist bandits could be accomplished in months or even weeks because the military power of the Nationalist army was much stronger than that of the poorly equipped communist troops.

Before Chiang Kai-shek formally ordered his troops to attack the communist forces in late 1945/early 1946, three militant movements, the anti–Chinese collaborationists movement, the anti–verification/reselection movement, and the anti–civil war movement, initiated in former occupied areas had become new social problems. Since these movements were considered by the authorities as seditious activities analogous to the communist revolution, all of them encountered harsh suppression from the Kuomintang government. Several thousand people who participated in these movements were apprehended and sent by secret police and security agents to concentration camps between September 1945 and June 1946 (Zhang, 1996: 145).

The anti–Chinese collaborationists movement (*fan han jian yun dong*) was a purging campaign organized by people who believed they had been deprived economically and/or politically during the Japanese rulership. It originated primarily from the reality that many social elites (most of whom were industrialists, entrepreneurs, high-level educational administrators, financiers, and university faculty members) had supported or worked in partnership with the Japanese and puppet regimes before and during the Sino-Japanese War. Nevertheless, after the Chiang Kai-shek government came back to Nanking from Chungking in late 1945, the Nationalist authorities, except for executing some notorious former high-ranking civil officials of the puppet governments, did not take any actions to put those economic/educational elites cum collaborators on trial.[38] Accordingly, many people who had experienced economic injustice or educational discrimination because of the pro–Japan acts of these Chinese traitors simply could not tolerate the Kuomintang government's inaction. Under the mobilization and leadership of the communist agents hiding on campus or in professional associations, numerous persons (particularly university students) joined demonstrations/parades with the goal of pushing the Chiang administration to do something to penalize those people who had betrayed national interests during the war.

Unlike the anti–Chinese collaborationists movement that focused on social justice, the second movement, the anti–verification/reselection movement (*fan zhen shen yun dong*) centered on the protection of individual rights and interests. This movement rose chiefly from the fact that in late 1945 when the Kuomintang government reopened its offices in Nanking, it proclaimed that the Nationalist state would not recognize the validity of the diploma issued by any high schools or colleges installed or administered by former puppet regimes.[39] This meant that unless someone had taken a series of political courses (especially the Three People's Principles and the speeches of Generalissimo Chiang Kai-shek) and passed allegiance tests, those who graduated from former puppet high schools or colleges would either lose their jobs (if they had already served in public institutions) or no longer be qualified to find government positions or to be hired by KMT-affiliated enterprises. The policy frustrated and angered many people who had received what the Chiang government called servant or slave education. Numerous graduates of former puppet schools believed that they had been betrayed by the Chiang regime. Therefore, with the help of underground communist agents, scores of people in almost every major city took to the streets to express their opposition to the reevaluation (of education background) policy made by the Nanking authorities. The Nanking government, needless to say, mobilized secret agents, troops, and police forces to counterattack. These suppressive measures resulted in many protesters' being beaten and arrested. Some demonstrators taken into custody even disappeared without leaving any clues.

The third movement organized by underground communist agents, students, liberal intellectuals, and many other social actors before June 1946 was the anti–civil war movement. As will be discussed below, this movement was "the most important student struggle of the 1940s" (Wasserstrom, 1991: 240). It laid a foundation for many student demonstrations and large protests in 1947, 1948, and early 1949.

According to Zhang (1996: 119–25), the root cause of the anti–civil war movement could be traced to late 1945/early 1946 when Chiang Kai-shek and his Nationalist government prepared to launch a total war against the communists. Having suffered years of economic hardship and political turbulence during the Sino-Japanese War, the Chinese public simply could not tolerate the news that the Nationalists would wage a new war. College students and liberal intellectuals were especially upset about this. Firmly believing that the Nanking government should devote itself to the task of reconstructing postwar China (specifically, developing the economy and reducing rampant corruption) instead of starting another war, campus activists (the great majority of whom were probably communist agents and communist sympathizers) and some of what the Chiang regime called extreme professors (such as Wen Yi-duo and Li Gong-pu; both of them were assassinated in 1946) brought students and progressive groups together to advance the idea that the Nationalists and the Communists must work out their disputes peacefully, cooperate with each other, and share political power — in other words, the Nationalists and the Communists should set up a joint government.

The continual street demonstrations, marches, protests, rallies, and strikes, almost without exception, provoked the Kuomintang's suppressive reaction. By assaulting and arresting students and certain intellectuals who firmly opposed the Chiang Kai-shek government's communist suppression policy, the Nanking authorities, at least in appearance, cracked down successfully on the anti–civil war movement in mid–1946.[40] The suppression of the anti–civil war movement, however, did not last very long. In 1947, when the armed struggle between the Nationalists and the Communists entered a new stage (in which the communist troops began to gain an upper hand), the anti–civil war movement reappeared.

The reemergent anti–civil war movement, just like the previous one, focused on the issue of restoring peace in China. On the other hand, since inflation had become one of the most serious social problems and threatened the livelihood of millions of urban residents during the civil war years, numerous people (including government employees) were forced to find ways to survive (one of the most common ones was to sell personal clothes or private belongings). Under this condition of great economic panic, an anti-hunger campaign (*fan ji e yun dong*) began to spread among teachers at public schools, lower-ranking government workers, and public agency staff who depended on state funds to make a living.[41] Anti-hunger also became another major appeal of the anti–civil war movement.

The 1947 anti–civil war and anti-hunger movements grew into a national movement in only a few days. Hundreds of thousands of students, college professors, school administrators, peasants, blue-collar workers, and unemployed people participated in the parades, protests, or strikes connected with the anti–civil war/anti-hunger movement to express their indignation over the status quo and to make demands. Facing such large-scale upheavals on campuses and in the streets, the Nanking authorities promptly sent armed forces to suppress all anti-government demonstrations, meetings, rallies, or strikes. In the eyes of decision makers in Nanking, these protest acts were nothing but rebellious and treacherous activities. Most senior high schools, technical colleges, and universities that student leaders or communist agitators of the anti–civil war/anti-hunger movement attended were besieged and searched by secret agents, policemen, and troops of the Kuomintang. Under this normless milieu in which the use of physical assaults had become legitimate, an unknown number of students, high school teachers, and college professors were beaten, intimidated, or harassed sexually by security agents and uneducated soldiers. Besides oral threats and physical menace, at least two thousand people (both men and women) were rounded up because of their connections with the anti–civil war movement (Zhang, 1996: 170–202).[42] All of these apprehended persons, aside from a few lucky ones who were released after paying ransoms or bribes, were sent to concentration camps in southern and southwestern China. In those camps, prisoners, as remarked earlier, became totally defenseless and helpless. It was not unusual that detainees were beaten to death shortly after they were imprisoned. In addition to physically weak persons, it was not rare that some mentally frail prisoners committed suicide due to the violent and sadistic actions of prison guards. No matter how people locked in death camps were treated and how they responded to ordeals, the fate of a portion of caged young females was unknown to their families after the Nationalist (or Blue) government was overthrown by the Red adversary in late 1949.

The repression of the anti–civil war cum anti-hunger movement inevitably caused many clashes between the KMT agents (including pro–Kuomintang occupational students, viewed by average students as the claws and teeth of the Nanking authorities) and the movement participants. Some of these conflicts turned out to be very bloody because heads of national security branches in Nanking consented tacitly, if not authorized, secret agents and military forces to use knives, grenades, machine guns, armored vehicles, or even tanks to attack demonstrators. As the casualties among those civilians who took part in the anti–civil war and anti-hunger movement continued to rise, movement leaders stopped temporarily mobilizing people to protest. The vanishing of the anti–civil war/anti-hunger movement did not mean that anti-government protests were dissolved. On the contrary, in late 1947 when Yu Zi-san, the chairman of the Student Autonomous Society of Zhejiang University, was arrested and executed secretly by secret agents, a new wave of demonstrations opposing the despotism of the Chiang Kai-shek regime began to come into sight.

Like previous anti–civil war movements, the parades, strikes, and other anti-government assemblies triggered by the Yu case centered on the issues of economic reconstruction, democratic reforms, and peaceful settlement of the dissension between the KMT and the CCP. However, since the former leaders (including underground communists) of the anti–civil war movement maintained the mobilization networks they had depended on earlier, the Yu incident attracted even more dissidents to join the rank of protests. The Nanking government was not able to crack down on this new wave of demonstrations until early 1948, probably because a substantial portion of the Kuomintang forces had been sent to Manchuria to fight against the communists. That gave organizers and followers of the Yu Zisan movement several months to discredit and demonize the Nanking government. In the face of widespread criticism and pervasive feelings of dissatisfaction, Chiang Kai-shek did not adopt a conciliatory policy to alleviate public condemnations and discontents. Instead, he chose the violent practice of oppression to put the legal holidays enjoyed by demonstrators to an end.

The hostility between anti-government protesters and the Nationalist regime reached its zenith in late 1948 and early 1949 when the People's Liberation Army defeated the Nationalist troops in three great battles: one in Manchuria, one in North China, and one in Central China. Given that these three decisive campaigns prepared the foundation for Mao Tse-tung and his Communist Party to overthrow the Nationalist rule and to transform China into a communist country, they stimulated the Nanking authorities to launch desperate arrests in big cities (especially in Beijing, Kunming, Nanking, and Shanghai). Because of these wide-ranging and random captures, another three to four thousand urban residents were taken away by security agents or undercover police without a formal trial. Some of these scapegoats for the breakdown of the Chiang Kai-shek government were executed publicly on the streets to warn city residents not to support the communists. The others were sent to labor corps or concentration camps to undermine the mass bases of the CCP. (Many of these unlucky detainees might have been slaughtered before Chiang Kai-shek and his regime fled to Taiwan in late 1949.)

In any event, it seems fair to conclude that during the civil war years, lots of political protesters became political prisoners because they took to the streets to challenge the authority (or to denounce the legitimacy) of the Nanking government. It was estimated that several thousand people got caught during the two-year interval from late 1945 to late 1947. In late 1948/early 1949, when signs of the collapse of the Nationalist regime became apparent, desperate apprehensions were carried out by security agents and armed police of the KMT. Three to four thousand more people were arrested and sent to concentration camps. Overall, at least twenty thousand troublemakers, ranging from teenagers to elders, were jailed during the final years of the Nationalist rule in China.[43]

IV. The Era of Refugee Regime (1950–1987)

For Chiang Kai-shek and his state managers, the breakdown of the Kuomintang regime appeared to be the least likely thing to happen in late 1945/early 1946 when the Nationalists, with the assistance of the American forces, began to take over former occupied areas and become the only legitimate regime of China. For Mao Tse-tung and his Red cadres, the establishment of a communist state in China probably was equally inconceivable because America had provided a huge amount of military aid to the Nanking authorities beginning in the early 1940s. That made it quite obvious that the communist troops could not match the military strength of the Nationalist armies (especially since the communist troops did not have any naval or air forces before 1949). No matter how confident or humble Chiang Kai-shek or Mao Tse-tung was, the final result of the armed struggle between the KMT and the CCP did reveal that military power was not the only factor that caused the fall of the Nationalist government and the victory of the communist insurgents in late 1949. Other non-military factors (such as hyperinflation and financial mismanagement in big cities, widespread corruption, bankruptcy of the peasant economy, political dictatorship, and student movements) also played a significant part in the rise and decline of these two rival camps. In this regard, since Chiang Kai-shek put all his stakes on the military side and believed that he could overcome the communist challenge exclusively by military superiority, the military setbacks of the Chiang forces in late 1948 and early 1949 clearly indicated that the Chiang dynasty in China was doomed to end.

The disastrous experiences endured by the Nationalists during the civil war years unquestionably taught Chiang Kai-shek some bitter lessons. These lessons stimulated Chiang to reform the security, party, and military apparatuses of the Kuomintang regime in Taiwan in the early 1950s when the Korean War was in progress.[44] With these political and military renovations, along with the Truman administration's resumption of economic and military aid to Taiwan, the highly unstable Chiang government luckily could recover gradually from the immense military losses of 1948 and 1949. The disappearance of an otherwise almost certain communist invasion therefore allowed the Nationalists to secure their governing status in Taiwan. All of these dramatic developments, shortly after the Korean War, gave the Taipei authorities the power and economic/military resources to essentially turn Taiwan into a state. Furthermore, since Chiang Kai-shek was the only political strongman on the island,[45] Taiwan was ruled as an authoritarian country. This repressive political atmosphere did not change fundamentally until 1987 when martial law was lifted. (Although political control became less rigid after Chiang passed away in 1975, Taiwan was still a police state under the reign of Chiang Ching-kuo, Chiang Kai-shek's older son and successor.)

The first measure taken by Chiang Kai-shek and his state managers to secure the supreme position of the Nationalist Party in Taiwan during the 1950s was to freeze all the civil rights–related articles stipulated in the Constitution of the Republic of China (ROC). That rendered the Constitution of the ROC (the framework of which was patterned after Sun Yat-sen's idea of a five-branch system of government) a hollow and worthless instrument in defending human rights. Put more explicitly, the Constitution of ROC was modeled on the U.S. Constitution (Copper, 1996: 92).[46] Therefore, it includes articles concerning the protection of the basic rights of the citizens. For instance:

Article Eight stipulates that, except criminal suspect(s) who were caught at a criminal scene, no citizens of the ROC can be arrested and incarcerated randomly by law enforcement authorities.

Article Nine specifies that, with the exception of servicemen, no civilians of the ROC will be tried by the military court.

Articles Ten to Fourteen point out that citizens of the ROC have the freedoms to travel, deliver a speech, lecture, publish, communicate, exercise religious belief, and associate.

Articles Fifteen and Sixteen state that citizens of the ROC have the right to live, work, keep private property, and make appeals as well as file lawsuits.

All of the above-noted articles, virtually without exception, were suspended in 1949/1950 when the great majority of defeated Nationalists arrived in Formosa. What replaced these civil rights–related articles of the ROC Constitution were the so-called Temporary Provisions Effective during the Period of National Mobilization for Suppression of the Communist

Rebellion (Copper, 1996: 85), and at least sixteen emergent rules, judicial precedents/interpretations, decrees, and executive orders (Tien, 1989: 108).[47] By giving the panic-stricken Chiang regime power to deal with all possible dangerous situations, these provisional laws successfully granted Chiang Kai-shek and his government absolute and unlimited authority: They were above the law. In this political environment of hard authoritarianism, the civil society of Taiwan was put under close military control throughout the 1950s and 1960s: no students or peasants were allowed to initiate (let alone to join) anti–Kuomintang demonstrations, parades, and protests; no workers were approved to organize labor unions or to strike; no entrepreneurs were permitted to establish companies related to the mass media (especially newspapers); no publishers or academic institutions could publish books about Marxism or socialism; no writers who wanted to publish a book (whether fiction or nonfiction) or drama/film script were exempt from state censorship; no civilians who wished to change their residences could do so without registering at local police stations; no civilians could go abroad without passing strict family background inspections; and, most important of all, no people were permitted to organize an opposition (or Taiwanese-directed) party.[48]

After enacting martial law and contingent regulations to justify a military rule on Taiwan in 1950, the Chiang government took actions to reorganize and expand security apparatuses. These reorganization and expansion practices (see the next paragraph), in just two to three years, refurnished secret agents and their informants with claws and teeth to terrorize people. With such roaring lions patrolling almost every corner of Taiwan's society (especially on campus and within armed forces), Taiwan became a politically quiet, culturally destitute, and intellectually docile society during the 1950s and 1960s.

As the previous three sections have shown, the Nationalist government's security apparatuses before 1950 were composed of two major organizations: the Military Commission's Bureau of Investigation and Statistics (MCBIS) and the Central Executive Committee's Bureau of Investigation and Statistics (CECBIS). Despite the fact that they could not get along with each other very well, these two secret service authorities were believed widely to be the chief plotters and perpetrators behind numerous cases of assassination, massacre, and political imprisonment in mainland China in the 1930s and 1940s. These outstanding capacities and trainings in purging enemies were extremely valuable for the Kuomintang at large and President Chiang Kai-shek in particular because the political situation of Taiwan (Formosa) in 1949 and early 1950s was remarkably precarious.

It was necessary for the Nationalist leaders to depend on the special talents possessed by secret agents to eliminate the communist elements on Formosa (who otherwise would serve as the liaison agents and agent provocateurs for the People's Liberation Army). Based on this policy of using secret service agencies to maintain social order and to consolidate the power of the Nationalist regime in Taiwan, both the MCBIS and the CECBIS experienced significant organizational adjustments.

First, the MCBIS was renamed *bao mi ju* (the Bureau of Secrecy Preservation or BMJ) in 1946.[49] Then, in the mid–1950s, *bao mi ju* was reorganized as the Military Intelligence Bureau (MIB), which functioned as a subordinate department of the Ministry of Defense. Unlike its precedent organizations, the MCBIS and BMJ, the newly created MIB was no longer in charge of investigating and suppressing political opposition movements. Instead, the MIB's chief task focused on the transportation of Taiwan's underground agents to communist China to collect military intelligence, to sabotage communication and industrial facilities along coastal China, and, if possible, to assassinate members of influential communist cadres. In addition to these espionage and sabotage activities, the MIB was responsible for tracking down the underground radio stations operated by communist agents in Taiwan as well as managing the Kuomintang-affiliated intelligence stations in North America, Japan, Southeast Asia, and western Europe (Tang [Su], 1997).

As for the CECBIS, it was renamed the Bureau of Investigation (BOI) of the Republic of China. The Ministry of Internal Affairs (*nei zheng bu*) first served as its superior office. This organizational transformation, at least ostensibly, meant that the Bureau of Investigation was no longer a military organization (which otherwise tended to act in an overt, crude, or even barbarian fashion when it was enforcing a law or an executive order). But in reality, the BOI, just like the MIB, still enjoyed unbridled power because, in spite of working merely as an official institution among many government agencies, few government divisions could monitor, let alone regulate, its acts. Anyway, after being supervised by the Ministry of Internal Affairs for a short period of time, the Ministry of Judicial Administration (*si fa xing zheng bu*) became the immediate commanding department of the BOI. This hierarchical relationship, as just mentioned, was not truly meaningful (it was probably meaningful only in textbooks about public administration or human management) because the minister of the Ministry of Judicial Administration, as a civil official appointed by the political strongman (that is, president Chiang Kai-shek, 1950–1975, and chairman Chiang Ching-kuo, 1978–1988), did not have the authority to ratify or alter any policy related to national security. All he could do in regard to anticommunist endeavors was to endorse the actions of the BOI— (i.e., he would serve simply as a rubber stamp). Given that the BOI was granted the special authority to detect every dubious aspect of civil society, the position of the BOI was seldom challenged by administrative, economic, technical, and street-level bureaucrats. This invincible status allowed the BOI to utilize various means (house arrest, intensive stalking, kidnapping, midnight apprehension, and so on) to round up communist agents. For that reason, the BOI acted similarly to the U.S. Federal Bureau of Investigation during the Cold War.[50]

The reforms of the BMJ and the CECBIS, however, were just two of the most important steps taken by the Chiang regime to safeguard the security of the Kuomintang state in Taiwan. In addition to these two organizational rearrangements, three independent (but closely interconnected) national security units — namely, the Security Command of Taiwan Province (SCTP, or *tai wan sheng bao an si ling bu*); the Political Work Department (PWD, or *zheng zhi gong zuo bu*); and the Data Group of the Confidential Office of the Presidential Palace (DGCOPP, or *zong tong fu ji yao shi zi liao zu*)— were installed in the late 1940s and early 1950s. (The SCTP, PWD and DGCOPP were established respectively in 1949/1950, 1950, and 1950/1951.) Just like the above-noted Military Intelligence Bureau and the Bureau of Investigation, these supplementary national security authorities were the chief planners and implementers of Taiwan's national security policy. On the other hand, since these security/secret service organizations also enjoyed the unparalleled power of adjudication before martial law was lifted in 1987, the BMJ/MIB, the BOI, the SCTP (which was restructured as the Taiwan General Garrison Command in 1957), the PWD (which was expanded as the General Political Warfare Department in 1963), and the DGCOPP (which was upgraded as the National Security Agency in 1955) were called the *wu da qing zhi xi tong* ("great five systems of security agencies") of Taiwan (Sun, 1985: 53).[51]

From the angle of preventing the Chinese communists from taking over Taiwan, the "great five systems of security agencies" were without a doubt very successful (Sun, 1985: 52). However, as all of these security and intelligence agencies were watchdogs of state security and vigilantes of factors that might instigate mass movements, each of them had a long record of violating human rights. One of the institutional practices that allowed these agencies to keep national security a sacrosanct goal as well as to engage in deliberate arrests was the system of household registration. According to this system (established around 1952), each household had to keep a listing booklet called *hu ko ming bu*. In this booklet, the demographic characteristics (i.e., name, age, gender, occupation, and relationship with household head) of all permanent residents of a household were to be recorded accurately (and modified regularly). Local policemen would go to each household in their jurisdictional district once or twice every month (sometimes it was even more frequent) to see if any household head failed to obey the rule. Violators, needless to say, would be punished. In addition to household control, security offices (the Nationalist government called them personnel offices) were installed in all administrative institutions; political commissars were deployed in every military unit and academy; and military instructors were sent to all colleges and senior high schools. All of these population control and crime prevention measures, step by step, let security and secret service agents create an information storage system or a national data bank of allegiance intelligence.[52] With this system, the national security networks functioned as invisible filters. Tens of thousands of people were identified as hidden enemies (for instance, people who had allegedly been involved in communism-related activities or the Formosa Independence Movement) or conspirators (such as those who provided shelter to political radicals) because they could not pass through the seemingly ubiquitous security webs.

Simply speaking, during the autocratic years (especially during the 1950s and '60s), the actions and/or social relationships of almost every person (older than sixteen years old) were screened every day in Taiwan. By virtue of this oppressive political environment, secret agents and security officers (including plain-clothes police and informants) tended to act like an omniscient and omnipresent Big Brother. At least 100,000 innocent Chinese Mainlanders and Taiwanese were arrested and kept in detention centers, military prisons, and political dogma-instructing reformatory schools before 1987 (as a rule, such prisoners would have to produce food for themselves and participate in obligatory or non-compensated community services). Of these victims of political imprisonment, some were merely working-class or peasant women. Yet they were regarded as revolutionaries or communist-organized guerrilla forces because security agents, by making up evidence, claimed that these women had joined the communist-led February 28 Uprising of 1947. This absurd situation can be exemplified by the *Lu Ku* (the Deer Cave) incident of 1952 (Zhang & Gao, 1998; Zhang & Chen, 2000). In addition to women of the grassroots, some female "rebels" were actresses or singers (Dai, 1998: 201–220). Technically, these art workers should have enjoyed an autonomous/undisturbed working environment because their jobs involved innovation of ideas, creation of cultural capital, and cultural exchange (for instance, introducing fashions from overseas, especially from the U.S., into Taiwan). But in reality, just like government or corporation employees they were required to follow numerous rules and stipulations when they were performing. Since some of these performers were not cautious enough in staying away from red elements (for instance, singing songs that implied communism or interacting with movie producers or directors from communist countries, specifically China), certain female entertainers (particularly less famous ones) were imprisoned and treated like true criminals.

If art workers (none of them could make the Nationalist government vulnerable) were not immune from political imprisonment, then business and factory owners (particularly affluent ones) tended to face much higher risk of getting into legal troubles for these entrepreneurs, at least in theory, could use their financial resources to sponsor anti-government acts. This situation can be exemplified by the case of Wu Han Grand Hotel, the largest in Taipei in the 1950s. In 1959, one of the hotel employees was found dead inside the building. While this event was proved by forensic experts to be an accident, agents of the Bureau of Investigation (who wanted to take over the hotel to enjoy free lunch) declared that this incident was a political murder. Based on this prearranged ruling, the hotel owner, his wife, and several others were sent to jail on charges of homicide. The hotel, as agents of the BOI expected, formally became a property of the government after years of closure (Huang, 1995).

In any event, hundreds of thousands of women and men (whether they were Chinese Mainlanders or Taiwanese) were accused of being redheads (communists) during the Chiang Kai-shek/Chiang Ching-kuo epoch. With so many victims of political imprisonment who could not prove their innocence by means of legal channel, several lawyers, magazine editors, and publishers, in the late 1970s when the political environment of Taiwan seemed to have become less oppressive, decided to break political taboos to assist political victims in acquiring the compensation they ought to get. One of the most important actions taken by such human rights activists was to mobilize people to take part in the *mei li dao* (Formosa Parade or March) held in Kaohsiung in December 1979. It was the first demonstration that drew tens of thousands of people (the Kuomintang government called these participants rioters) in martial law Taiwan,[53] so the security agencies of the KMT, needless to say, paid close attention to this illegal gathering. Soon more and more people attended mass meetings to listen to speeches about the poor human rights records of the Nationalist regime and the illegitimate ruling status of the Chiang government. President Chiang decided to use extraordinary means to solve this great crisis. With such a determination to suppress the Formosa March, thousands of well-equipped military police forces were dispatched to Kaohsiung to subdue "rioters" (Xin Tai Wan Yan Jiu Wen Jiao Ji Jin Hui, 1999). After this insurrectionary event was quelled, all movement organizers were arrested and treated like felons. Then, just like Aung San Suu Kyi and her backers in contemporary Myanmar, all of these criminals were sentenced and locked in jail for years. Two of the most famous and probably luckiest ones were Annette Lu and Chen Ju; the former became the first female vice president of the Republic of China in 2000 and the latter was elected as the first female mayor of Kaohsiung city in 2006.

Based on the statements above, it seems fair to conclude that nearly all (female) political prisoners in martial law Taiwan, like their counterparts in mainland China, had to engage in unpaid or exceedingly exploitative jobs after they were confined. Besides hard labor, political prisoners would, more often than not, experience total isolation and illegal violent acts (including murder). This dangerous living environment, together with the political culture dictating that security agents of the Nationalist government would destroy confidential documents or fabricate personal records whenever necessary (these cover-up practices would, in one way or another, prevent family members/friends of certain political prisoners who died by accident in prison from questioning the authorities or finding out the true cause of death), made political prisoners very liable to suffer indeterminate prison terms or to undergo fortuitous death. With this in mind, people locked in Kuomintang prisons for political reasons normally could not ascertain whether they could survive in detention centers/political schools or would be released after they had served the formal jail time. These prisoners had few channels to make contact with their families (let alone get in touch with the mass media or international human rights organizations). They could not obtain necessary treatments when they became critically sick, could easily get additional sentences if they violated certain regulations or orders (including offending prison guards), and were not allowed to keep a diary, memoir, or any written records (such personal documents usually were destroyed if found). Many women and men, during the de facto lawless years of the 1950s and 1960s, became missing after years of confinement.

The human rights practices of the Nationalist government began to improve in the 1970s and 1980s. Although no investigative writers report that the Taipei authorities waged a dirty war of the Argentine style (Lewis, 2002) against political radicals (such as sending death squads to clandestinely execute political liberals or slaying political dissidents in a flying airplane and dumping their bodies into the sea), certain people were still attacked, intimidated, or even assassinated by KMT-affiliated political extremists (Kaplan, 1992: 303–306). These underground criminal behaviors perpetrated by ultra–Nationalists (such as kidnapping women and girls with biological or common-law relationships with political dissenters and selling them to brothels) might be responsible for some cases of lost females.

The Communist State and Political Imprisonment, 1950–2000s

For Taiwanese in the new century, political imprisonment is no longer a sociopolitical taboo: not only has this term become out-of-date, if not a cliché, in public discourses, but nongovernment actors can advocate any political ideologies (as long as they do not lead to violent acts), criticize politics (particularly the performance of government officials, including the president), and publish books about the history of political persecutions linked with the White Terror without having to worry about midnight arrest or secret interrogation. Two of the key factors which made authoritarian Taiwan rapidly grow to be a joyful and tumultuous island are, first, political power was no longer dominated by a political strongman after president Chiang Ching-kuo died in January 1988; second, shortly after martial law was lifted in 1987, the previously mentioned great five systems of security agencies were either abolished, such as the Taiwan General Garrison Command, or reduced in power to the point that no security units can intervene in activities engaged in by civilians.

For people of modern China, the jubilant political atmosphere enjoyed by people of Taiwan is amazing and enviable: unlike democratized Taiwan (where freedom of speech has become a solid part of civil society, democracy), autonomy of ethnic minorities, and safeguard of human rights continue to be highly sensitive subjects, if not taboos, for the Beijing government. One index for this is that even communist China has become a capitalist society in the twenty-first century, American and European companies which have denounced the human rights records of the Chinese communists will either be attacked by Chinese hackers or lose commercial contracts which otherwise should be acquired by such corporations.

Since political policing remains prevalent and cannot be separated from civil life (Dutton, 2005), contemporary China, in spite of the fact that certain provinces (especially coastal ones, such as Jiangsu, Zhejiang, Fujian, and Guangdong) have experienced rapid economic development and urbanization in the past three decades, is still a transparent society: inside this society, individual privacy usually is not well respected. Accordingly, personal space (whether home or private office) can be visited or shared easily by outsiders (perhaps high-ranking government officials and military commanders are the only minorities who can enjoy privacy).

In addition to insufficient respect to personal life, civilians are monitored closely by national security agents, such as armed police, or street bureaucrats, such as *cheng guan*, or city patrol officers. Even workers in public transportation and tourism industries (for example, taxi drivers and hotel clerks) are responsible for reporting suspicious behaviors to the authorities. All of these social control measures make collective actions (particularly those related to political liberalization and social democratization) all but impossible. In other words, after the Tiananmen Square massacre, civil and political rights movements are still defined by the Beijing authorities as antisocial behaviors; hence, it is virtually impossible for such movements to arise, let alone grow.

I. Defensive Suppression[54]

In terms of stopping political dissidents from organizing democratic movements, all communist regimes in the modern world have resorted to mass execution or comparable measures to uproot "wicked" citizens (see Courtois et al., 1999). The Chinese communist regime was one of the leading actors in this regard because compared with its counterparts in Southeast Asia, Eastern Europe, and Central America, the Beijing government has a much longer history in slaying civilians. This feature can be divided into the following stages (see Table 2-1).

In the first place, before the Chinese Bolsheviks (whether they were described as social justice seekers, humanists, or fanatic Marxists) took over China in late 1949, Chinese communists were radical land reformers. Because of that identity, numerous landlords and those described as rich peasants were charged with felonious offenses and executed when the so-called Soviet areas were created in Jiangxi and adjacent provinces in the 1920s and 1930s (Bryon & Pack, 1992). After the People's Republic of China was established formally in October 1949, the communists, under the leadership of Mao Tse-tung, decided to redistribute farmland among peasants on a national scale so that no farmland owners or so-called upper-class farmers could continue to be masters (that is, no tenants or lower-class farmers would remain as serfs). Based on this designated course of action, the Land Reform Movement (LRM) was initiated in 1950.

TABLE 2-1. POLITICAL MOVEMENTS AND SUPPRESSIVE ACTS DIRECTED BY THE CHINESE COMMUNIST PARTY, 1950–2000s

Period	Political Movements	Major Targets of Suppression	Defensive or Offensive Suppression
1950–1953	1. Land Reform Movement 2. Oppression of Counter-revolutionaries Movement	1. Landlords/Wealthy Peasants 2. Counterrevolutionaries 3. "Nationalist Spies"	Defensive
1956–1957	Hundred Flowers Movement	"Right-Wing" Intellectuals	Defensive
1958–1961	The Great Leap Forward	Political Moderates	Defensive
1959–	Anti–Tibet Independence Movement	Supporters of the Free Tibet/ Tibet Independence Movement	Offensive, then Defensive
1966–1976	The Cultural Revolution	1. "Treacherous" Government Officials 2. Buddhist Monks/Nuns 3. Christians 4. Intellectuals 5. People Who Have Relatives Living Overseas 6. "Subversive" Red Guards	Defensive, then Offensive
1990s–	Anti–Uighur Independence Movement/Anti–East Turkestan Islamic Movement	Supporters of the Uighur Liberation Movement	Offensive, then Defensive
1990s–	1. Anti–"Evil Sects" Movement 2. Anti-Superstition Campaign	1. Members of Fa Lun Gong 2. Affiliates of "Evil" Cults 3. Christians	Defensive

*People such as journalists and investigative writers sent to "black jails" because they reported the corrupt acts of communist officials ought to be considered political prisoners as well. Nevertheless, such cases are omitted from this table because, according to available data, few female reporters were involved in these anticorruption efforts.

Aiming to eradicate every class enemy in rural areas, the Land Reform Movement was full of passion and wrath from its emergence. Thanks to this movement, several million peasants (including impoverished lease-holders who happened to be more affluent than certain tenants) were convicted of being local thugs or bloodthirsty property owners.[55] A large amount of these "bad elements" were shot to death in public shortly after they were found guilty in "accusation meetings" (Hsu, 2000: 653) attended by local villagers. For those lucky ones who were not executed right after the accusation meetings, they still could not escape from the shadow of death: such bullies or scoundrels, at the mercy of collective violence, usually were sent to labor camps located in extremely barren provinces, such as Qinghai and Heilongjiang, for thought reform or taken to uninhabited places, such as jungles, swamps, canyons, or deserts, for execution. No matter which penalty took place more frequently, innumerable people labeled as enemies of socialism went missing: people transported to the wild West and Manchuria, found it virtually impossible to enjoy high-quality medical services or to be paroled for medical reasons. Therefore, when they became seriously ill, suffered severe injuries, or were attacked by fierce creatures, the weaker and the less fortunate ones generally would lose their life silently and unnoticeably. Dying convicts, as a rule, would be buried or abandoned in the wilderness and, of course, no memorial services would be held. The bodies of people who were slain in unpopulated locations would, more often than not, be devoured by wild animals or obliterated by forces of nature (avalanche, earthquake, inundation, mudslide, and so on). That made the finding of these persons almost impossible after the Land Reform Movement.

The Land Reform Movement persisted for three years and has been listed as one of the most atrocious man-made calamities in the history of modern China (Rummel, 1994: 96–97). Regrettably, the incredible death tolls caused by this extreme agrarian reform did not prompt Mao Tse-tung and the other extremist communist leaders to adjust their radical-ism-oriented policy line. On the contrary, since the communist rulership was believed to have been challenged directly by liberalism and democratic movements (such as those in eastern Europe), Chairman Mao, starting in the mid–1950s, waged a series of political movements and suppression campaigns (see Table 2-1) to prevent the governing status of the communists (which had become virtually absolute after the LRM) from being questioned and undermined. Although they differed in duration, all of these crusades focused on eliminating individuals considered to be opponents of communism.

The first Mao-directed anti-rightist crusade was the Hundred Flowers Movement (HFM). During the brief period of this movement (approximately late 1956 to the summer of 1957), Chairman Mao claimed that his party welcomed suggestions from every stratum of society. As a result, people (especially intellectuals and artists) were encouraged strongly to advance their opinions about politics in general and the Communist Party in particular ("Let a hundred flowers bloom [and] let a hundred schools contend" [MacFarquhar, 1974: 51]). Under this atmosphere of freedom of speech, many scholars and well-educated people who had been absolutely forbidden from denouncing Leninism/Marxism since the communists came into power began to express "politically incorrect" opinions, whether overtly or privately (Domenach, 1995: 48–50). After enjoying the political right to condemn the communist regime for a few months, almost all persons who had publicly criticized the Communist Party (for instance, specifying the errors perpetrated by the Communist Party since 1950) were identified as rightists (that is, capitalism supporters) and arrested. (Chairman Mao called this drawing snakes out of their dens, meaning having people reveal their true political stance). Then all of these apprehended rightists, just like those peasants classified as people's enemies during the days of the Land Reform Movement, were either executed or sent to *lao gai* (reform through labor) camps. In those camps, prisoners experienced inhuman treatments such as nonstop interrogation, physical punishments, underfeeding, and inferior medical services (Wu & Vecsey, 1996). Unfortunately, since rightists behind bars were prohibited from contacting outsiders (especially Western reporters and investigators from Amnesty International), it was tremendously difficult for investigative writers to reveal the typical life of rightists in *lao gai* camps (or any Chinese gulags) and to estimate how many (female) prisoners died miserably in those mysterious environments.

Soon after the Hundred Flowers Movement, not only could politically improper voices be heard no more, but certain intellectuals who were fortunate enough to pass the allegiance trial of HFM began to publish articles and commentaries praising the success of the Land Reform Movement and the bright future of China. Under the inspiration of this political environment full of congratulations, praises, and gratitude, Chairman Mao and extreme left-wing communist leaders drew the following conclusions: first, the Chinese peasants have been liberated; second, the communists have gained extensive support in rural areas; and third, problems historically linked with unequal distribution of rural land (which had been the origins of social chaos for numerous generations), such as rural bankruptcy and blind migration of unemployed peasants, have been essentially solved. Based on these conclusions, Mao decided to mobilize peasants through the establishment of communes in order to transform China into an industrialized, modernized country. With this ambition, the Great Leap Forward (GLF) was launched in 1958.

In terms of pursuing the goal of turning underdeveloped China into a modernized nation, the success of the Land Reform Movement undoubtedly provided Mao and his right-hand men with concrete evidence that social problems (including inadequate industrialization) can be solved within a short period of time. (This also proved that the communists were much more competent and efficient than were traditional social reformers because the latter could not solve the long-term problem of land monopolization within three years.) In addition to having witnessed the power of revolutionary means in eliminating social inequalities, Mao and his orthodox Marxist cadres also believed steadfastly that the strength of Chinese peasants is unparalleled and unshakable. One typical example was that although the communist-directed peasant guerrillas possessed limited military resources and substandard weapons, they still defeated the well-equipped Nationalist troops in 1948 and 1949. These political experiences and beliefs caused Mao to treat peasant power as the shortcut, if not panacea, to realizing the objective of *chao yin gan mei* (that is, surpassing the United Kingdom and catching up with the United States in industrial/agricultural production and national power).

After choosing peasants as the engine behind express industrialization and modernization, Lysenkoism was adopted as the guiding principle or theoretical foundation for peasants' actions (Becker, 1997: 64–70). From the viewpoint of modern science, this decision is incredibly irrational and reckless. This is because the core concepts advocated by Russian biologist Lysenko (that agricultural crops can grow in extremely inferior environments and super grain production is feasible) in the 1930s and '40s totally violated the laws of nature (that is why Lysenko's viewpoints, at least before the 1950s, were not buttressed by any empirical example in the Soviet Union or any country in the world). Therefore, when radical and anti-intellectual notions derived from Lysenkoism (such as colossal grain production can happen overnight, the production of jumbo crops is possible, and prompt industrialization can be completed within an allocated period of time) were put into practice by Chairman Mao, the People's Teacher, the Chinese people were programmed to pay extremely high social costs for this utopian cum anti-nature movement.

Put simply, because Mao believed that China could become a modernized country within a designated short period of time, millions of peasants were required to take part in the jobs of increasing grain harvest and augmenting steel production. Both jobs, in just two to three years, caused great famines in several provinces because the agricultural methods suggested by Lysenko (such as close planting and deep plowing) were proved to be totally erroneous: not only could these methods not create extraordinary plants and animals, but immeasurable agricultural crops were devastated (Becker, 1997: 70–79). In addition, since numerous peasants were ordered to establish homemade furnaces to produce high-quality steel (these efforts ultimately were demonstrated to be futile as well), a million acres of farmland became badlands as most peasants were redirected from farming to the valueless job of refining steel. (This job also constituted a huge environmental disaster because peasants had to deforest to keep furnaces burning.)

Despite the hope of Chairman Mao and his fanatic henchmen that China could become a superpower within several years, the Great Leap Forward proved to be a cataclysm shortly after it was initiated: millions of people starved to death because of scarcity of food (before they died, lots of these refugees had nothing to eat but wild plants, bark, and earth); an unknown number of deceased babies and young children were eaten by their relatives in a desperate attempt to survive; tens (or hundreds) of thousands of young women and children (especially girls) were sold in places far from their hometown; and numerous children were abandoned and became homeless and/or drifters.

The calamities caused by the Great Leap Forward motivated a number of high-level communist officials to inspect famine-stricken provinces. After viewing a variety of horrible scenes, some moderate communist leaders (such as Liu Shao-qi and Deng Xiao-ping) began to carry out emergency plans in a few rural areas to rectify Mao's extremely irrational policies (Liu seemed to be especially popular among peasants in this regard). In addition to these remedial actions, certain university professors, writers, and art workers also criticized the raison d'être of the GLF (some of these cultural elites even suggested that Mao should be held responsible for the massive deaths brought about by his militant strategy of modernization). All of these revisionists or deviationists of orthodox Marxism and socialism, starting in 1960, made Mao believe that his leadership was shaky.

In an attempt to safeguard his ruling status and to make sure that China would continue to be the leader of the international communist movement and revolution,[56] Mao called several conventions and organized numerous public meetings from 1961 to 1965. At those conventions and meetings, Mao delivered speeches asserting that the task of turning China into a socialist society was far from being finished. Therefore, everybody must be dedicated to the holy mission of class struggle so that the peasants and the workers would not be governed by bloodthirsty bourgeoisie all over again. Under Mao's encouragement and sponsorship, the Cultural Revolution was launched in 1966.

From the perspective of social movements, the Cultural Revolution is a typical example of a collective violent and state-endorsed terrorist movement: from the time when this campaign became a routine part of Chinese society, everyone was required to hunt for class enemies. Since few people (including high-level government officials) were exempt from this Great Judgment, the Cultural Revolution, on the whole, revealed the following characteristics.

Mao used this revolution to purge his designated successor Liu Shao-qi as well as the other moderate communist cadres (these state managers appeared to have become more and more popular among the general public after the Great Leap Forward). To ensure that this clean-up crusade could develop into an institutionalized practice of annihilating betrayers of social-ism, Mao (among others) adopted two strategies. The first was that he organized students (particularly high school and university students) all over the country as Red Guards. (Mao's wife, Jiang Qing, called them the "Little Suns.") Then by defining the Cultural Revolution as a proletarian battle against propertied people, who were labeled as symbols of corrup-tion, exploitation, and social injustice, Mao, the "Great Helmsman," gave the Red Guards the authority to wipe out the "Four Olds" (namely, old cultures, old ideas, old customs, and old routines) on every campus as well as in public agencies. Under the full support of Mao and his hatchet men (among them Kang Sheng and the so-called Gang of Four), teenage stu-dents started to enjoy ten years of moral and legal holidays.

During the turbulent and frenzied years of the Cultural Revolution, the Red Guards had the power to tear down everything and to judge every person deemed an obstacle to change or innovation. Because of this author-ity, the Red Guards could do anything necessary (such as burning classic books and art pieces, destroying temples, demolishing historical buildings, and the like) to get rid of old or bad things and persons. The only exception was the unwritten but precise rule that they could not confront the People's Liberation Army, which was still under Mao's tight control. This nearly unrivaled status let the Chinese politics and society reveal the following features during the "Little Red Devil" years, 1966–1976:

First, given that the Red Guards were granted the jurisdiction to oust incompetent government officials (particularly Liu Shao-qi), almost all communist cadres labeled as pro-capitalism bureaucrats or opportunists — people who failed to show total commitment to the Great Leap Forward or earlier movements — were subject to political inspection. Since these inspections were rife with perjury, fabricated documents, and baseless accu-sations, numerous civil servants (including Liu Shao-qi and certain senior officials) were locked in squalid and isolated places, such as pig pens, cow sheds, or horse stalls. Not surprisingly, some of these ruling elites who had been turned into victims of political cleansing committed suicide due to spiritual pressure or died in places totally segregated from outside world due to deteriorating health problems.

In addition to inept state managers and street bureaucrats, innumerable Buddhist monks and nuns, Christians, intellectuals (artists, high school teachers, musicians, poets, university professors, writers, and the like), employees of national enterprises, and people with overseas connections were classified as *niu* (cow), *gui* (demon), *she* (snake), or *shen* (deity). Since these persons were regarded as social evils, the process of getting rid of these all too conspicuous enemies was extreme and appalling: tens of millions of "thugs" were humiliated publicly and beaten severely (often resulting in permanent injuries). Several million families were devastated when heads of household, as chief economic supporters, were detained or beaten to death. (This atrocity also resulted in millions of children becoming orphans, homeless, or drifters, especially vulnerable to human trafficking, the manipulation of beggar rings, slavery, and other criminal activities.) Finally, hundreds of thousands of professionals and scientists were sent to labor camps to do menial or dangerous jobs, as Wu's (1993) case clearly demonstrates.

As a progressive movement directed by Mao Tse-tung to remove his disloyal comrades from office, the Cultural Revolution gave students unprecedented authority to serve as crime investigators, political prosecutors, and judicial adjudicators. Under the terror reign of student politics, the legal system of China became totally chaotic: career judges and professional lawyers were replaced by students; student-managed courts and torture chambers were created nationwide; and different student groups, because of their self-governing status, could enact varieties of legal codes. All of these bizarre phenomena made political imprisonment a fact of daily life.[57]

After creating tons of political imprisonment cases and turning the sociopolitical affairs of China upside down for nearly a decade, the Red Guards began to fight frequently and fiercely against one another for political power in 1974 and 1975. As the political situation became more and more anarchic (which put China on the verge of revolution and directly threatened the ruling status of the Communist Party), the People's Liberation Army (PLA) was mobilized all over the country to suppress the Red Guards. Hundreds of thousands of the "Little Suns" were killed in direct battles with the PLA. The remaining "Little Red Devils," just like people whom they had persecuted, were sent to labor camps in barren regions.

Many of them never went back to mainstream society. Only a very small number of the former Red Guards were fortunate enough to escape to Hong Kong, Southeast Asia, or other areas.

If the previously mentioned movements represent efforts to suppress potentially defiant social members (including some communist cadres), then banning people from joining *Fa Lun Gong* (literally Wheel of Law Exercise) provides another example of defensive suppression. Founded by Li Hong-zhi in the early 1990s, *Fa Lun Gong*, at least in activity, is simply a recreation and research group: first, it allows people to get together to practice meditation, *tai chi chuan*, or *qi gong* (according to Li, the main purpose of these exercises is to help people stay healthy, instead of training people to be martial arts experts or street fighters); second, members can attend seminars to share their ideas about the Buddhist tenets taught by Li; and third, it can aid members to explore many complicated issues related to corporal existence or soul (for instance, aging, disease, karma, and transmigration). All of these trainings and studies are meant to improve quality of life. They do not involve political ideologies or contain serious political implications.

Although advocates and adherents of *Fa Lun Gong* unanimously argue that they are not promoting political doctrines and have nothing to do with politics, the Beijing authorities insist that *Fa Lun Gong* is far more dangerous and aggressive than its leaders would like to admit. This assertion contains two parts. First, public security officials maintain that *Fa Lun Gong* is an underground delinquent cult because besides practicing *tai chi* and *qi gong*, members are indoctrinated constantly with apocalyptic ideas. Since these future-oriented notions embrace millenarian messages (which will undermine the legitimacy of the communist government as the "lifespan" of the Beijing regime becomes predictable), *Fa Lun Gong* (which functions as an "enlightenment" movement) must be put down so that the general public will not be enticed to take part in anti-government activities (Chang, 2004: 46–50). In addition to spreading the rumor that the Chinese politics is going to change dramatically in the near future, Fa *Lun Gong*, as a well-structured entity, is considered a modern version of the rebellious cults of the nineteenth century (Chang, 2004: 51–58). To prevent *Fa Lun Gong* from evolving into an insurgent bloc like *Bai Lian Jiao* (the White Lotus Sect), *Tai Ping Tian Guo* (the Heavenly Kingdom of Great Peace), or *Yi He Tuan* (the Boxer), precautionary measures must be taken so that national security will not be threatened while social order can be retained.

Based on these appeals to higher loyalties (see Sykes & Matza, 1957), tens of thousands of people who have membership of *Fa Lun Gong* were apprehended in the 1990s and early 2000s. No one knows exactly how many of them were kept permanently in labor/concentration camps, detention centers, or prisons affiliated with mental hospitals. No one can decide precisely how many of these caged *Fa Lun Gong* members were beaten to death, either.[58] By the same token, many Christians and affiliates of "heterodox" religious societies/"evil sects" have been arrested in the past two decades. Many are still behind bars at the total mercy of the prison staff because they are accused of spreading "reactionary ideas" or engaging in "heretical/seditious activities" (see Chang, 2004: 124–158).

II. Offensive Suppression[59]

Compared to the above-noted exemplars of defensive suppression (which involve deliberate and methodical steps taken by the Beijing authorities to eliminate all possible class enemies and political opponents), cases of offensive suppression tend to be infrequent, if not uncommon, in the history of the People's Republic of China. One important reason for this is that political movements in the 1950s allowed the communists to wipe out tens of millions of conservatives and intransigents. That made armed struggle an unappealing course of action for political dissidents who wished to challenge the Beijing government in the past half century.

Although countrywide uprising has not occurred in communist China since 1950, popular unrest did take place in some regions. One of the most noteworthy ones was Tibet. As a protectorate of China since the seventeenth century, Tibet was a de facto independent state before 1950. This highly autonomous status did not change a great deal until 1957-58 when the conflict between the People's Liberation Army and Tibetan monks became increasingly intense. Shortly after new China was established in late 1949, Mao Tse-tung claimed that the Dalai Lama's politico-religious authority would be fully respected and that the aristocracy of Tibet will be kept intact. This assurance turned out to be merely lip service as Buddhist activities in East Tibet, starting in 1956, were policed tightly by the PLA. As a result of that policing, some monks tried to drive out the Chinese troops by launching guerrilla fights:

> Despite Mao's initial promise to respect Buddhism, the normal activities
> of the monasteries of Eastern Tibet were severely curtailed. Later they
> would be shut down, or blown to bits. Head lamas, monks, and nuns
> were publicly humiliated through forced fornication, torture, imprisonment,
> and execution.... A guerrilla was ensued [Dunham, 2004: 5].

In addition to clashing with monks, the political power of Tibetan nobles (most of them were landlords as well) was replaced step by step with Chinese representatives or counselors sent by Beijing. In the end, these power switch measures allowed the communist authorities to carry out the land reform program in East Tibet. The outcome of putting this project into practice, like the one implemented in 1950 (see above), was destructive:

> Chinese land reforms in Eastern Tibet included the catastrophic replanting of barley crops (Tibet's most important agricultural staple) with the Chinese-favored wheat. The crops failed, and approximately 500,000 Tibetans ... starved to death as a result. It was the first time in recorded history that Tibet had experienced famine [Dunham, 2004: 5].

Given that land reform brought nothing but death and crisis to their communities, tens of thousands of Tibetans (many of them were women) gathered at the foot of the Potala in March 1959 to voice disapproval of Beijing's suppressive policy (Dunham, 2004: 280). This mass rally in just a few days evolved into a large-scale armed struggle in Lhasa. That triggered the Beijing government to dispatch hundreds of thousands of PLA troops into Tibet. With the appearance of these people's troops, tens of thousands of Tibetans fell victims to arbitrary arrest and random killings and were not seen again (Jackson, 2004).

After Tibet formally became a part of China in 1959, Tibetans who dared to propose the idea of Tibetan independence in public or to organize separatist movements were classified as "rebels" and became targets of the purge. Since then, many of these rebels, or what Harff and Gurr (2003: 19) called "ethnonationalists" (including the Dalai Lama), have taken refuge in India and adjacent countries. It is virtually impossible for the Indian government (as well as other administrations involved) to manage or supervise effectively these floating populations or, from the Chinese viewpoint, missing persons.[60]

Suppressing the Tibetan independence movement is still a principal job for the Beijing authorities in the twenty-first century. Another analogous task is the repression of the East Turkestan Independence Movement in Xinjiang. As an area occupied by the Uighur people and miscellaneous ethnic groups (the imperial Chinese government called them barbarians) for over a thousand years, Xinjiang's self-sufficient and self-governing situation was not ended until the mid-eighteenth century, when a frontier war was launched by Emperor Qianlong (r. 1735–1796). After that war, Xinjiang became a province of China and remained a tranquil place for the next one hundred and fifty years. Xinjiang's subordinate status changed considerably after the Republican revolution of 1911 as warlords became the main players in China's politics (see previous section). As a result of this transformation, Xinjiang, step by step, turned out to be a substantially independent region after the Manchurian emperor in Beijing was deposed by the Nationalists in 1911.

The self-determining and self-regulating status of Xinjiang was maintained by warlords (such as Sheng Shi-cai) and international forces (especially Russia/the Soviet Union) from the 1910s to the 1940s. These political and economic adventurers did not lose the opportunity to preserve their power or to hunt treasures until 1949 and 1950 when the newly established communist regime sent hundreds of thousands of PLA, armed police, and street bureaucrats into Xinjiang. Because of these military-cum-political actions directed by Chairman Mao, the warlord-cum-international politics of Xinjiang became history in a brief time. That allowed Beijing to reclaim its sovereignty over Xinjiang and to retransform this massive and spectacular land into China's westernmost domain and nuclear test site.

While Xinjiang has been reincorporated into China for more than half a century, the subsequent factors still make modern Xinjiang a troublesome district for Beijing:

In the first place, like the territories possessed by Native Americans before European incursions of the nineteenth century (the areas now called Arizona, California, New Mexico, and Oregon), Xinjiang has been the home of Uighur people (as well as miscellaneous other racial/ethnic groups) for over two thousand years. Accordingly, the Beijing authorities always have to take measures (such as encouraging Han settlers or interracial/interethnic marriage) to turn this racially and ethnically heterogeneous area into a society dominated by the Han Chinese (these efforts can also be found in Tibet). In addition to racial/ethnic diversities, the Uighur communities are shaped by the Islamic culture (which appears to be incompatible with Confucianism, the dominant philosophy and orthodox thought of the Han society, because the former is God-focused while the latter is man-centered). Thus, the process of converting Uighur Muslims into a submissive part of a gigantic politico-economic entity is full of resentment and hostility. (The Uighur Muslims tend to believe that this process of assimilation is a form of cultural suppression or ethnic purification.)

Political geography is another factor that prevents the Uighur settlements from totally becoming Sinicized: as just mentioned, the Han Chinese and the Uighur population belong to two different racial/ethnic and religious groups. For that reason, inhabitants of the Uighur Autonomous

Region and residents of Central Asian countries have much more demographic and cultural features in common than those shared by the Han Chinese and their Uighur counterparts (i.e., the former groups look far more like brothers and sisters than the latter parties because in terms of religious belief/custom and physical appearance, the social distance among Uighur and Central Asian Muslims obviously is much shorter than that involving the Han Chinese and the Uighurs). All of these social and religious similarities make Afghanistan and adjacent Islamic countries perfect sanctuaries for Uighur persons forced to leave their native land due to political and/or religious causes (in this regard, Afghanistan and adjoining Islamic states can function as transfer countries for activists of the East Turkestan Independence Movement, if these dissidents plan to head for Turkey/Europe; or as safe havens for Uighur refugees).

Finally, in terms of economic development, South Xinjiang is one of the poorest areas in China. This economically backward situation not only turns Aksu and neighboring regions into a major source of female trafficking (see Chapter 6), but numerous Uighur youths are reduced to what Harff and Gurr (2003: 19) called ethnoclasses.[61] With such an economically inferior status, along with the seemingly irreconcilable racial differences and ethnic prejudices, it is not surprising that anger and anti–Beijing sentiments spread widely among the Uighurs. These exceptionally discontented feelings could be observed time after time in the 1990s and early 2000s when inter-ethnic/interracial conflicts, which led to a series of urban riots and mass demonstrations, became more and more intense (see Tyler, 2004: 155–180). All of these furious passions motivate some Uighur militants (or extremists) to join the ETIM (the East Turkestan Islamic Movement) or other similar organizations to establish a sovereign Islamic Republic of Uighuristan. Since these freedom fighters are functional in giving the Uighur public an image that the status quo of Xinjiang can be/ will be changed, the ETIM and the other equivalent associations, at least among Uighur exiles living in the Middle East or Europe, are greeted fervently.

To contain the proliferation of all separatist organizations (including the ETIM, tens of thousands of Uighur teachers, cultural workers, civil rights campaigners, or even businessmen were arrested by Chinese security agents in the past decade. Of these Uighur rebels taken to police stations or detention centers, some might be fined and locked in jail for a few days or weeks if they do not have any criminal records of getting involved in anti–Chinese or pro-independence activities. On the contrary, if persons are found to be recidivists (that is, they had once engaged in separatist activities), then these habitual offenders are very likely to experience what Tyler (2004: 173) called judicial shortcuts:

> Judicial shortcuts are common ... in China. Current practice includes: arresting suspects' families, jailing suspects without trial, dispensing with defence lawyers, reaching verdicts in secret "adjudication committees," handing down long sentences for political dissidents ... and hunting down pregnant women (Tyler, 2004: 173).

From the angle of human rights, all of these practices of judicial contingencies are means of social control outside the law. They are used by the Xinjiang authorities to warn and to retaliate against those Uighurs who attempt to alter the status quo. Since all of these terrorist techniques are inherently ruthless and cold-blooded, thousands of Uighur demonstrators and campaigners, like their Tibetan counterparts, have gone missing. This condition can be exemplified by the Yining riot of 1997 (see Tyler, 2004: 168–172).

In any event, numerous missing persons cases in Xinjiang are pending. As it is hardly possible that the public security and prison authorities of Xinjiang will disclose information concerning vanishing Uighur insurgents, the criminal justice agencies of Xinjiang, in the eyes of countless Uighur civilians, seem to have become symbols of injustice. This may explain why Xinjiang is still racked by ethnic conflicts in the 2000s (the most recent one took place in the summer of 2009), despite the fact that the ETIM and certain radical Uighur groups have been classified by the United States as terrorist organizations after the September 11, 2001, attacks on the U.S.

Concluding Remarks

Political imprisonment is an oppressive practice sponsored or directed by state managers (particularly security authorities). Since this measure is a form of secret violence (just like the comfort women system; see Chapter 5), people detained for political reasons always are extremely vulnerable to police brutality and sadistic acts committed by security officials.

Based on the Chinese/Taiwanese cases examined in the previous sections, the characteristics and implications of political confinement can be summarized as follows:

First, before political imprisonment can become an institutionalized measure of social control, it is necessary for political circumstances to display a certain degree of stability. An exceedingly turbulent political milieu (such as countries ruled by multiple regimes because of civil war) will make state managers unable to engage in political policing.

Second, according to Schafer (1974: 13), almost all societies "have a version of some ideal state of affairs, sometimes expressed in religious terms, at other times in secular ones." That means political prisoners are those people who have committed (or are believed to have the motivation to commit) behaviors that deviate from certain political/religious ideals. Given that this deviation will undermine the legitimacy of a political system, political prisoners, more often than not, are treated as public enemies (this may explain why political prisoners normally will get harsher treatments than average criminals).

Third, compared to governments of liberal and less repressive societies, ruling bodies of close and (highly) regulated countries usually will convert certain ideology or dogmatic thought into a sacrosanct behavioral yardstick. This criterion not only makes people of authoritarian/totalitarian states constantly face the risk of being labeled as outlaws if they fail to show sheer allegiance to the status quo, but persons rounded up for involving in antigovernment activities have few opportunities to avoid arbitrary violence and indefinite sentence.

Finally, although males, in terms of quantity, tend to be far more numerous than females, female political prisoners (no matter whether they are scapegoats or have engaged in antigovernment activities in the past) seem to face a higher probability of disappearing in prisons than their male counterparts. This gender inequality might be connected to the facts that females, generally speaking, are physically weaker than males and are the chief targets of sexual assault (in other words, females tend to be more vulnerable than men when they face atrocious acts). With this in mind, it seems plausible to infer that in dictatorial/oppressive countries, cases of women who go missing from prisons, state-controlled mental hospitals or sweatshops, and other institutions would be more prevalent than those of males.

CHAPTER 3

Slain Baby Girls

Female infanticide or "gendercide" (see *The Economist*, 2010, March 6: 11) has been practiced in China for more than two thousand years. This social custom, like its counterpart in modern India or Pakistan, is generally considered a by-product of patriarchy and sexism. It is believed to be inseparable from the cultural ideologies of gender differences (in terms of intelligence, physical strength, and "reliability" of work), gender hierarchy (that is, male superiority vs. female inferiority), and gender preference (Fairbank, 1992: 18–19). Because of these prejudices, which endorse male domination, male chauvinism, and the idea that females are inherently weak or inferior, it is estimated that at least five million of unborn or newborn baby girls have been slain every year in Greater China in the past thirty years.

In this chapter, girl infanticide will be examined within the paradigm of homicidal behavior (the selection of this paradigm is based on the fact that infanticide involves the killing of a totally defenseless person). This paradigm, according to the *Crime Classification Manual*, or CCM (Douglas et al., 1997: 17–18), can be divided into four themes or fields of study:

1. Criminal enterprise homicide is triggered by material rewards. It includes eight types of murderous behaviors.
2. Personal cause homicide is caused by interpersonal conflict or negative emotions. It comprises nine varieties of killing acts.
3. Sexual homicide is provoked by anomalous sexual desires. Its form can be organized, disorganized, mixed, or sadistic.
4. Group cause homicide is ignited by an emergent communal norm. This category embraces cult murder, extremist murder, and group excitement homicide.

All of these typologies and relevant murderous behaviors can be seen in Table 3-1 on page 72.

TABLE 3-1. TYPOLOGIES OF KILLING BEHAVIORS

Criminal Enterprise Homicide	Personal Cause Homicide	Sexual Homicide	Group Cause Homicide
Contract Killing	Erotomania-Motivated Killing.	Organized Sexual Homicide	Cult Murder
Gang-Motivated Murder	Domestic Homicide (which includes spontaneous domestic homicide and staged domestic homicide)	Disorganized Sexual Homicide	Extremist Murder (which includes paramilitary extremist murder and hostage extremist murder)
Criminal Competition Homicide	Argument/Conflict Murder	Mixed Sexual Homicide	Group Excitement Homicide
Kidnap Murder	Authority Killing	Sadistic Murder	
Product Tampering Homicide	Revenge Killing		
Drug Murder	Nonspecific Motive Killing		
Insurance/Inheritance-Related Death	Extremist Homicide (which includes political extremist homicide, religious extremist homicide, and socioeconomic extremist homicide)		
Felony Murder (which includes indiscriminate felony murder and situational felony murder)	Mercy/Hero Homicide		
	Hostage Murder		

Based on the nomenclature suggested by the CCM for homicide, it seems appropriate to assert that the underlying motivations of all homicidal acts are either related to economic/instrumental incentives (that is, the pursuit of economic benefits/material rewards) or expressive/psychological urges (that is, the manifestation of emotional factors).

Inspired by the idea that murderous behaviors can be instrumental or expressive, girl infanticide will be examined in the instrumental or expressive contexts in this chapter. Two central questions will be analyzed:

• Why and how do economic considerations or material advantages motivate certain mothers or parents to destroy their infant girl?
• Why and how do emotional factors (which can be negative ones, such

as anger and anxiety, or positive ones, like pity and compassion) stimulate certain mothers or parents to slay their baby girl?

After these two contexts have been inspected, some remarkable social problems generated by girl infanticides will be summarized.

Female Infanticide As an Instrumental Homicide

Killing baby girls has a very long history in China. As early as the Zhou dynasty (1045–256 B.C.), this crime appeared to have already been perpetrated (Mungello, 2008: 4–5). While no statistics (official or unofficial) are available regarding the demographic features and prevalence of girl infanticide before the twentieth century, it seems that this secret execution is strongly related to certain economic institutions. One such factor is the dowry culture, which, in pre-modern China, not only could ruin a working-class family; it also could be a financial disaster for a wealthy household.

I. Dowry Culture

According to Hudson and den Boer (2004: 136), the dowry culture had become customary in China as early as the Song dynasty (960–1279). No matter how institutionalized this custom was during the Song years, it is apparent that this culture became formalized and assumed more power after the Song era. This evolution eventually culminated in the Qing dynasty (1644–1911), when parents of brides (regardless of their socio-economic status) were required to offer handsome gifts to their in-laws. One deep-rooted tradition in Chinese society tended to play an extremely significant role in keeping the dowry culture normal during the Qing period, Republican years, and other ages: the social necessity of maintaining good interpersonal relationships.

For traditional Chinese, sustaining harmonious interpersonal relationships is not merely an expression of etiquette. What is far more critical is that these efforts allow people to survive in a highly bureaucratic or even corrupt society. More specifically, China was a highly authoritarian society. Therefore, authority figures, whether they were street bureaucrats or high-ranking government officials, always enjoyed unparalleled power in local events and national affairs. That means traditional Chinese society was ruled by a small group of political power holders, intellectual elites-cum-civil servants, and military commanders. In this society, people who did not enjoy political power (or did not possess sufficient political power) always faced the risks of wrong accusation, random arrest, indefinite incarceration, or even the death penalty. Under this exceedingly autocratic environment, average people as well as certain government officials (especially middle- and lower-ranking ones) must maintain or construct good social connections so that they can find help or seek asylum whenever they encountered a legal or political trouble, financial crisis, or natural disaster. To preserve or to form legally valuable and/or economically beneficial social ties, however, was a highly skilled task. It required people who believed they were not powerful enough to employ procedurally subtle but psychologically impressive methods to obtain the friendships they were looking for. One such method was gift-offering.

Like modern American enterprises that evaluate the demographic background of every job applicant before hiring someone, people of traditional China also had to consider someone's socioeconomic status if a goodie was going to be given to that individual. That means gift-givers in Old China must take components like social occasions, collective parties, and possible societal reaction(s) into account if they decided to take actions to create a friendship. These efforts might allow gift-givers to realize their intended goal(s) and to save face if all (or at least most) relevant interpersonal networks are taken good care of. In contrast, if the gift presented was deemed to be socially or culturally unacceptable (whether in quantity or quality), then not only would the givers lose face, it is also very likely that such persons would become stigmatized: they might be labeled as foolish, irresponsible, or shameful, or even bring troubles upon themselves.

Simply speaking, gift-conferring behavior was a sophisticated art and culture in Old China: not only was this behavior considered a moral imperative (Yang, 1994: 141) as well as a symbol of "social honor and self-respect" (Yang, 1994: 141), it also entailed delicate information, implications, and/or (economic) interest which could not be discerned easily by outsiders (this situation, to an extent, still holds true in present-day China). Given that gift-offering was a functional, strategic, or goal-oriented behavior in traditional China, it was utilized by people to consolidate, extend, or repair interpersonal relationships on numerous occasions. One such occasion was the engagement/marriage ceremony.

Just like its counterpart in modern American society, engagement or marriage was a remarkably vital event in China. As a result, parents always had to follow strictly a complicated set of procedures and rituals for a daughter's or son's engagement or marriage ceremony (particularly for a daughter). It was crucial for parents to hew to the requirements of the dowry culture so that they and their daughter would not become laughingstocks among neighbors and in-laws. It was not uncommon that newly married women were physically and emotionally abused by their in-laws because their parents did not or could not fulfill all the obligations designated by the dowry culture; inability to bring satisfactory amount of money and goodies to the groom's household was probably the most serious offense. Some married women even committed suicide, believing the humiliations they faced would never end.

Under this enormous social pressure, the culture of dowry actually functioned like a "procrustean bed": all parents, regardless of their socioeconomic position, must stick to established social standards and publicly recognized norms when they held a wedding for their daughter. Since these standards and norms, no matter how arbitrary or even ludicrous they might look, had tremendous social control power in punishing people who failed to meet the minimal requirements, low-income parents always had to find ways (such as making loans) to increase their financial height so that they could fit the procrustean bed and avoid social sanctions. For parents in wealthy families (who, more often than not, had to maintain a private relationship with local officials to safeguard their property), meeting the expectations of dowry culture was a big challenge too. This was due to the fact that these fat cats always were expected to hold a luxurious wedding ceremony whenever their daughter got married. Accordingly, it was not unusual that these upper-class people lost a certain (or even a significant) portion of their assets after holding a century wedding (which often were attended by local ruling elites, who usually got a handsome amount of gifts as gratitude; and numerous unheard-of relatives or friends, who came to help and celebrate).

In brief, holding a wedding ceremony in traditional China (especially during the period of the eighteenth century to the 1940s) was a time-consuming and costly matter. So, despite the fact that the preliminary purpose of the dowry custom was to help the bride (as well as the groom) to adapt to a new environment, this social practice, at least in the past three to four hundred years, evolved into an arena of exhibiting personal honor. People had to follow only one rule: they must show off their wealth to demonstrate their love for their daughter. In the same way, only through the display of individual riches could sincere interpersonal relationships be established. All of these mores left parents (including low-income ones) few spaces in negotiating the dowry they had to pay.

As the dowry culture turned out to be nothing but a catastrophe of spending all one's personal property, baby girls naturally became more and more undesirable: from the viewpoint of economic benefit or financial deficit, infant girls are simply *pei qian huo* (literally commodities that are doomed to cause monetary losses) or a short-term family member who could not bring in any fortunes but used up family resources instead. Based on these gender prejudices (which, from the perspective of symbolic interactionism, are self-fulfilling prophecies), many parents and grandparents did not want to have a daughter/granddaughter. If they did have a daughter/granddaughter, they would either donate the baby to a household or brothel looking for a female member or simply put the infant girl to death.[1] If the latter option was chosen, then the subsequent five methods would be frequently employed (Mungello, 2008: 9, 57):

- drowning: plunging the head of a newborn girl into a container loaded with water and keeping her head underwater until she died by suffocation[2]
- choking with ashes: pushing the head of a newborn baby girl into a container filled with ashes and keeping her head under the ashes until she died by suffocation[3]
- starving to death: supplying no food to a newborn girl, or if the girl was a toddler or older, locking her up in a chamber, without water and food[4]
- throwing the baby girl into a river or lake[5]
- abandonment: leaving a newborn baby girl in wilderness, such as an unpopulated mountainous area, and letting wild creatures "take care" of her.[6]

In addition to these appalling behaviors, strangulation and burial alive were also employed in putting an infant girl to death (Mungello, 2008: 2). All of these unspeakable behaviors in getting rid of young females (whether they were infants, toddlers, or even older girls) not only precipitated opponents of the practice to issue publications (in the form of broadsheets, pamphlets, flyers, morality books, and so on) concerning karmic retribution to warn people of the horrible outcomes of committing girl infanticide (Mungello, 2008: 14–44), these homicidal behaviors also turned numerous households into killing fields. Due to these practices, millions of young girls disappeared wordlessly and covertly.

II. One-Child Policy

While the influence of the dowry culture has lost its significance in producing missing female babies in present-day China, the behavior of killing infant girls (including unborn ones whose gender has been confirmed) for economic reasons, unfortunately has not vanished. More specifically, girl infanticide, starting in the late 1970s, seems to have become more and more popular. Since female infanticide has been a hidden phenomenon in one of the world's largest societies in the past three decades, it is very challenging for scholars to report precisely the magnitude and severity of this problem.[7] In spite of the fact that it is not possible to measure accurately the scale of gendercide in China, it is obvious that the one-child-per-married-couple policy (implemented by the Chinese communist government in 1979 as part of a family planning strategy) plays an extremely important role in preserving this Chinese tradition. The original goal of this policy was to restrain China's fast population growth so that the potential fruits of economic growth would not be offset by the immense demands of extra populations (Hudson and den Boer, 2004: 152):

> By 1978, China's population was thought to be closing in on the one billion mark, with 65 percent estimated to be under age thirty. This demographic structure, which resulted from the baby boom of the 1950s and 1960s, meant that an extremely large cohort of young couples was or would be bearing children during the last two decades of the twentieth century. If these couples were allowed to have two or more children ... the ripple effects would last throughout the twenty-first century, pushing the population ever upward and fatally retarding the prospects for economic advancement [White, 2006: 1–2].

Although the initial motivation of the officials who enacted the one-child policy (which implies no gender priority) was to prevent "economic advancement" from being "fatally retarded," innumerable married couples still express "son preference" (Hudson and den Boer, 2004: 154).

In the first place, boys in traditional China were deemed to be far more valuable than girls because daughters, after they have married, cannot provide labor for their biological family, carry on their family name, or help parents accumulate wealth. As a result of these rational evaluations or scientific calculations, raising a baby girl usually was regarded as an economically risky and financially foolish behavior:

> In Chinese culture, children are viewed as the means of family continuity, the basis of prosperity, and the source of care for the aged. Caring for the financial needs of parents is one of the primary roles of sons. Daughters do not play a role in carrying on the family name, nor is their labor thought to be equally valuable, although in some cases women produce and earn more than men [Hudson and den Boer, 2004: 155].

All of these feudal ideas and backward concepts were suppressed during the days of the Cultural Revolution (1966–1976). Nevertheless, it is clear that these old values outlast the fanatical years of the Red Guards. One index for this is that numerous women in China (as well as in Hong Kong and Taiwan) in the past two decades carried out gender-discriminatory/sex-selective abortions (Croll, 2000: 35–37; Hudson and den Boer, 2004: 172; Johnson, 2004; Kristof & WuDunn, 1994: 227–240). Because of these acts, it was estimated that, in less than ten years (mid–1980s to 1990), at least 1.5 million female fetuses were deliberately aborted in China (Hudson and den Boer, 2004: 172).

In terms of aborting female babies, Greater China, just like India and the Arab world, is one of the least regulated regions in the modern world (Kristof & WuDunn, 1994: 232). This societal trait, of course, does not imply that the majority of Chinese women are pro-choice supporters. However, it does denote that abortion is widely tolerated.[8] In this regard, some social routines do encourage or even coerce women to have an abortion. The first one is that in China, ultrasound scanners are extensively employed in testing the gender of an unborn baby: "One Chinese demographer has estimated that 100,000 ultrasound scanners were in place around the country by 1990" (Kristof & WuDunn, 1994: 229). With so many machines that can assist parents to determine whether their unborn child has a penis and with perhaps the same number of medical doctors (including unlicensed and illegal ones, like "barefoot doctors") who can perform abortion, it is no surprise that aborting babies in China is fairly easy, compared to America, for instance, which may have the strictest abortion regulations in the world. The sterilization measure enforced by street bureaucrats, from time to time, makes abortion even easier:

> The family planning authorities routinely force young women to undergo abortions and sterilization. The township authorities send teams into the villages once or twice a year to collect all the women who are due to be fitted with an IUD [intrauterine device] or to be sterilized. Some run away, in hopes that they can remain fertile and have another baby, and the authorities then send goons to the women's relatives in other villages, even in other provinces, to find and sterilize them. Usually they do not have to drag a woman to the operating table; when half a dozen young men surround her home and order her to come out, she may not see much sense in fighting back [Kristof & WuDunn, 1994: 233].

Another factor that gives pregnant women incentive to abort a female infant is that the one-child policy is not absolute. On the contrary, it does embrace some exceptions or exemptions, which allow qualified couples to have a "bonus child" (or even extra children). These exceptions or exemptions can be summarized as the following five "ifs" (see Hudson and den Boer, 2004: 153):

A gynecology and obstetrics clinic in Taipei, Taiwan.

- if the couple lives in a rural area where labor is in severely short supply
- if a married couple has a (severely) physically or psychologically disabled child
- if both parties of a married couple are the single child of his/her parents
- if both parties of a married couple are racial/ethnic minorities within racial/ethnic minorities
- if a married couple are overseas Chinese who return to China for permanent settlement.

Of these ifs, the first two items seem to have a direct impact on fostering abortion: according to the first if, married couples who live in a big city and have their own child are, of course, not qualified to have the second child. To make themselves qualified or to avoid heavy fines stipulated by the one-child statute (suppose these parents have an infant girl already and are eager to have a son), certain pregnant women or young mothers resort to abortion (or even infanticide) to get another chance of having the first child.

The second if, to a considerable extent, is an insurmountable challenge for numerous parents, particularly working-class ones: for such parents, having a child with physical deformities or psychological disorders means that they have to spend a lot of money on medical treatments. To avert this avoidable financial responsibility, some pregnant women, in light of the information (whether it is accurate or prejudiced) provided by the ultrasound scanner technician, abort their "deformed" or "psychologically handicapped" baby.[9] After this potential financial crisis is solved, such "intelligent" women will try at another time to give birth to a normal child.[10]

An additional practice that enables pregnant women (including teen-age mothers) to abort their unwanted baby easily is the slack law. This feature can be exemplified by Taiwan's Eugenics and Health Protection Law (*you sheng bao jian fa*), or EHPL. Enacted in 1984, EHPL's main goals are to "enhance population quality, to safeguard the health of the mother and her child(ren), and to promote family harmony." In order to achieve these objectives, the health authorities of Taiwan passed several stipulations which authorize gynecologists/obstetricians to perform abortion for pregnant women if the latter face "critical" conditions. One such condition can be found in the third item of the ninth clause.

According to this regulation, an elective abortion can be carried out if "pregnancy or delivering a baby will, based on medical reasons, cause danger to mother's life or threaten mother's physical/mental health." Technically speaking, this article is not controversial because in certain cases, pregnancy or delivering a baby does entail "danger to the mother's life or threatening the mother's physical/mental health." What is arguable is the phrase "medical reasons": as an overarching concept, this term virtually gives gynecologists/obstetricians autonomous, if not absolute, power in determining the necessity or appropriateness of performing an abortion. Since the exercise of this power is essentially boundless, abortion surgery in Taiwan generally has the following four characteristics:[11]

- it can be performed in almost all gynecology and obstetrics clinics because abortion is essentially legal (one such clinic can be seen on page 79)
- numerous gynecologists and obstetricians in Taiwan view abortion as a "treatment"
- since abortion is widely regarded as a "treatment," hundreds of thousands of abortion surgeries (including unnecessary ones) might have been performed each year
- an unknown number of these operations, however, were not reported to the authorities partially due to tax reasons.

No matter whether gynecologists and obstetricians in Taiwan can become prosperous because of helping women to get rid of redundant or unwanted girl babies, some Taiwanese women who have aborted their baby believe that they must do something to pacify the infant spirit. Otherwise, the spirit will retaliate and bring unanticipated disaster to the mother. To soothe this little ghost, many bereaved women install a tablet that has different sizes and can be purchased from a funeral articles supplier for an infant spirit. (See photograph on page 82.) Once this tablet (which will function as cradle for a dead baby) is ordered and personalized, it will be placed in a joss house that becomes the infant spirit's permanent abode. (See photograph on page 84.) Then the mother of the tablet must go to that joss house and pay respect to her daughter (sometimes son) once or twice a year.

Another alternative for regretful women to demonstrate their "love" or "solicitude" for the aborted fetus is to go to a feng shui or geomancy agency (run by an astrologist, fortune-teller, or sorcerer, see photograph on page 87). In that place, the women can get various suggestions for comforting their invisible daughter or son. Then, based on the counsels (which involve spirit beings, bizarre or even chilling advice), these women can take necessary measures to soothe the invisible child.

III. Famine

Apart from the dowry culture and the one-child population policy, another factor that can lead to girl infanticide is famine. For numerous

An exhibition hall of tablets for adult or infant spirits.

Chinese (especially those born after the 1970s), famine is a remote or even strange concept. This is because China has not been stricken by a nation-wide food crisis for decades. Accordingly, the collective memory in connection with the difficult time brought about by the severe food shortage of the 1950s and earlier years seems to have faded.

Whether or not China will ever again undergo a countrywide famine, it is obvious that during a large-scale food deficiency, certain defenseless populations are always hit hardest. Female infants, unfortunately, are one of them. This trend, to an extent, is inseparable from the inferior social status of traditional Chinese women.

Traditionally, females in China were taught and required to submit to three males in their life: single girls must obey their father; young women, as soon as they were married, must comply with their husband; and elderly mothers have to submit themselves to their son(s). This life path, of course, was not fixed and invariable (for instance, some women did not have a father, never married, or did not have a son). Nevertheless, it is clear that compared to males, the destiny of females was "weaker" (Croll, 2000: 1–20). And young or teenage girls, as *mooi-jai* ("little sister"; see Jaschok, 1988), were significantly more likely than young boys to be abandoned (Johnson, 2004) or sold (see Chapter 6).

Given that women were valued less than men, it became apparent that whenever a famine took place, those parents who had both sons and daughters had a choice between two evils: save food for all children (that is, no gender discrimination), but risk losing one child; or save all food for son(s), but risk losing a girl (or girls).

In Old China, most parents in famine-stricken regions tended to choose the second option. This tendency might be irrational and hard to comprehend for most white Americans and Europeans. But as Kristof and WuDunn (2000: 119) indicate, such a "spirit of ruthless drive and flexibility" (i.e., the will to sacrifice one person to save the others) allowed numerous East Asian families in general and Chinese families in particular to survive when they encountered excessively difficult times (whether they were produced by a man-made calamity or natural disaster). This determination can be exemplified by the behavior of selling a girl to a brothel to help a family overcome economic hardship (or other difficulty):

> Asia, more than other continents, is a temple of pragmatism. Other cultures put primacy on God, on individual rights, on sacred principles, while Asia by and large has been more accepting of terrible solutions. Western mothers only very rarely would sell their daughters into slavery.... Asian mothers sold their daughters, wept, and prospered [Kristof & WuDunn, 2000: 120].

A joss house that can help people to handle infant spirits.

If East Asian or Chinese parents, to an extent, possessed a stronger "spirit of ruthless drive and flexibility" than their Western counterparts, then it should not be surprising that when a great famine occurred, female infants and little girls who had siblings constantly had to depend on good luck to survive because their "parents [generally would save] the rice for their brothers" (Kristof & WuDunn, 1994: 232).

In brief, China (or more precisely, North and Northwest China) was stricken by three big famines in the first half of the twentieth century. The first one, caused by a severe drought, lasted for three years (1929–1931). No one knows for sure how many people starved to death in this catastrophe: estimates range from three million (Snow, 1968: 216) to twenty-five million (Clubb, 1978: 186). No one can ascertain how many young children perished in this tragedy. Only one thing is certain: an unknown number of baby girls were abandoned or sold. Of these deserted or auctioned infant girls, some might have been killed and eaten by starving people who desperately sought all possible measures to survive.

The second famine (triggered by exceedingly unreasonable taxes) occurred in Henan province in 1943 (Becker, 1997: 19–23). This horrible event, like the earlier one caused by drought persisted for years (partially due to slow reaction by the authorities). During the years of this "Great Hunger," it was estimated that at least five million people died (Becker, 1997: 22), including numerous baby girls. Given that countless rural residents could not find any means to live, cannibalism was practiced once again (Becker, 1997: 20). In this environment of "Hunger Terror," certain infant girls, born at the wrong time in the wrong place, were put to death and became the only food for their relatives or even parents.

The third famine happened in the late 1950s/early 1960s after a series of militant utopian policies affiliated with the Great Leap Forward (GLF) were carried out in almost all rural areas of China (Becker, 1997; Domenach, 1995). As mentioned in Chapter 2, the GLF was an ideological, radical, and enchanted movement founded on a pseudo-science. Therefore, not only were the goals set by the Beijing authorities impossible, but the movement turned China into a bizarre society in which extremely inefficient production behaviors were justified by an exceptionally optimistic social ethos. Given that the GLF completely violated natural law, approximately thirty to forty million people perished as a result of food shortage (Becker, 1997: 272–273). Of these famine victims, "nearly a quarter ... were peasant girls, who appear[ed] to have been deliberately allowed to starve to death or were killed by their parents" (Becker, 1997: 271).

Overall, hundreds of millions of baby girls (including full-term fetuses and newborn infants) were eliminated in China in the past one-hundred-plus years because of their "inferior economic value." These missing females tend to have three qualities in common: first, they were forced to break away from their family because of disadvantageous external factors, such as gender prejudice and great famine, that could not be controlled by individuals; second, such girls, before being put to death, were not old enough to become slave laborers; and third, once these children disappeared, they would become missing permanently.

Female Infanticide as an Expressive Homicide

Compared to murdering an infant girl on the assumption that it is economically unwise and financially burdensome to nurture a daughter, killing a baby girl for emotional reasons tends to entail far more complicated motivations. (It should be noted that this killing behavior can be committed by the victim's mother, father, or both.) These motivations, according to studies (for instance, Boswell, 1988; Hausfater & Hrdy, 2008; Holmes & Holmes, 2010; Meyer & Oberman, 2001; Piers, 1978; Schwartz & Isser, 2000; Shreeve, 2008), might originate from abnormal psychological structures (including psychiatric illnesses and psychopathologies), biological/genetic makeup, distinctive social customs, evolutionary processes, or religious rituals. No matter which reason is cited as a root cause by researchers who seek to explicate the etiology of female infanticide in Western societies, it seems reasonable to claim that in Greater China, all of those expressive forces that result in trigger girl infanticide are more or less related to two socio-psychological paradigms: rejection (which is negation-based) and "rebirth" (which is sympathy-oriented). After these two arch-paradigms are inspected in the next pages, female infanticide in China will provide social scientists with evidence of "the labile nature of human parenting" (Piers, 1978: 25).

I. Rejection

In the past century in Greater China, an unknown number of young single women unexpectedly assumed motherhood under culturally unacceptable or socially forbidden circumstances. Since this new identity of unmarried motherhood, a symbol of dishonor, disgrace, and degradation in conventional China, could bring punishments to females, certain women who became mothers unwillingly, chose to abort their baby or to kill their newborn child to avoid the shame.

From the perspective of life-course theory (suggested by criminologists like Samson & Laub, 1993), everyone will experience certain depressing or discouraging turning points at some time in their life: attempting to quit using drugs, bankruptcy, demotion, divorce, dropping out of school, extramarital affairs, getting infected with a chronic or incurable disease,

A *feng shui* or geomancy agency that can help people to pacify infant spirits.

legal trouble, severe financial crisis, job loss, permanent physical injury, running away from home, and so on. Surviving these crises in a culturally acceptable and socially endorsed manner, however, is by no means stress-free or trouble-free because people (including the most mature and resourceful ones) are very likely to become mired in an emotional or financial predicament even they enjoy supportive interpersonal relationships or possess considerable individual resources, such as personal savings. In other words, life course theorists (such as Benson, 2002; Piquero & Mazerolle, 2000; Samson & Laub, 1993) suggest that watershed events can result in complicating difficulties or traumas. If people are able to cope with those tests or adversities in a socially or legally approved style (with, for instance, family networks or private wealth), then the shock generated by unanticipated, undesirable, or unspeakable episodes in life might be minimized. On the contrary, people might be motivated to resort to antiestablishment or antisocial means (whether violent or nonviolent) to deal with their crisis if they cannot find an outlet accepted in mainstream values.

As an emerging theory in criminology, the life-course theory is not perfect because of its causal framework. For example, almost every individual will experience certain breaking events in life. Since these events have cumulative effects in shaping behavior, it is not easy to ascertain the causal relationship between a specific incident and a given deviant or delinquent act that occurs after that incident. In spite of the fact that the life-course theory is not flawless, advocates of this theory do propose a valuable argument: turning points in life are sources of personal pressures; consequently, they can stimulate people to commit immoral or illegal acts if they feel they are unlikely to overcome the adversity.

For single women, unexpected pregnancy is undoubtedly a highly stressful turning point in their life. This new experience can take place in numerous socially and culturally incorrect settings and contexts, among them extramarital affair, incest, one-night stand, and premarital sex. Of these settings and contexts, three situations seem to have enormous power in precipitating a young mother to kill her baby in an attempt to obliterate the negative social evaluations associated with wrong motherhood.

1. War/Military Conquest

The first (and the most cruel) situation is war. For females, war always is a catastrophe. Unlike men who probably could take advantage of the chaotic moments (or lawlessness) generated by a war to become economically prosperous, politically powerful, or even historically prestigious, women, partially due to their weaker physical strength, always face the danger of sexual assault when a war occurs (see Chapter 5). As women, whether they are attractive or not, constantly live in the shadow of rape, which can be perpetrated by a familiar person or by a stranger, and frequently confront the threat of involuntary pregnancy, girl infanticide inevitably serves as a "happy" solution for unhappy mothers who want to get rid of their unexpected or unsolicited child to resume their "normal" life. This phenomenon can be exemplified by two wars in China.

The first one took place in the thirteenth century: in the 1250s and 1260s, the invincible Mongol armies invaded China proper, defeated the imperial troops of the Song dynasty (960–1279), and established the Yuan dynasty (1271–1368). Because of this military conquest, numerous young females of the Han tribe (the dominant group of China) were compelled to marry Mongol males (who, despite their ruling status, were racial/ethnic minorities). These interracial or interethnic marriages for conquered Han Chinese were irresistible because Yuan China, just like the Nazi Germany of the twentieth century, was a racist state. Within this state (where the distribution of social resources was directed by the ideology of racial hierarchy), the socioeconomic and political statuses of social members were determined largely by their racial and ethnic background.[12] As the Han Chinese (specifically people of South China) were classified as the most "inferior" human ethnic group within the empire (i.e., the relationship between Han Chinese and Mongolians was the same as that between masters and slaves; see Zheng, 1996: 76–77), any choice in the matter was beyond the control of Han Chinese families.

No matter how many Han women were forced to give birth to a half-Mongolian baby, a brutal social custom called *shuai tou tai* (meaning forcefully hurling the firstborn to the ground) was developed (secretly) in South China (Wang, 2010: 123). According to this ruthless ideology, babies with mixed or multiple racial background were sources of "racial pollution." This was because their blood was thought to contain the Mongolian genes of barbarity, belligerence, and bloodthirst. Therefore, these "born criminals" could spread their mean or criminal genes among the Han Chinese if they grew up to marry Han.[13] To prevent the noble blood of the Han peoples from being contaminated, such wicked babies, it was believed, must be destroyed.

Under the impact of the custom of *shuai tou tai*, an underground "racial holy war" (Perry, 2001: 163) or hate movement was waged, during which an unknown quantity of baby girls was slain. This tragedy took place again in the 1930s and 1940s when North China, Central China, and most parts of South China were governed by Japan-backed puppet governments.

Beginning in late 1938, because of the Sino-Japanese War China was managed by two competing camps: one was Japan and its Chinese collaborators; the other was the Chungking-based Nationalist government. Within the territories dominated by the Japanese and *han jian* (Chinese who cooperated with the Japanese), certain young women were made to intermarry with the Japanese males (whether they were soldiers or civilians) or to establish intimate relationships with the Chinese collaborationists (probably because of economic pressures). Many such women, however, were abandoned by their Japanese/Chinese partner after a period of time as the men did not treat seriously the relationship he established with a Chinese woman (after all, finding a female, whether married or unmarried, as a substitute was extremely easy).

Given that countless gender relationships ended up being false in wartime China, many pregnant women betrayed or discarded by their Japanese/*han jian* "husband" or *han jian*/Japanese "lover" had to abort their daughter, son, or even twins, for if they were born, they must be thrown away. Otherwise, it would be really difficult for these mothers to stay in orthodox Chinese communities (this tended to be especially true shortly after the end of the Sino-Japanese War in August 1945). As tens of thousands of stigmatized women took desperate measures to remain single, it was inevitable that a deserted population composed of abandoned children was created. Estimating, let alone precisely determining, the size of this population is impossible because so many cases went unreported or unrecorded.

2. ABORTION WAVE OF SEPTEMBER

Ever since the early 1990s, China seems to have become a synonym of economic change: commercial buildings and skyscrapers were built in big cities; industrial parks were founded in coastal provinces; shopping malls and theme parks, just like mushrooms shoot up after a spring rain, were established nationwide; railroads were laid in Tibet and West China; new and spectacular facilities (such as the Bird's Nest Stadium and the National Aquatics Center) constructed for the 2008 Olympic Games appeared in Beijing; and large-scale urban renewal programs were carried out in Shanghai for the 2010 Expo. In addition to these dazzling infrastructures, the economic growth and technological power of China are equally impressive. In the past two decades, it was the fastest growing economy in the world; in 2003, it sent its first astronaut into space; and in 2010, it became the second largest economy on the planet.

While the above short list might be sufficient to demonstrate that China is a rising star of the modern world in the twenty-first century, this

"Middle Kingdom" is also confronting many challenges (or even crises). One of them is sexual liberation.

As China was a Confucian state for more than two thousand years (especially during the Ming and Qing dynasties), sex always was portrayed by Confucian scholars and government bureaucrats as a dirty and decadent behavior (although these scholars and bureaucrats frequented brothels; see Wang, 2006). Based on such teachings, it was believed that sexual behavior must be regulated firmly so that people can maintain "spiritual civilization." Unmarried females were strictly prohibited from dating single men before getting married, let alone engaging in premarital sex. The same philosophy was applied to widows, too. For these single females, regardless of their age, the only way to avoid trouble was to remain celibate (Zheng, 1996: 78–79). Those who could resist the temptation of love would be praised and/or obtain material rewards. In contrast, those who could not maintain singlehood (for instance, dating a single male) would be stigmatized and treated like adulteresses. None of these ascetic criteria and requirements really changed until the feminist movement emerged in Beijing, Shanghai, and a few other big cities in the 1920s.

The feminist movement of China, as a part of the May Fourth Movement (see Chow, 1960), did make some unprecedented ideas (such as women's political and marriage rights) known to the Chinese public in the 1920s and 1930s. However, those concepts were circulated and talked about largely among college students and intellectuals only because as "heretical ideas," they were rejected entirely by social elites such as local gentry. Besides the opposition of traditionalists, another obstacle that prevented the feminist movement from becoming widespread was that in the 1920s, at least 90 percent of Chinese women were illiterates or semi-illiterates. With so many women who could not read and write, it was essentially impossible for feminists to promote their ideals or to recruit followers.

In any event, after the transitory period of the May Fourth Movement, sex was again demonized in China. It was, to a considerable extent, considered an equivalent of moral degeneration and "spiritual pollution." As a result, people (including married people) always had to repress their passions (especially the desire for romantic love) to get positive social evaluations, to impress others that they were not lewd persons, and to prove that they were pure in heart. This culminated in the Cultural Revolution (1966–1976) when China became a genderless and sexless society: all social members, regardless of their age and gender, "wore the same style of clothes, made the same comments, exhibited the same facial expressions, and displayed the same movements" (Zheng, 1996: 97).

Described as a period of "the demise of sex" (Zheng, 1996: 97), the Cultural Revolution not only turned sex-related publications and activities into a taboo, it also made people hate beauty, for physical attractiveness always could bring someone political troubles. This black-and-white world began to change gradually in the late 1970s/early 1980s when the Beijing authorities (led by Deng Xiao-ping) started to reduce extremist political doctrines in economy and adopted a pragmatic approach to promote economic development. Under the stimulus of this big transformation, the economy and commerce of China grew more and more. That allowed various sex-related and other businesses (such as dance halls, massage parlors, karaoke bars, night clubs and pubs, sauna baths, and so on) dormant for decades to reappear in the late 1980s.

After more than twenty years of growth, sex-related industries are no longer strange to the Chinese public in the 2010s. One indicator for this alteration is that sex-connected enterprises are ubiquitous: not only can people in urban areas find a variety of opportunities to buy sex, but rural residents can get access to sex-associated messages without great difficulty. Several social problems are generated because of this sexual revolution. One is that adults can find occasions to engage in non-orthodox, if not abnormal, sexual behaviors. This "social welfare" can be exemplified by the Ma case: in 2009, Ma, a professor at Nanjing University of Technology, was arrested for "organizing group sex parties" (Wang, 2010). Professor Ma eventually got a three-and-half-year sentence, partially because the court, in the light of widespread corruption among government officials, had to make a guilty verdict in order to better the public image of the communist government (see the next section). This case, from the angle of the wedding cake model of criminal justice (that is, the number of persons who commit a punishable behavior always is far greater than the number of arrested persons who perpetrate that behavior), did suggest that certain people in present-day China have taken part in promiscuous sex (which was unimaginable before the 1980s).

Sexual revolution does not bring sexual liberation to adults only. This social movement also gives adolescents channels to become involved in premarital sex. One such channel is *wang ba*, or Internet bars.

For foreign tourists, the exterior of Internet bars usually is plain: no magnificent decorations, no elegant entrance, and, of course, no doorman. Despite Internet bars' pedestrian appearance, the activities engaged in by teenagers (particularly unsupervised ones) inside Internet bars are somewhat uncommon: teenage boys and girls can use these places to chat, to share indecent pictures, and to search for dating targets. As long as these minors have found their "true love," they may engage in one-night stands if they feel that this ulterior behavior is simply a game.

Numerous juveniles maintain a quasi-marital relationship with their *wang you*, or friends met via Internet. As these teenagers, may not take seriously these sexual relationships, millions of teenage girls in China, in the past decade, have elective abortion surgery in order to avoid dropping out of school, to evade peer pressure, to prevent bringing disgrace to family, and/or to stay away from potential legal trouble: in this regard, "good girls" may have an abortion once a year while "bad girls" may undergo the same process five or more times.[14] No matter how many pregnant teenage girls abort their pregnancies, cases of teenage abortion in China (as well as in Hong Kong and Taiwan) peak in September, shortly after the school vacation.

3. EXTRAMARITAL AFFAIRS

As mentioned above, modern-day China has become an economically liberalized country. As a result, elements of sex industries, in the name of developing local economy or attracting foreign investment, obtain miscellaneous opportunities (whether legitimate, semi-legitimate, or even illegitimate) to grow and expand. Given that these tertiary economies are rampant (not only are they abundant in cities, they are active in rural districts as well), 21st-century China, at least during nighttime, has grown to be a sexually porous society: on the one hand, minors, compared to their counterparts of previous generations, enjoy far more opportunities to get involved in pre-marital sex; on the other hand, (married) adults can enrich their life by developing sexual relationships outside marriage. In both situations, girl infanticide is bound to happen. But this homicidal behavior entails much more complicated social and interpersonal contexts if it occurs in the adult world.

The first context is that, compared to average married couples, government officials (including military officers, national security agents, and members of local communist cadres) find it much easier to engage in the so-called *bao er nai* (keeping a mistress in a love nest), *bao san nai* (keeping two mistresses in two love nests), or even *bao si nai* (keeping three mistresses in three love nests). This advantageous position basically cannot be separated from the fact that in China, power holders (as well as their family members) have far better chances than average people to enjoy social resources, such as obtaining a government-subsidized residence, entering an elite university, getting a high-paid job, acquiring choicest medical services, and traveling overseas. While this does not mean that all communist officials and their family members get involved in extramarital affairs, it does suggest that corrupt government agents can use their power to build up polygamous relationships, accumulate personal wealth, or both. In terms of creating polygamous affiliations, crooked officials can utilize some nasty techniques to make their life "full of joy and good memory" (see Shi, 2002; Zi, 1999).

The most systematic and efficient technique is that in many cities and rural towns, delinquent administrators and street bureaucrats (particularly law enforcement agencies, prosecutors, and tax collectors) can establish a mutually beneficial relationship with owners of local sex industries (Shi, 2002: 173–185). Based on this transaction, government agents can abuse their power and provide economic benefits or extra protection to their clients (that is, the former can introduce customers for the latter or the former can create a safe and secure environment for the latter to run business). In return, owners of sex industries must offer free sexual services to their guardian angels so that they can enjoy eternal peace. This symbiotic association makes it evident that the sex industry in China has grown to be state-sponsored. On the other hand, this business makes corrupt state agents assume two identities on immeasurable occasions: during daytime, they provide state-appointed services to the public; after sunset, they obtain sexual services from the public. With so many male public servants (particularly those who are married) becoming involved in casual sex, it seems to have become an "iron law" that whenever these very important persons let showgirls, bar girls, massage girls, or other sex workers become pregnant, the latter usually have to abort the baby so that no one will get into legal or political troubles (Zi, 1999: 312).

Another technique frequently employed by crooked officials to enjoy free sex is that they can coerce female applicants or petitioners to provide sexual services in exchange for official assistance (such as acquiring a Ph.D. degree, moving, finding a job, getting an identification card, obtaining a business license, and so on). This trading behavior can be exemplified by incalculable hidden agreements or secret deals (Zi, 1999), which, though they involve different players, scenarios, and work places, tend to reveal the following characteristics:

- the perpetrator was, by and large, a married male
- the perpetrator typically was a male power holder (who could be a senior agent of a public security agency, a court judge, a prosecutor, a magistrate, a mayor, a manager/director of a TV station, an executive officer of a national enterprise, a professor of a university, a mili-

tary officer, a warden of female prison, or even a high-ranking official of the Beijing government)

- the perpetrator usually enjoyed "supreme authority" or tremendous decision-making power in the institution with which he was affiliated (i.e., the perpetrator, as a king-like figure, firmly controlled certain social resources, both material and symbolic)

- the perpetrator generally took part in sexual adventure in an orderly and deliberate way: first, he would target females nearby (such as female subordinates); then, if the victims did not resist desperately or "call the police," he would start to organize his own sex parties made up of his "female friends" or *gan nu er* (nominal daughters)

- the perpetrator normally had an excellent work history (which enabled the perpetrator to take advantage of his reputation to nullify any accusations against his immoral personal life)

- the perpetrator always would demand that his lovers (who could be the perpetrator's colleagues or *gan nu er*) to have abortions if they became pregnant (it was not unusual that the latter aborted a baby more than once for the former).

- the perpetrator, more often than not, would use public funds to keep up his personal expenses (which, compared to average income of the public, was appalling).

Sexual immorality perpetrated by authority figures inevitably precipitated the Beijing authorities to implement a series of anti-corruption campaigns in the past twenty years. None of these movements, however, lasted very long (roughly from a few days to a few weeks). As these moral-reconstruction crusades did not persist long enough to eradicate erotic businesses, the effects of these wars against *huang liu*[15] and *san pei*[16] appeared limited/temporary. One possible factor that caused the Beijing authorities to take merely a nominal/symbolic approach to suppress the sex industry was that the latter played a vital role in drawing investors from Hong Kong, Macau, and Taiwan (particularly Taiwan) in the 1990s and 2000s. Starting in the early 1990s, it became clear that Taiwan was no longer a favorable environment for manufacturing (or labor-intensive) industries because of continually rising wages. Facing this irreversible structural transformation, tens of thousands of Taiwanese businessmen (of the secondary economy) left Taiwan and established/re-established their career in China, where labor costs were far lower than Taiwan's.[17]

These waves of Taiwanese exodus, despite their magnitude and regardless of the enterprises (workshops, production centers, processing/reprocessing factories, and so on) which Taiwanese founded in China, seemed to have one feature in common: the great majority of Taiwanese manufacturers, factory owners, and entrepreneurs who migrated to China to pursue economic profits were celibate males. More precisely, most of them were married persons in Taiwan; however, they stayed in China alone because they wanted their children to receive a Taiwanese education or for other private reasons). These single males, just like Chinese laborers who came to the United States in the late nineteenth and early twentieth centuries, would separate from their family for a period of time. As a result, some of these Taiwanese immigrants (probably due to emotional causes) created a new family as their temporary home in China. This act (called *bao er nai*; see above), of course, must be committed behind closed doors because, according to the laws of China and Taiwan, it was illegal.

No matter how many Taiwanese (as well as Hong Kongese and Macauese) businessmen had extramarital affairs in China in the past twenty years, it is certain that not all mistresses (whether they were *er nai*/the first lover, *san nai*/the second lover, *si nai*/the third lover, or even *wu nai*/the fourth lover) could become the formal spouse of their Taiwanese boyfriend or fiancé. While some conscientious Taiwanese businessmen might marry their new sweetheart after divorcing their wife in Taiwan, it was not uncommon for *er nai* (or *san nai*/*si nai*/*wu nai*) to be abandoned when she became pregnant. If the latter situation did occur, many women aborted the baby in the hope that the father would be psychologically punished — in other words, abortion was turned into a means of reprisal.

In short, certain abortion cases in China resulted from the desertion of Taiwanese, Hong Kongese, and Macauese males. Such cases probably exceed one thousand per year because more than 100,000 of these men are currently doing business in China. Correctly estimating these cases, however, is not feasible because many relevant instances are not registered by the health authorities.

II. Rebirthing

Unlike the above-noted situations in which girl infanticide takes place in the context of rejection or negation, murdering baby girls is sometimes perpetrated out of sympathy or empathy. While this positive typology may look infrequent, it does not imply that it is insignificant, for it is a category of mercy homicide: according to the definition in the *Crime Classification Manual* (Douglas, et al., 1997: 111), mercy homicide is committed by someone who "believes inducing death is relieving the victim's suffering." Based on this definition, a medical professional who kills a patient who has suffered a chronic disease for years is usually considered the "typical example" of mercy killing.

No matter whether medical murder is really the standard pattern of mercy homicide, what we are concerned with in this chapter is the issue of why and how girl infanticide can be viewed as mercy killing. From the angle of eternal life, most Chinese (both traditional and modern) accept two things as true. One is that human life is endless: after someone dies, his/her spirit will go to an underworld and stay there for a while; living persons, through specifically devised methods, can interact with the spirit of a dead person. The other is that human life is regulated by the laws of karma and reincarnation: after someone passes away, the spirit of this person will go to a Plutonic world, but it will not stay there forever. Instead, the person will be reborn. In the meantime, the family and country this person will go to are determined by his or her conduct in previous life. Benevolent, kind persons will be born into a wealthy and caring family and/or economically advanced country, while people who spent most of their previous life on iniquitous things or activities will be born into a poverty-stricken or abusive family and/or economically underdeveloped region. In addition, depending on the rewards or punishments someone deserves, the genders of this individual may switch according to the cycle of reincarnation: a courageous woman might become an Eisenhower-like military commander, while a racist and sexist male might be born as a less-educated minority female in a white country.

Taking these beliefs together, it seems plausible to declare that the following three types of parents are most likely to slay infant girls in the context of hope:

- penniless ones, who can be considered "the poorest within the poor"
- those who have a baby with severe physical disability, such as cerebral palsy
- those who have a baby with an incurable disease (especially AIDS).

For these parents, raising a baby girl is essentially meaningless because the future of the child is predictably miserable. To prevent the child from suffering, some parents, on the assumption that their child will be reborn to a wealthy family or with a healthy body, take the life of their baby. This act is precisely the same as that committed by married slaves and servants during the imperial years. Immeasurable unemployed or bankrupt peasants were sold (or sold themselves) to well-to-do families as slaves or bonded servants (see Chapter 6). Once these marginalized populations became movable properties, their life, just like black slaves who worked on plantations in North America in the seventeenth, eighteenth, and nineteenth centuries, was occupied with toil and moil. However, these walking assets were allowed to marry. But these marriages were arranged by the slave owner; then all children produced by slaves would keep providing labor (including child labor) for their master. With a future of servitude, a "dead-end" life path let some parents choose to slay their infants in hope that death would enable their child to get a better destiny in the next life cycle (Ma, 1999: 43–44).

Concluding Remarks

Girl infanticide has a long history in China. Due to this custom, China is experiencing some serious social problems.

The most obvious one is that the sex ratios become highly distorted. That makes numerous young males unable to get married (particularly those in underdeveloped inland provinces) due to a shortage of unmarried females.

If males in their twenties or thirties cannot find a spouse, then it becomes clear that only sex businesses can assist these surplus single males to enjoy family life. This social function not only gives sex industries legitimate raison d'être, it also enables the sex industry to enjoy firm support among a huge crowd of playboys (controlling this population, however, is impossible because it is dispersed and hidden).

Given that the sex industry is buttressed solidly (at least in private) by the male masses in general and unmarried men in particular, it is inevitable that components of the sex industry will compete among themselves in order to survive and prosper. To win this commercial war, owners of sex businesses, as a rule, must devise new programs to entertain their male customers. One such program (which probably is the most crucial element) is to introduce new faces (especially young women in the sex industry) to male patrons. This task, however, is not always easy because the demand for young stars might be (much) greater than the supply. To make up this difference, managers of sex businesses usually have two options. One is that they can publicize the hiring news by disseminating flyers or newsletters. These messages usually will give women who are looking for a better-paid job the misapprehension that they can make high income in the hotel, restaurant, or tourist industry, making the possibility very appealing to rural women who plan to go to a city to become wealthy. The other alternative is that operators of sex industries can covertly buy trafficked women (particularly those from the poorest rural towns) to satisfy their need for human resources. This choice, nominally speaking, might offer a stable job to trafficked women. However, such women (as victims of human trafficking) might turn into human traffickers if they become acquainted with the law of survival of the trafficking world (see the section on repeat victimization in Chapter 6).

Another important problem caused by the sex industry is that numerous places connected with commercialized sex become the meeting places for good guys (that is, government agents; see previous section) and bad guys (underground elements). This magnet effect not only obscures the boundary between law enforcement and law-breakers, it may also undermine the reputation or even legitimacy of the Beijing authorities: for the public, the convergence of these two incompatible camps in criminogenic settings simply implies that government officials are corrupt and untrustworthy.

In sum, due to the practice of girl infanticide, tens of millions of males are forced to remain single (although this problem, at least in theory, can be solved through a Chinese version of polyandry called *peng guo*, or, literally, "sharing a pot"; this solution, a local custom, is negligible because it is practiced among biological brothers in North China only). With so many men facing forced singlehood, it seems reasonable to believe that the sex industry will keep growing in China. Both government and non-government actors will also have plenty time to have fun in the next ten to twenty years.

CHAPTER 4

Ghost Brides

For Westerners and non–Chinese, some Chinese customs appear bizarre and inconceivable (if not preposterous). One such custom is ghost marriage. In Chinese, it is called *ming hun* (marriage of the netherworld), *yin hun* (Plutonic marriage), *gui hun* (spirit marriage), *yin pei* (matchmaking for the dead), *pei gu* (matching bones), *jie yin qing* (forming Plutonic marital relationship), *qu gan gu* (marrying dry bones), or *qu gu nu* (marrying female corpse).

As a part of Chinese marriage culture for more than two thousand years, the practice of arranging a wedding ceremony (which, as will be examined in the following, is largely performed at midnight or before dawn) for a living individual and a deceased person (sometimes two dead persons) still can be seen in some areas of China and Taiwan in the twenty-first century.[1] Since this custom creates a demand market (which, for the most part, is underground and cannot be measured) for female corpses, it motivates some outlaws to abduct and murder young women in order to supply fresh and first-rate ghost brides to people who want to find a spouse for their deceased son (sometimes father, brother, or uncle).

In this chapter, the following two issues will be scrutinized:

- What are the typologies of ghost marriage in China and Taiwan?
- Why and how can this tradition (especially the custom of finding a wife for a dead male) lead to cultural homicide (or serial killing)?

After these issues are examined, the criminological and sociological implications of *yin hun* will be summarized.

100

Typologies of Ghost Marriage in China and Taiwan

As mentioned above, ghost marriage has been a part of the Chinese marriage system for many centuries.[2] According to extant literature concerning this peculiar tradition (Bao, 2006; Huang, 2008: 37–68; Jordan, 1972; McGough, 1981: 183–184; Yao, 1991, 1999), ghost marriage in China/Taiwan includes four leading patterns. (The other two patterns — having a male deity and a female god get married or having a living person marry a deity — are not examined in this chapter because they are anthropological topics, which are beyond the scope of this book.):

- Pattern I: both husband and wife are deceased minors
- Pattern II: both husband and wife are deceased (young) adults
- Pattern III: husband a living person, wife a dead individual
- Pattern IV: husband a dead person, wife a living individual

Each of these versions is described as follows.

I. Both Husband and Wife Are Deceased Minors

In the past three thousand years, Chinese people have generally believed that every individual is made up of two parts: body and spirit or soul. Body is perishable because no one can live forever. Unlike the body doomed to perish, the soul can stay alive without end: soul is an ageless and boundless being because it is not constrained by time and space. Since the spirit is not regulated by the law of nature (including the force of death), this element, despite its invisible nature, can outlive all mortal creatures and material things.

Based on the belief that spirit is timeless and endless, Chinese traditionally assume that after someone dies, his/her spirit will leave the earthly world and go to an immaterial domain called *ming jie* (Plutonic territory or Sheol). During the period of staying in Sheol, spirits will be judged: good spirits (whose owners exhibited upright qualities while they lived on earth in physical form) will go to *ji le shi jie* (the Elysian fields) to enjoy eternal happiness; on the contrary, evil spirits (whose holders committed numerous wicked acts before they left the earthly world) will go to *shi ba ceng di yu* (eighteen-tiered hell) to suffer never-ending punishments.

In addition to good and bad spirits, numerous people die (whether naturally or accidentally) before the age of twenty (according to traditional Chinese customs, twenty is the turning point that separates childhood/

puberty from adulthood). These young, immature spirits, generally speaking, have not yet demonstrated their genuine character because they did not live long enough. As a result, such souls will not be judged by *Yan Luo Wang* (the King of Death). As an alternative, they will exist and wander, aimless and lonely, in *ming jie*, which will become their permanent abode.

For some parents whose child passes away before the age of twenty, finding a spouse for their deceased son or daughter (who is supposed to keep getting older and eventually will become an adult in *ming jie*) is crucial.[3] This is because Plutonic marriage can keep departed youths, when they become adults, from living in the netherworld without a companion. It also has the function of extending the family tree. More specifically, ghost marriage can help wandering young souls to settle down in Sheol: if boys and girls stay in a place inaccessible to their parents, then these little ghosts will travel from place to place, just like teenage runaways or thrownaways living in the material world. For parents, such a life is miserable. Having these young kids get married when their *ming sui* (that is, their age on earth if such youngsters were still alive) is around twenty will terminate their singlehood and allow the married couple to provide emotional support to each other: according to news reports, the majority of departed young persons will get married in their late teens or early twenties. Some late bloomers will not find their spouse until their thirties, and it is rare for dead children to establish their family in their forties or even later.[4]

Besides the benefit of mutual care, some parents believe that if their children can establish a household in Sheol, then they must have children of their own: if the child was a boy, his fatherhood can help his family in the material world to continue the patrilineal genealogy. (Although this continuity occurs in the netherworld, this fact seems extremely important for those parents who have only their deceased son to carry on the family line.) If the child was a girl (who, according to the patrilineal tradition of China/Taiwan, is not eligible to carry on the genealogy), she will be remembered and worshipped by her offspring.

In a word, certain parents are enthusiastic to end the celibacy of their young ghost son or daughter. To achieve this goal, parents looking for ghost bride must find their counterparts who are searching for a ghost bridegroom. In this regard, these parents (especially those who have comprehensive interpersonal networks) usually can find potential in-laws without great difficulty (after all, such parents can acquire the information they need from neighbors, relatives, friends, or even friends' friends). What is more complicated as well as important, however, is whether they can find suitable in-laws: that is, almost no wealthy parents (whether they were merchants or nobles of ancient China or businessmen or bankers of modern China and Taiwan) will accept a mate from a peasant family for their ghost son or daughter; by the same token, almost no poor parents (whether they are farmers or laborers) can find a mate for their deceased child from a prominent family.[5] Given that this process of mate selection is, to a considerable extent, determined by factors related to social status (income, education level, occupational prestige, power, and the like), few parents seeking for a ghost bride or ghost bridegroom will become in-laws if they do not belong to the same socioeconomic group. This phenomenon is called *men dang hu dui* in Chinese, meaning choosing a son-in-law/daughter-in-law from families of equivalent social rank.

If parents trying to find a ghost spouse through whatever channels meet and agree to hold a wedding for their ghost son and ghost daughter,[6] then this marriage ceremony usually will be performed as follows.

First, an auspicious date according to the Chinese lunar calendar for the wedding will be chosen. This date normally is determined by an experienced astrologist or fortune-teller.

Second, after the date has been decided, two representative images (one for the bride, the other one for the groom) will be created. In ancient China, such images could be effigies, made out of straw, thatch, or bamboo, or spirit tablets; in modern China and Taiwan, they can be effigies, spirit tablets, and/or framed photos (at times, the effigies are not three-dimensional but simply two figures or silhouettes cut from cardboard or other material). These images will be placed in different altars (one in the house of the bride, one in the house of the groom) before the official wedding ceremony is held.

When the day of marriage comes, the images are brought to a joss house called *yin miao*, like the one pictured on page 104.[7] In that ghost temple, Buddhist or Taoist shamans (who are paid in advance) perform the rituals of *chao du* (which can help wandering souls leave the Sheol) and *lun hui* (that can help wandering souls find the paths leading to the afterlife).[8] After these betrothal rituals have finished, the shamans will throw several things [e.g., a piece of red paper with the name and horoscope of bride and bridegroom on it; several pieces of rectangular spells, which can be yellow or white; and betrothal money, in the form of *ming bi* (joss notes, see photograph on p. 104) or *ming zhi* (joss paper, see photograph on p. 105)] into a burner to prove that the young couple are no longer unattached and will live as husband and wife in the underworld. As soon as these things are

Yin miao (ghost temple) in Tainan, Taiwan.

Sample of joss note.

reduced to ashes by fire (which means the marriage license and dowries[9] have been transferred to the netherworld), the images of the couple will be put together in the temple and/or in the houses of the newlyweds.

Once the aforementioned rites of passage have been completed, a small party, which normally is held in the nighttime, usually follows. Members of the two families officially become in-laws after the whole program has finished. With the establishment of this common-law relationship, parents of the bride and groom typically believe that their daughter or son has already started a family and will no longer live nomadically in *ming jie*.

Sample of joss paper.

II. Both Husband and Wife Are Deceased Young Adults

Strictly speaking, when a wedding — which, for outsiders, looks like a funeral more than a matrimonial ceremony — is staged for two deceased minors (who, more often than not, did not know each other while they were alive), this wedding, no matter how ceremonial it may look, is symbolic only.[10] This is because the bride and groom were strangers (that is, they did not establish any emotional ties). Therefore, except assuming that the couple would act like husband and wife in the otherworld (supposing this invisible place does exist), no one can ascertain whether this couple will stay relevant to each other (for instance, whether they will divorce if they find a better spouse) or whether they can get along (that is, whether they can maintain a vital relationship).

Unlike the marriage arranged for departed young persons (which is theoretical or imaginary in nature), holding a wedding for two deceased adults tends to be much more meaningful. This is due to the fact that before these young adults died, they had already founded a stable emotional affiliation.[11] As a result of this link, it seems reasonable to make this pair of lovers a genuine couple for this effort is compensatory, similar to the posthumous honor conferred on certain notable or talented persons such as artists, combat heroes, composers, scientists, and writers. With such a measure, the nominal relationship between quasi-bride and quasi-bridegroom can be transformed into a formal and legitimate bond.

More specifically, this type of ghost marriage includes the following characteristics:

First of all, before they died, the bride-elect and bridegroom-elect were not strangers but acquaintances: they might be work colleagues, classmates, partners in the same activity or business (which can be intellectual or physical), or good friends who have dwelled in the same neighborhood for a long period of time (all of these suggest that the couple had shared a given working or living space for years).

Second, besides having become acquainted with each other, the couple had already established a mutually dependent connection: they could be fiancée and fiancé; or, if not engaged, they have already treated each other as a "trouble-shooter" (for example, providing emotional or monetary support to the other person when she/he faced a thorny problem). Because of this total or hard-to-substitute emotional bond, relatives and close friends of the couple have determined that these two persons will definitely get married some time in the future: it is only a matter of time.

Third, given that the private relationship between the couple had grown to be exclusive, it becomes virtually impossible for the third party to alter that status quo (in other words, this relationship is irreplaceable for outsiders).

Finally, as the emotional tie between the couple became unshakeable, relatives and close friends of the couple might have opportunities to interact with one another. It is not uncommon that these interactions became more and more frequent; as a result, family members of the couple did expect that a new relative, sooner or later will join their family. In this regard, family members of the couple probably have formed an in-law relationship.

From the above, it should become clear that if the couple had not passed away, they would definitely have become husband and wife at some time in their life. On the other hand, given that they have perished (or gone missing) due to a traffic accident, natural disaster, or other unanticipated events, the firm relationship they had established suddenly becomes a "beautiful sorrow" to their parents and relatives. The relationship has already been deemed similar to that of a wedded couple since it is just one step or a few simple steps away from becoming official. It is the status of near-completeness that precipitates some parents to take actions to make this incomplete and informal marital affiliation complete.[12]

Once parents of a deceased couple decide to have this pair get married, it follows that a ghost wedding will be orchestrated. This wedding, while it may vary from district to district in content and scale, usually embraces the following features (some of these characteristics can also be seen in the previous section):

To begin with, a propitious date for the wedding will be selected by a fortune-teller or "qualified" medium/psychic.[13] After that date is picked, two paper effigies representing bride and groom will be manufactured: depending on the social position and family background of bride and groom, the exteriors of these effigies differ. If both bride and groom are from well-to-do families, the effigies usually are life-sized.[14] Their faces are carefully drawn and colored (or the pictures of bride and groom can be pasted on them), and based on customers' requests, their clothes can be traditional Chinese style, modern Western fashion, or a combination of both. In sharp contrast, the effigies are usually minimal if both bride and groom are from working- or lower-class families; made out of cardboard, they normally are around two to four feet tall (they sometimes look like large paper dolls). Their faces are crudely (if not arbitrarily) drawn; and their clothes are commonly traditional Chinese fashion.

Shortly after the effigies/paper figures have been created, these images, according to their gender, will be placed respectively in the abode of the bride or groom (see previous section). They will be carried to the house of the groom on the day of the wedding ceremony, designated by a veteran fortune-teller.

Several traits can be identified regarding the nature and modus operandi of this absentee service (that is, a service without the protagonists, bride and groom). In the first place, this practice is considered an alternative of turning two deceased adults who had established a solid connection (see above) into *jie fa fu qi* (literally "entwined-haired husband and wife," meaning husband and wife who will live together everlastingly). Based on this faith, people who participate in this ritual, whether or not they know one another, generally are expected to treat one another as in-laws. (While this pseudo-relationship might be kept for a period of time, it seems rare that it will be sustained permanently.) These in-laws, according to prearranged scripts, must interact with one another enthusiastically and amiably, as if they had known one another for a long time.

In other words, despite the fact that this wedding is phony — purely a play because only "supporting actors" are in attendance — its configuration is essentially the same as a conventional nuptial ceremony: in this regard, most of the red tape surrounding the traditional marriage ritual can be observed in this fake wedding (this perhaps is the reason why this type of ghost marriage gives outsiders an impression that it is indistinguishable from a real wedding). For instance, adults in attendance, as remarked above, have to greet one another sincerely and ardently, in spite of the embarrassing situation that some of them might be totally unknown to one another. As for children, they normally will be required to call certain grown-ups grandpa or grandma, grand-uncle or grand-aunt, and so forth, even though these grown persons are complete strangers. Under these mechanisms of impression management (or laws of interaction order), everybody, according to his/her hierarchal status, is given a role to play.[15] As a result of this role assignment, every person has to show verbal manner when he/she is presenting himself/herself. This interaction fashion not only can help strangers recognize one another, it also can prevent unwelcome and offensive behaviors such as questioning the value of the wedding or calling the wedding a superstition. Furthermore, it can keep every role player from alienating from his/her part.[16] So, just as the following paragraph describes, acts considered to be rude or provocative usually can be dodged (or at least minimized):

> Unmeant gestures, inopportune intrusions, and faux pas are sources of embarrassment and dissonance which are typically unintended by the person who is responsible for making them and which would be avoided were the individual to know in advance the consequences of his activity (Goffman, 1959: 210)

Another convention that people must follow when they are invited to participate in a spirit wedding is the wearing of appropriate formal attire. Women usually have to choose a crimson or bright-colored outfit (according to traditional Chinese customs, these colors are symbols of joyfulness and pleasure), and men have to put on smart Western-style clothes or traditional Chinese garments, as if they are attending an important meeting. This practice, in the light of Goffman's (1966) analysis of how people behave in public settings, contains at least two functions. First, it is a way for known persons to display visual etiquette. Partially because of this presentation, the unstructured or ambiguous relationship between acquainted parties (some are from the bride's side, the others are from the groom's side) may become structured and definite. In addition to helping familiar individuals transform their bonds (whether loose or informal) into an enduring kinship, formal wear (including a uniform) can give unacquainted people a reason (Goffman, 1966: 124) for interaction (that is, all of these unfamiliar persons become obliged to congratulate a loving couple for their wedding). Given that this shared reason paves a way for unacquainted persons to engage in focused and directional interaction (which can be exemplified by the exchange of private information like name, residence, organizational affiliation, marital status, and so forth), this communication, as soon as it starts, will remind all parties involved of the fact that this wedding is not a game but a serious event. Under this context, a ceremonial atmosphere for the wedding normally can be created.

Some additional features regarding this wedding can be summarized as follows.

In the first place, people asked to attend have to offer gifts (which can be real or symbolic) to the bride and groom (the purpose of doing this, needless to say, is to congratulate the couple on their marriage). If these gifts are real objects (for instance, the three F's: flowers, fruits, and food), then such items are set on an altar or incense table so that the souls of the bride and groom can come to smell or taste them. By contrast, if the presents are symbolic (such as a paper car, paper clothes, paper furniture, paper jewelry, paper notes, paper stereo, or even paper "mansion"), then they are piled up in a room before the wedding rite is over. After the rite is over, all the gifts are taken to a spacious place or Buddhist temple to burn. This norm is based on the presumption that both the bride and the groom are "jobless persons." Therefore, it is necessary to send them items essential for daily life to help them survive. (This practice is regarded as a way to support the newlyweds; accordingly, objects that have instrumental value and are "usable" for dead people usually are preferred.)

After the ritual of presenting gifts, it is time for the banquet. This family gathering, just like other festivities and private meetings, gives people an opportunity to engage in interpersonal interaction. However, this party is not a feast in the traditional sense because compared to, say, a lavish American wedding, this social event always is small (generally speaking, no more than forty persons will become involved). Furthermore, according to present-day Taiwanese tradition, this feast must be held after dark: while identifying the standard time for this party is not easy because it varies from region to region, it seems that this private assembly is often held after 9:00 P.M. (10:00 P.M. to 4:00 A.M. tend to be the peak hours). One plausible factor that motivates people to choose this time interval to celebrate is that nighttime is much quieter than daytime. That can keep curious spectators (such as news reporters or anthropologists/sociologists) from disturbing the marriage ceremony, especially the hour when the bride-elect and the groom-elect have been scheduled to establish formal a marital relationship.[17]

In addition to keeping potential troublemakers from creating commotion, this midnight dinner is fairly quiet, compared to a typical Chinese wedding (which, more often than not, is tumultuous for it is normally held in a public place like a hotel or tea house, where disorderly behaviors caused by binge drinking are common). A key factor in keeping this late-night meal from growing boisterous is that neither distilled beverages including beer nor a square meal are served. Instead, only soft drinks, tea, and snacks will be furnished. Under this alcohol-free and ascetic situation, it is very unlikely that someone will become drunk and, accordingly, show undesirable behaviors.

On the whole, this banquet tends to function subtly.[18] Therefore, it can be held in residential districts after the bedtime hour. (As a matter of fact, it is customarily held in residential areas instead of public places, or *yin miao.*) What should be noted is that since this feast is usually held in a private space, the interior of that space (which, fundamentally, is an apartment in Taiwan) always will be decorated as if a traditional wedding is being held. Moreover, this party is not merely attended by relatives and friends of the bride and the groom. Two crucial figures have to be there as well: one is the matchmaker, the other a Buddhist or Taoist monk. The former will serve as "ring announcer," analogous to that for a boxing or martial arts event. The matchmaker's major job is to introduce the demographic background of the bride and groom and to explain why these two young persons were born to stay together. This speech usually does not exceed ten minutes. The monk acts as a medium. His chief job is to help the couple live together in the otherworld. To achieve this goal, this monk will perform a series of rites (which embrace components of both the funeral and wedding) to draw the souls of the bride and the groom together. Of these rituals, the most critical is to cremate the following things in a small burner (which can be utilized inside a house):

- tokens of the bride and groom (such as their nails, hair, pictures, or clothes)
- a piece of red paper with the name and horoscope of the bride and bridegroom
- amulets (written on several pieces of white paper)
- joss paper and joss notes (which function as dowries and gifts)

When all of these things have been reduced to ashes, the spirit tablets, effigies, and/or pictures of the newlyweds will be put together in the house of bridegroom's parents. Then the matchmaker, who tends to play a role similar to that of a pastor at this moment, will proclaim that Mr. X and Miss Y have legitimately become husband and wife.[19] After all of these religious procedures have finished, attendees of the party will leave silently. Since this departing act generally is noiseless, people who live in the surrounding quarters usually will not realize that a ghost marriage has just been held in their neighborhood.

III. Husband a Living Person, Wife a Dead Individual

The third category of ghost marriage — husband a living individual while wife a deceased person — includes two varieties. The first one is similar to the typology portrayed above: the couple were fiancée and fiancé before their marital relationship became official (if they were not engaged, a very personal relationship still could be found between them). The only difference between these two typologies is that in the former case, bridegroom is a living person.

The second variety is totally different from the typology examined in the preceding section: not only were the couple not fiancée and fiancé (that is, they did not create an exclusive private bond), but the groom, as a living individual, had never met the bride while she was still alive. It is this type of ghost marriage that will be inspected in this section.

From the viewpoint of family sociology, having a living male take an unknown and deceased female as wife is very unlikely, if not totally impossible. The reason is obvious: few males are willing to be bound by a substantially imaginary marriage relationship and to live solitarily as if he were a widower. Given that having a living male marry a dead female is essentially impossible, parents in northeastern or southern Taiwan who want to find a son-in-law for their deceased daughter (who could be a little girl, a teenager, or a young adult at the time of death) usually will use one of two techniques to find a husband for their daughter (Yao, 1991: 77–80).

The first method is to have two family members, a child and an adult, place a red envelope on a street corner or under a tree in early morning. Inside the envelope are money and a piece of red paper with the name and birthday of the bride-elect on it. After this "trap" is set, the child and the adult will wait in a place where they can hide and keep an eye on the red envelope. If a naïve man picks up the envelope (whether this behavior is driven by curiosity is not discussed here because it is beyond the scope of this chapter to list all possible psychological motivations that might lead to this behavior), the child will immediately run to the man and call him uncle. (If a woman, a minor, or an elderly man picks up the envelope, the adult hiding nearby will come out and ask this "unqualified" candidate to put the envelope back where it was.) The adult accompanying the child will also appear and greet the man with a smile and friendly words. Then the innocent man will be told that he has been chosen by a given deity to be the husband of a deceased young lady. Therefore, he must accept this offer and prepare to marry his fiancée.

After hearing this unexpected "good news," most fortunate men will agree to marry the deceased woman whom they have never met before. This obedient act, to an extent, can be explained by the fact that Greater China, while it is not a politically unified entity, is a society dominated by Buddhist thoughts. As a result of this cultural homogeneity, people generally believe that all good and bad things (whether they are man-made accidents or supernatural events) that have happened/will happen to them during this life are causally related to certain personal behaviors of the previous life. Such a karma-centered mindset, under most circumstances, also makes those "blessed" men who collect the red envelope accept the theory that they are predestined to have a ghost wife. Denying or trying to alter this predetermined destiny will displease deities and could bring about disasters.

Although placing an unattended red envelope in an inconspicuous location to have a simple-minded adult male play the matchmaking game enables certain dead females to find their husband, this method, no matter how successful it was in helping female ghosts get married, has a serious flaw: namely, it is too random/unsystematic to filter the background of the groom-to-be. In other words, with the exception of the previously mentioned "unqualified" persons, this game allows all adult males (if they look younger than sixty years old) to play. Thus it is not unusual that parents (especially desperate ones) choose a social outcast (for instance, a carrier of the AIDS virus, a beggar, drug addict, fugitive, homeless person, individual with physical deformities, or mentally retarded person) as son-in-law for their daughter.

Given that the red envelope approach is, to an extent, risky (for the selected groom may bring troubles to the bride's family), this method, while it is still utilized by some parents in contemporary Taiwan, has become less and less visible in the past two decades. In contrast, choosing a *gui mei ren* (ghost matchmaker) and having this person do the job of searching for an appropriate candidate seems to have developed into the mainstream modus operandi (one ideal place to find a ghost matchmaker is Ilan, a prosperous town in northeastern Taiwan).

In terms of helping parents get a good husband for their deceased daughter, appointing a ghost matchmaker appears far more satisfactory. This is because the red envelope trick, as indicated, depends solely on pure luck. That gives parents of the bride-elect few opportunities to avoid getting a son-in-law whose horoscope is believed to be totally incompatible with their daughter's. In contrast, a ghost matchmaker can carefully check the family background of all possible players. Then, based on the information collected, the matchmaker can recommend the finest candidate to her/his clients. This goal-keeping task, while it might be time-consuming, can prevent disqualified or unwelcome males (especially those with delinquent records) from entering the ghost marriage market. Consequently, more and more parents in Taiwan who want to engage in type III spirit marriage select a ghost matchmaker to take care of things. (This probably is why *gui mei ren* has become a professional occupation in current Taiwan.)

What should be pointed out is that if the man selected to marry the unwed girl is single, then on the day of the engagement, this man must let a ghost matchmaker carry his betrothed gifts (wedding cakes, dried fruits, food, and the like) to the house of his would-be father-in-law/ mother-in-law. In return, this man will receive a variety of presents from his prospective father-in-law/mother-in-law (the value of these presents is greater than the betrothed gifts, whether the bride is from a wealthy clan, which usually will give the groom-to-be handsome dowries, or from a working-class family, which probably can afford only plain and simple stuff). Shortly after the engagement, parents of the bride-to-be must finish two required assignments. One is to seek advice from a fortune-teller about the auspicious day for the wedding; the other is to order an effigy for the bride. When these two tasks have been completed, the parents of the bride-elect will invite certain relatives and friends to participate in the wedding. This wedding, no matter how many economic benefits the groom can acquire from it, shares a number of qualities with its counterpart described in the previous section. For example:

- both weddings are a mixture of funeral and marriage
- both weddings are held on a designated day considered to be the luckiest
- both weddings involve effigy construction
- both weddings call for attendees to wear formal attire
- both weddings are merely a show (that is, attendees will play a certain role and are required to treat one another as in-laws as well as to engage in earnest interaction)
- both weddings, in spite of the fact that they are simply a drama, allow two families to establish a permanent relationship (at least in theory)

In addition to having the above traits in common, both weddings entail a late evening dinner. This social gathering, as mentioned earlier, is the final stage of the spirit marriage (in which the groom and the bride will be pronounced by a matchmaker or monk as legitimate spouses) and is not easy for outsiders to observe. Thus, after the wedding, the groom can escort his wife home without having to worry about unexpected interruption. This is particularly true in modern Taiwan because the groom can hire a taxi or use his own car to carry his wife home right after the dinner. After reaching the groom's house at midnight or in the early morning hours, the bride, as an effigy, will be placed on an altar along with the tablets of her husband's ancestors. Then she will officially become a member of her husband's family (that is, her name will be written into the genealogy of her husband's family).

One more feature of this wedding is that according to Taiwan's custom, the groom must go to his wife's house on the fourth day of his marriage. The purpose of this visit is to have the groom pay respect to his father-in-law/mother-in-law as well as to give him an opportunity to know clan members whom he has not met before (Yao, 1991: 79). As soon as this visit is over, the groom will become a permanent member of his wife's family.[20]

As an ingenious wedding system which enables living men and dead women to create a marital relationship, type III ghost marriage does not involve unmarried (young) males only. As a matter of fact, eligible married men, under certain circumstances, can be implicated in this type of wedding as well. One example took place in Taiwan in 2009. In June, 20, 1964, an airplane crashed in a rural area of central Taiwan. All fifty-seven persons on board were killed. After this incident, many villagers reported that certain victims of the accident appeared in their dreams and requested them to provide help. One of these villagers, a married woman, stated that, in 2006, a long-haired woman who lost her life in the 1964 disaster arose in her dream and told her that she wants to marry the villager's husband. She ignored the request at first, but the dream recurred in 2007 and 2008. In the end, the village woman agreed that her husband can take this female ghost as another wife. The wedding was held in 2009. After that, the female ghost never emerged again (You, 2010).

No matter how bizarre (or credible) the above story may sound, marrying a ghost bride due to the enlightenment of a vision appears uncommon and atypical. What appears "common" and "typical" is that some wedded men firmly believe that dead people (whether they are known or unknown parties) can act as "guardian angels." Therefore, the men believe, if they can marry a female spirit, this otherworldly wife will help them stay away from calamity, offer them covert protection, and bring them good luck.

Another factor that motivates a few married men to find a ghost partner is that some (especially those who do not have a stable job or reliable income) want to acquire dowries (which, as indicated earlier, could be generous) to support their life. Believing that marrying a deceased daughter of a wealthy family will allow them to acquire quick money, these men, once they can convince their wives, will ask a ghost matchmaker to help them find an appropriate spouse. Then they will get married again.

Compared to those men who desperately want to remarry to gain *rong* (glory), *hua* (splendor), *fu* (wealth), and *gui* (nobility) overnight, some married men get involved in spirit marriage because of spouse encouragement. Generally speaking, men authorized to engage in extramarital affairs are entrepreneurs or company owners. As successful businessmen, they naturally have the financial ability to frequent sex business like brothels and strip clubs. Since this way of life is likely to turn these males into womanizers, their wives, needless to say, must find ways to rectify the condition. One option is to convince their husbands to marry a deceased female (who, as noted previously, can function as a guardian angel). So despite the fact that the human soul cannot be seen by naked eyes, these angry or anxious married women believe that if they can find a Miss Ghost as supervisor, the latter will dissuade their womanizing husband from dating young girls and teach him a lesson if he keeps committing disloyal behaviors.

Simply speaking, ghost marriage of the third typology can be divided into three subcategories: dream-inspired, dowry-induced, and deterrence-initiated. No matter which factor triggers a wedded man to take a dead woman as his wife, this woman, technically speaking, will become his legitimate spouse. By contrast, his current wife, according to the custom of *min nan* (South Fujian) and Taiwan, will become concubine: right after the tablet or effigy of the ghost bride, the legal wife, has been placed on the family altar on the day of marriage, the concubine must burn joss sticks to greet her and call her big sister. Based on this new family relation/hierarchy, married males cannot sleep with their living wife for three days after they bring their newlywed wife home. Instead, during that three-day period, the groom must sleep with a set of clothes which his "new wife" had ever wore. The groom, before the wedding, must get the dress from his in-laws and arrange it on a bed to resemble a sleeping woman. The concubine, no matter how she feels, has to stay in a different room (Yao, 1991: 83).[21]

After the separation interval is over, the groom must go to his in-laws' house with his concubine to pay his respects to senior family members and to meet unfamiliar relatives (this tradition is called *gui ning* in Chinese, meaning a woman goes back to her paternal family for a visit shortly after she is married). On this occasion, the concubine has to serve as surrogate bride and do all the jobs (such as proposing a toast) which a bride is supposed to do at a normal wedding. When this visit (which normally is performed at night) is finished, the kinship between the groom and his in-laws, like the one mentioned above, will become perpetual.

IV. Husband a Dead Person, Wife a Living Individual

The last type of ghost marriage examined in this chapter involves a dead male and a living female. This particular style of wedding did exist in ancient China because before the twentieth century, China was an authoritarian patriarchal society.[22] That gave males virtually unlimited power to dominate females: not only could males (whether married or unmarried) frequent red-light districts, legally become involved in polygyny, and purchase female victims of natural disasters as concubines, maidservants, singers, or prostitutes (see Chapter 6); but females were deprived of the right to make decisions about their marriage. Under this social ethos, females must submit themselves to their husband and demonstrate absolute allegiance to family life after they were engaged or wedded. This extremely unjust marriage system can be exemplified by the ingrained tradition that when a married female became a widow, she was expected to remain single for the rest of her life, even if she was still young. Those who could fulfill this cultural expectation (which, for many modern American/Western women, is hard to believe) would be extolled as role models. On the contrary, if they failed to comply with this social norm (for instance, by engaging in an illicit love affair), these women would be labeled adulteresses. Predictably, they would be humiliated relentlessly (whether verbally or physically). Numerous unfaithful women committed suicide because of enormous social pressure.

Fearing that disloyalty to marriage/gender relationship could bring infinite humiliation and would dishonor their family, conventional Chinese women usually had to show commitment as long as they were betrothed to a male chosen by their parents, grandparents, and/or clan seniors. This tradition could be disastrous for certain young females if the groom-to-be died unexpectedly before the wedding. If this did happen, then such women could be compelled by their parents to marry a dummy representing their husband in order to preserve personal chastity as well as to maintain family honor. It is impossible to determine the degree to which this mode of family creation prevailed in pre-modern China (partially due to the dilemma that in traditional China, few intellectuals addressed this subject matter systematically), but it appears appropriate to infer that the closer the relationship between the parents of bride-to-be and groom-to-be, the higher the possibility that type IV ghost marriage would be pursued.

If a spirit marriage as described in this section was performed, then the bride (who would become a young widow right after the wedding) would be doomed to live alone permanently. One decisive factor that kept this tradition alive was that married women in traditional China were no longer regarded as a member of their paternal family. Therefore, unlike those Western young adults who still live with their parents because they cannot become economically independent after finishing higher education, the bride basically had to live by herself and could not return to her birth family for emotional support (obtaining economic assistance, however, was possible). She could enjoy family life only by adopting an orphan or "extra child" from her fiancé's family.

From the perspective of feminism, forcing a young woman to marry a male effigy and to live as a widow for decades is undoubtedly a ludicrous practice. To use modern criminal justice terms, this custom is a spiritual punishment without parole. An unknown number of married young women in traditional China took their own life to end unbearable emotional torture. Fortunately, ghost marriage that coerces women to keep permanent widowhood has been no longer visible in China for many years as numerous old and corrupt social customs were suppressed by the communists in the 1950s and 1960s. Thanks to this social change, females in China, starting in the late 1980s and 1990s, enjoy more and more opportunities to hold up half the sky (Tao et al., 2004).

Ghost Marriage, Cultural Murder, and Missing Women

As portrayed at the beginning of this chapter, spirit/ghost marriage in China and Taiwan can be divided into four prototypes:

- type I: both husband and wife are deceased adolescents
- type II: both husband and wife are deceased young adults
- type III: husband a living individual, wife a dead person
- type IV: husband a dead individual, wife a living person

Of these prototypes, the first three categories, to a varying extent, still can be observed in a few places in modern-day Taiwan (as well as certain Chinese communities in Indonesia, Malaysia, and Singapore). As for type IV, it seems to have disappeared completely in Greater China.

Although spirit marriage has not been seen in contemporary China for decades, the vanishing of this custom appears merely temporary. This tradition has resurfaced in some parts of North China, such as Shanxi, Hebei, and Shangdong, in the past ten years. Factors that prompted the reemergence of this custom include rapid economic development, massive population migration, and tolerance of local bureaucrats. As a result, it is possible that an unknown number of missing young women might have been murdered to satisfy the need for female remains: like the organ trade, drug transactions, and other contraband dealings, forcing a living female to marry to a lifeless male is illegal in China. However, despite prohibitions by law, some peasants (a few of them are street bureaucrats as well) still want to find a wife for a deceased family member (particularly an unmarried male) so the genealogy of that member can continue. To achieve this goal, certain peasants secretly buy female corpses from "dealers." These dealers, in turn, will use whatever means they can think of to ensnare young females, especially drifting peasant women from impoverished inland provinces. (These women desperately want to migrate to a big city to obtain a stable job, but many of them cannot settle down in the city because they lack legal documents.) After such women are under the control of the "dealers," they will, almost without exception, be slain and sold. The wedding ceremonies portrayed in the previous sections will then be performed to prove that these murdered women and their boyfriend or fiancé have become married couples. One of the most dangerous places that migrant peasant women fall victim to these horrible experiences is railway stations (particularly in big cities; see photograph in Chapter 6). These stations usually are high-crime locations and even become lawless during the Chinese New Year and Labor Day holidays, chiefly because of the influx of millions of travelers and the shortage of law enforcement agents. These seemingly innocuous sites where human traffickers conduct business enable female-corpse dealers to seize wandering women as prisoners without attracting police notice. Sadly, the disappearance of these women is permanent.

For criminologists, the act of slaughtering women to make them ghost brides differs from average homicidal behavior in several aspects. One of them is that the former is precipitated and, to an extent, justified by a social belief. As a result of this rationalization, the former can be regarded as a cultural murder (for other versions of cultural crime, see Ferrell & Sanders, 1995, and Oldenburg, 2002). According to the example examined in the next pages, murderous behavior triggered by ghost marriage appears to have the subsequent qualities:

- it involves multiple players ("dealer"/"supplier," "customer," and victim)
- it involves carefully designed acts ("dealer"/"supplier" cautiously selects his target and meticulously devises his method of execution as well as a cover-up technique), which, as a whole, function as an underground mechanism of taking women's life
- it involves the economic law of demand and supply
- it is very likely to develop into a series of killings because, under the sway of the law of demand and supply, the dealer will keep slaying simple-mined women and won't stop until he is caught

In any event, in the 1990s and 2000s, some murder cases related to spirit marriage took place in Hebei, Shanxi and several provinces of North China (Huang, 2008: 40–41; Wang, 2007). In those cases, a few peasant families offered high rewards for female corpses to help their deceased brothers, sons, or fathers get married or remarried. This demand, however, could not be met easily because, according to the law, all female bodies (unless they are historical relics or national treasures) must be cremated. Since female remains are extremely difficult to obtain through lawful channels, suppliers usually will find that they have few options but kidnapping to satisfy the market for female corpses. In this way certain women were abducted, killed, and sold as commodities.

Regardless of the bounty that suppliers of female bodies can obtain, such murderers usually will use the trick of cajolery to acquire the "merchandise."[23] More specifically, brokers of female remains generally will make potential victims believe that they can find a stable, better-paid job or travel everywhere without expense. Women who agree to follow their "helpers" or "sponsors," are soon killed and sold to those (peasant) families that still practice spiritual marriage.

The homicide cases mentioned above show that some women in China are erased (Strong, 2008) when they are persuaded to go to some unknown but attractive place. In those unfamiliar places, these females will be deliberately assaulted, like penned pigs awaiting butchery, and have few chances to stay alive.

Concluding Remarks

As a peculiar marriage system, *ming hun* has existed in Greater China for numerous generations. The raison d'être of this system can be dated back to the Shang dynasty (1600–1045 B.C.), when early people believed that human souls, as their existence is never-ending, could establish marital relationships with spirits or living humans. Based on this traditional faith, some people in present-day China believe that if they can find a wife for a deceased member of their family, then this dead person should be able to prolong his own pedigree in the otherworld. On the other hand, finding a living woman as a wife for this dead person is effectively impossible, for if females enjoy more and more opportunities to hold up half the sky (see previous pages) in economically prosperous China, Taiwan, or even Hong Kong, then what woman would be willing to maintain permanent widowhood for an unknown deceased male? Facing this reality, certain peasants are driven to search privately for female dead bodies as substitutes. All of these covert acts increasingly let a demand market for female remains take shape in rural China in the past decade.

While it is hard to determine the size of this emerging market, three points can be proposed regarding the nature and operation of this hidden mechanism.

First, the emergence of this market is related not only to the economic law of demand and supply but to the Buddhist idea that human life is imperishable. Given that the latter provides a justifying ground for people to engage in odd mate-selection behaviors like the ones discussed in this chapter, the Buddhist theory of spirit immortality, compared to economic forces, tends to play a more profound and decisive role in generating and sustaining a female corpse market in Greater China.

Second, since the formation of this market is intellectually supported by an ingrained Buddhist philosophy, it will, at least technically, continue in the foreseeable future. It may not vanish until this Buddhist faith is challenged or rejected.

Finally, certain young females (particularly seasonal laborers) appear exceptionally vulnerable to become victims of ghost marriage-related murder: as can be seen in Chapter 6, social control in a number of places of modern China (such as railway stations located in large cities) have been weakened by two unprecedented events — extremely fast economic development and high population turnover. These new socioeconomic trends inevitably turn many rural young women who just arrived in big cities to find jobs into vanished individuals. Since these young females are isolated and friendless, they can easily go missing if they do not take steps to protect themselves.

To sum up, the instances of Hebei and Shanxi mentioned above are an example of a social problem which has been lying dormant in China for many decades. As this problem is awakening, it is all too likely that some women will keep falling into the traps set by female corpse hunters and become lost.

PART III

Missing Females with Some Chances to Re-Emerge

CHAPTER 5

Comfort Women

Coercing innocent Asian and European women to become *ianfu*[1] (literally, "comfort women") to provide sexual services to Japanese troops is one of the atrocities endorsed/supported by the Japanese authorities before and during World War II. According to unofficial statistics (Chung, 2000: 17; Edgerton, 1998: 16; Farr, 2005: 198; Hsieh, 1995: 154; Yoshime, 2000: 29), at least 200,000 Chinese and Korean females were compelled to become sex slaves.[2] Since nearly all *ianfu* were victims of gang rape, forced abortion, physical mistreatment/torture, and had endured psychological ordeals, sex slavery is considered to be one of the most horrific and malicious war crimes directed by the Japanese military in the 1930s and 1940s (Neier, 1998: 47).

In the past four thousand years, there have been innumerable wars on earth. Although wars (whether civil struggles or international conflicts) vary in cause, casualty numbers, duration, impact, magnitude, leadership, organizational pattern, and technological level, all wars seem to have one thing in common: they provide soldiers and paramilitary groups (such as "freedom fighters" and militias with opportunities to enjoy free sex and to engage in disorderly sexual behaviors:

> Rape, enslaved prostitution, and other sexual violence against women have been a part of war for all of recorded history — across all cultures, and in all kinds of wars, be they religious, colonizing, or revolutionary [Farr, 2005: 165].

This feature can be exemplified by those areas devastated by military clashes (especially ethnic wars and guerrilla movements), such as the disunited states of America during the Civil War (Lowry, 1994, 2006: 114–182), the Germany-annexed Belgium during the first World War (Zuckerman, 2003), the rural towns of Angola stricken by bandits/terrorists in the 1960s

(Teixeira, 1965: 100–101), the killing fields of Southeast/South Asia in the 1960s and the 1970s (Brownmiller, 1993: 31–113), villages controlled by contras in Guatemala and Nicaragua in the 1980s (Ciborski, 2000; Vukelich, 2000), the disintegrated Yugoslavia in the early 1990s (Stiglmayer, 1994), and the Darfur district of Sudan in the 2000s (Bales, 2005: 128–129).

In brief, despite the fact that wars involve diverse causes and take different forms, armed struggles always turn an ordered society into a chaotic and disorganized one. Anomie and anarchy then give delinquent armed males many chances to commit rape when women lose their homes and become refugees. These female refugees, even if they are accompanied by competent male guardians like a father or husband, usually become a free commodity or property without proprietor if they cannot break away from their rootless, defenseless status within a short period of time.

The seemingly predestined lot of females during war (that is, becoming prey of sex offenders) can be seen clearly from two circumstances. The first condition is that during the period of military conquest, conquerors can resort to sex crime to prove their superiority. Genghis Khan, after subduing countless cities and countries, provides a vivid description for this point:

> The greatest joy a man can know is to conquer his enemies and drive them before him. To ride their horses and take away their possessions. To see the faces of those who were dear to him bedewed with tears, and to clasp their wives and daughters in his arms [Lowry, 2006: 114].

The second circumstance (which tends to be far more common in the twentieth and twenty-first centuries) is that when the future of a war is unclear or when a war is transformed into a bloody stalemate, then raping the opponent's women more often than not becomes the norm. This characteristic can be demonstrated by the following statement:

> Women have always been raped in wartime.... Pares seem to be part and parcel of a soldier's life.... He rapes because he wants to engage in violence. He rapes because he wants to demonstrate his power. He rapes because he is the victor. He rapes because the woman is the enemy's women.... He rapes because the woman is herself the enemy whom he wishes to humiliate and annihilate. He rapes because he despises women.... He rapes because the acquisition of the female body means a piece of territory conquered. He rapes to take out on someone else the humiliation he has suffered in the war. He rapes to work off his fears. He rapes because it's really some fun with the guys. He rapes because war ... has weakened his aggressiveness, and he directs it at those who play a subordinate role in the world of war [Stiglmayer, 1994: 84].

To sum up, war-ravaged zones always become places full of violence. Since these areas sooner or later become criminogenic, it is typical that the sex industry there becomes more and more prosperous (which also means that the business of woman kidnapping, trafficking, and selling flourishes). In this regard, cities such as Beijing, Shanghai, Nanjing, and Hong Kong, as well as rural areas occupied by Japanese troops in the 1930s and 1940s, provide tons of instances for the interplay between war and sex (see the following sections).

Japanese Troops, War, and Sex

For women's rights campaigners and historians who study Sino-Japanese relations, one of the atrocities committed by the Japanese military during the Sino-Japanese War (1937–1945) was the creation of so-called comfort stations (*wei an suo* in Chinese or *ianjo* in Japanese) in the territories of the Empire of Japan (which culminated in the annexation of the South Pacific in 1942). Because of the establishment of these military brothels, hundreds of thousands of Asian and European females became sex slaves or victims of forced prostitution (Soh, 2008: 72). Not until the end of World War II did some of these unfortunate women regain freedom.

From the perspective of government crime or state terror, the emergence of *wei an* stations is not an unplanned or incoherent event in the war history of Japan. First, traditional Japanese warriors (*samurai*) had developed the custom of hanging around *yūjoya* (houses of sexual entertainers, equivalent to modern nightclub-cum-brothels) as early as the twelfth century (Chen, 2006: 9). Second, commercialized sex was supported and institutionalized by Toyotomi Hedeyoshi and Tokugawa Ieyasu, two of the unifiers of Japan (Jansen, 2000: 17–31), in the sixteenth and seventeenth centuries (Chen, 2006: 5–16). And, third, during the Meiji era (1868–1912), entrepreneurs and politicians formed the tradition of doing businesses, making decisions, and/or reaching agreements in *geigi* houses[3] (Chen, 2006: 24). The appearance of *wei an* stations thus should be viewed as an extension of the unique culture of sexual politics in Japan. In this regard, the system of *wei an* stations is unparalleled in modern military history because no regime was as considerate and sympathetic as the Japanese government in constructing brothels exclusively for military men.

Like *wei an* stations/*ianjo* which were popular in areas annexed by Japanese troops before 1945, indiscriminate sex assaults (almost all of which were sadistic and extremely violent) were ubiquitous in those regions as well. Although these incidents of bestial rape (Rabe, 1998: 121), which largely took place in anarchic areas (particularly severely devastated towns and villages located at the front), are very difficult, if not impossible, for contemporary criminologists, historians, and sociologists to report comprehensively and systematically, certain records about such brutal and barbarian acts are still obtainable (see Chang, 1997; Xie, 2005; Yamamoto, 2000).

In any event, historical literature and data indicate that the relationship between Japanese troops and sex crime (whether deliberate/organized or opportunistic/arbitrary) was inseparable before 1945. Partially because of this feature, Japanese troops were called blocs of beasts by Western reporters in the 1930s (Hsieh, 1995: 42). The phenomenon of how and why sex adventure or lust for women became a trademark of Japanese troops before the end of World War II will be examined in this chapter.

Japanese Troops and Organized Sex Assaults: The Evolution of the Comfort Woman System

I. SAMURAI AND YŪJO

As mentioned above, as early as the twelfth century, *samurai* had already developed the tradition of lingering on *yūjoya*. According to Goodwin (2006) and other scholars, the establishment of this tradition can be attributed to the following factors.

First, during the seventh century, the teachings of Confucianism (together with other cultural elements like architecture, art, and written Chinese) were introduced from China/Korea to Japan and were turned into laws (Feng, 2000:130–131). Since Confucianism is a philosophy that justifies gender hierarchy/male domination, the importation of this belief system was apparently disastrous for Japanese females in terms of civil rights. The following paragraph illustrates this point vividly:

> [One] relationship that Confucius spoke about was between husband and wife. Wives were to be completely subservient to their husbands. They were never to question their husbands nor show any sign of disrespect. A double standard existed in the sexual relationship between husband and wife. If it was discovered that a married woman was having an adulterous affair, the punishment was death. Meanwhile, men who could afford it usually had concubines or secondary wives. There was no penalty for this unfaithfulness [Woods, 2004: 31].

No matter how many married men got involved in affairs after gender roles were standardized and regulated by Confucianism and various laws,

Japan had grown to be a patriarchal society since the mid-seventh century. In this social system, males (especially those who belonged to the ruling class) enjoyed enormous power over females. In contrast, females (just like their counterparts in China and Korea) were regularly deprived of political power and economic rights as a consequence of "a change in family structures from a system with strong maternal rights and individual freedom of choice in marriage to a patriarchal system in which women were controlled by men and monogamy was expected of wives" (Goodwin, 2006: 14). Due to this institutionalized discrimination, unmarried women (particularly those from bankrupt peasant families) had few rights or opportunities for work except jobs related to public entertainment or the manufacturing industry (the former seemed much more common than the latter). Of those females who grew to be entertainers (most of them were dancers, singers, or both), some became the so-called *asobime* or *yūjo* (literally, "traveling girls"). Despite their diverse backgrounds and personal stories, these *asobime/yūjo*, have two traits in common. The first one is that, as the titles suggest, these women were wanderers. They had to move about to find an audience. Second, since these entertainers had to migrate constantly to look for spectators, they usually would concentrate in ports, courier stations, towns where festivals were held, or in other places that travelers and businessmen frequent.

After the emergence of *asobime/yūjo*, some itinerant performers began to engage in the sex trade,[4] often as sexual entertainers. Eventually, they no longer moved around periodically, instead concentrating in places like inns, taverns, or tea houses. They then gradually transformed into surrogate wives or concubines of *samurai* and other men (whether married or unmarried) who must leave their family for several months (or even longer) to handle a variety of businesses. This marital system was preserved for almost one thousand years. Then in the early 1600s, when Japan was unified by Tokugawa Ieyasu, it was accepted and normalized by the Tokugawa shogunate.

II. ORIGINS OF SEXUAL POLITICS

Before 1868, Japan was a feudal society. Pre–1868 Japan was composed of numerous fiefdoms, like China during the Spring and Autumn period, approximately 770 to 476 B.C. Because of this sociopolitical structure, political power was not enjoyed substantially by the emperor but split (although not evenly) among feudal lords/local sovereigns called *daimyo* and certain powerful *samurai* houses that assisted *daimyo* to rule. This condition motivated virtually all *daimyo* to get involved in the power struggle (especially armed conflict), for these very important persons enjoyed an autonomous status similar to the Chinese warlords of the early twentieth century. It was necessary for these provincial monarchs to overpower their opponents to avoid losing territories and political influence.

No matter what military strategies, political channels, and/or economic policies were used by *daimyo* to survive, it was common for competing lords to fight against one another repeatedly. On the other hand, since no one was strong enough to wipe out all enemies (that is, no one was weak enough to be annihilated), all fiefdoms functioned as de facto independent kingdoms. This chaotic and fragmented state of affairs did not change significantly until the sixteenth century when most *samurai* houses in Central Japan were defeated by Oda Nobunaga (Jansen, 2000: 11–17). Although Oda merely conquered approximately one-third of Japan (Jansen, 2000: 15), he did lay a foundation for his successors to create a centralized government.

Oda Nobunaga was succeeded by Toyotomi Hedeyoshi and Tokugawa Ieyasu. Both men continued to use military and political means to subdue their rivals. These efforts at last let Japan become a unified country in the early seventeenth century.

Japan had developed into a unified nation after 1610s, but some *samurai* houses (particularly those in southern Japan) were still unruly and posed a potential threat to the shogunate. With this in mind, Toyotomi and Tokugawa adopted several policies to suppress untamed warrior clans. One of the policies (or countermeasures) formulated by Toyotomi Hedeyoshi and Tokugawa Ieyasu was to construct entertainment districts called *yūkaku*.[5] These districts, in terms of helping Toyotomi and Tokugawa maintain the stability of shogunate, made the following contributions (Chen, 2006: 7).

First, *yūkaku* were high-class red-light districts. They had large and magnificent buildings, and every building had numerous dancers and singers/sexual entertainers). These places were deemed by and large as homes by *samurai* (whether single or married) who must leave their real homes to engage in a combat or to carry out certain military or commercial missions.[6]

Second, these luxurious amusement districts that functioned as substitute homes cost the *samurai* (including potentially defiant provincial lords) a considerable fortune. This condition was what Toyotomi Hedeyoshi and Tokugawa shoguns intended because, like modern-day casino resorts in Las Vegas, they could weaken considerably the financial might of insubordinate *daimyo* who might mobilize the masses to challenge the authorities. That means *yūkaku* could provide enormous taxes to the government by sucking away the wealth of *daimyo*. In addition to these financial advantages, owners of *yūkaku*, under the patronage of shogunate, were required to help the shogunate to monitor the suspicious actions of all customers and to arrest suspected rebels.[7]

Regardless of the profits which the Tokugawa regime obtained from *yūkaku*, the appearance of these men's heavens was undoubtedly a monumental event in the history of early modern Japan: it symbolized that the sex industry was formally endorsed and sponsored by the authorities. Since commercialized sex was accepted and, to an extent, encouraged by the Tokugawa shogunate, red-light districts were patronized frequently not only by businessmen and middle-ranking *samurai* but also by Toyotomi Hedeyoshi, Tokugawa Ieyasu, and the other top-ranking military commanders. This new lifestyle was continued by ruling elites in the subsequent two centuries and evolved gradually into a custom in politics. Ultimately, it became a deep-rooted political tradition/culture during the Meiji years (1868–1912). Throughout this period, numerous commercial deals and political decisions (including critical ones, such as initiating wars overseas), under the lubricating effect (Chen, 2006: 24) of feasts and courtesans, were made behind closed doors.

III. The Expansion of Japan's Sex Industry Overseas

During the nineteenth century (specifically during the Meiji epoch when Westernization had become an official policy and social ethos of Japan), it was common for politicians to negotiate or determine a course of action in recreation spots like *geigi* houses. Consequently, not only did such men's clubs increase remarkably in quantity, but the practice of woman trafficking was tolerated (or even disregarded) by law enforcement authorities of the Tokugawa/Meiji government. This social phenomenon was much condemned by Western diplomats and reporters in the 1860s and 1870s when campaigners of women's rights movement advocated a series of radical practices (including the abolition of prostitution) to protect politically and economically suppressed females.[8] Under strong international pressure imposed by feminists and other moral entrepreneurs (Becker, 1966: 147–163), the Meiji government took several measures to alleviate international waves of criticism, such as promulgating the Prostitute Emancipation Order (which, before 1950, was actually unknown to most sex workers and never implemented seriously) and changing the term *yūkaku*, which has explicit sexual connotations, to *kashizashiki*,[9] an implicit phrase for brothels (Chen, 2006: 42). Unfortunately, none of these practices proved to have substantial effects on preventing the prostitution business from growing, let alone eradicating the sex trade.

Compared to issuing the Prostitute Emancipation Order and inventing new terms to keep the prosperous sex industry low profile (or even to deny the existence of such an industry), an event not directly related to the efforts to suppress prostitution — encouraging bankrupt people to go overseas — was much more successful in limiting the expansion of prostitution in Japan proper. In the 1870s, many villages in Japan were stricken by severe natural disasters. Worried that these disasters might lead to large-scale revolts, the Meiji government adopted some emergency measures to help displaced people (particularly impoverished peasants) overcome financial hardships or find jobs. One of these measures was to encourage people to go to China (mainly Manchuria and Shanghai), the Far East (Russia, Korea, and Southeast Asia, especially Hong Kong and Singapore), Hawaii, or even South America (particularly Argentina and Brazil) to establish a business.[10] Inspired by this emigration policy, numerous lower-class and unemployed Japanese, including drifters and homeless people, went overseas to seek their fortune.

The emigration policy attracted not only low-income persons; many involved in the sex industry, such as brothel keepers, pimps, in woman traffickers and thugs who kidnapped and sold young women, were also drawn into this treasure-hunting movement. With the involvement of these sex adventurers, tens of thousands of brothels (euphemistically called bars, inns, massage parlors, tea houses, and so on) were created in Honolulu, Rio, São Paulo, and in all major cities of China, Korea, far eastern Russia, and Southeast Asia; (these included Dalian, Guangzhou, Harbin, Hong Kong, Hsin Ching, Jakarta, Kuala Lumpur, Manila, Pusan, Saigon, Seoul, Shanghai, Singapore, Vladivostok, and Wuhan) between the 1870s and the 1930s. All of these brothels (except those in Hawaii and South America) served as "refreshment" and "relaxation" centers for Japanese troops during the periods (see Table 5-1) when Japan was engaged in a territory-expanding war.

IV. THE CREATION OF COMFORT STATIONS

From the viewpoint of colonial history, Japan is clearly a latecomer: not only was Japan not involved in the Atlantic slave trade in the past five hundred years,[11] but the Tokugawa regime did not terminate the closed-door/seclusion policy until the 1850s when America began to establish an informal empire (Schumacher, 2007: 288) in the West Pacific. Although Japan was a late bloomer in terms of competing for settlements and maritime resources with European powers, the expansion of this nation was by no means less noteworthy than that of its European counterparts (for instance, the Napoleonic empire of the nineteenth century or the Third Reich of the 1930s and 1940s) because it did make almost all of Asia tremble in the first half of the twentieth century.[12]

As can be seen in Table 5-1, the Empire of Japan grew bigger and bigger after 1894. This Land of Sakura (which covered most of East and Southeast Asia and the South Pacific) ultimately became a mega-regime in 1942.

TABLE 5-1. JAPAN'S TERRITORY-EXPANDING WARS, 1890S–1940S

Period	Opponent	New Territory Obtained by Japan Before August 1945
1894–1895	China	Taiwan
1905	Russia	South Manchuria and southern Sakhalin
1910	Korea	Korea
1918–1922	Russia	East Siberia*
1931–1932	China	North Manchuria
1937–1938	China	North, Central, and coastal China
1941–1942	America	The Philippines
1941–1942	Great Britain	Burma, Hong Kong, and Malay Peninsula (including Singapore)
1941–1942	France	Indochina
1941–1942	Holland	Dutch East Indies and the South Pacific

*Under international and domestic pressures, Japanese troops withdrew from this region before the end of 1922.

During the process of expanding, Japanese fighting personnel of course faced challenges, tests, and dangers, ranging from bad weather to primitive living conditions to death. To motivate combatants to dedicate themselves totally to the emperor of Japan, to the so-called Holy War of Greater East Asia, and to help newly enlisted soldiers overcome anxiety and fear, the Japanese military took a virtually unrestrained stance toward military prostitution (this approach was modified after the Siberian war, see the next section). Under this lenient policy, not only were soldiers and low-ranking officers allowed to hang around brothels (specifically those run by Japanese or Koreans) and to hold parties in these men's clubs on weekdays, but it was prevalent that many high-ranking officers (including battlefield commanders) had maidservants who, besides performing routine chores, would serve as "wives" (Chen, 2006: 63–70). All of these signify that the relationship between Japanese military men sent overseas and *karayuki*[13] was close because the latter, as remarked previously, had spread steadily to almost every corner of Asia since the 1870s (reaching from far eastern Russia and Manchuria in the north to the Dutch East Indies in the south). Therefore, when Japan became involved in the expansion of the war after 1894, Japanese military men could always find extra energy in Japanese-styled vacation resorts; first in Taiwan, then in China, Korea, and the Russian Far East.[14]

This tradition did not change significantly until the interval of 1918 to 1922. During that four-year period, the Japanese authorities, at the request of U.S. president Wilson, dispatched about 70,000 men to eastern Siberia and northern Sakhalin to support the White Army and to prevent the communist movement led by the Red forces from disseminating to the West Pacific (Lai, et al., 2005: 35; Lincoln: 1989). Of the men who were sent to the Russian Far East, only 1,387 soldiers were killed (2,066 were wounded) on the battlefield (Senda, [1978] 1992: 25). In contrast, approximately 10,000 to 14,000 Japanese soldiers lost (or partially lost) their ability to fight, due to syphilis and other venereal diseases (Senda, [1978] 1992: 25–27).

The severe reduction in troop strength caused by sexually transmitted diseases taught the Japanese military a valuable lesson. The Japanese authorities now insisted that safety measures be taken to prevent disease among servicemen. Otherwise, they feared, Japanese troops would be wiped out not by enemies but by unsafe sex. To make sure that Japanese troops would not be destroyed by their own behavior, the Japanese military began to search for ways to avert massive contagion. After years of debate and research, the Japanese navy created the first military-controlled brothel (called *wei an suo* in Chinese or *ianjo* in Japanese) in Shanghai in late 1931/ early 1932 (Hicks, 1995: 45; Tanaka: 2001: 8). Soon after that, scores of "comfort stations" were established by the Japanese military in that city. The Kwantung Army in Manchuria also followed this model and constructed lots of *wei an suo* or *ianjo* in that region.[15]

Compared to private brothels run by madams, pimps and/or woman traffickers, brothels supervised by the military seemed more effective in stopping sexually transmitted diseases from proliferating. This achievement, according to studies of comfort women (Chen, 2006; Hsieh, 1995; Kim, [1976] 1992; Kim-Gibson, 1999; Lai et al., 2005; Senda, [1978] 1992; Suzuki, 1992; Taipei Women's Rescue Foundation, 1999; Tanaka, 2001; Yoshimi, 2000), was connected with the following precautionary practices:

First, in military brothels, both Japanese and non–Japanese prostitutes (or more accurately, sex slaves) were examined regularly: nearly every comfort woman testifies that medical examinations in the comfort stations were fairly routine (Kim-Gibson, 1999: 39). Women who were sick would be suspended temporarily from work.[16]

Second, all military officers, rank-and-file soldiers, and authorized persons who patronized these places were required to wear a condom. No condom, no woman.

Third, after sexual intercourse, both comfort women and customers were required to wash their private parts.

Finally, by means of arrest, coercion, deception, or kidnapping, managers of comfort stations acquired countless Chinese, Korean, and Taiwanese teenage girls (or even married women) as employees. Since these female civilians were by and large healthy, they provided pure sex to fighting men as well as high-ranking generals. These unfortunate females, almost without exception, would be abandoned on the battlefield or murdered within the comfort stations if they were regarded as a military materiel that had no more value.

V. COMFORT STATIONS AS PLACES OF STATE-ENDORSED SEX ASSAULTS

As a way to guard against the spread of venereal diseases, the Japanese military authorities established the first comfort station in Shanghai after the Siberian war. Then facilities like this were set up swiftly all over Shanghai[17] as well as Manchuria, Korea, Taiwan, and the Far East of Russia. After 1942, as Southeast Asia had become a part of the empire of Japan, such stations were also built in areas governed by Japanese troops. They were located in big cities, medium-sized towns, rural villages, and even fortresses located in isolated small islands. (See Soh, 2008: 138 for a map.)

Although no figure is available regarding the precise number of comfort stations, they have some features in common:

First of all, all comfort stations were created and overseen by the Japanese military. Therefore, comfort women (whether Japanese or non–Japanese) were defined as a military necessity and a strategic asset for the imperial army (Lai, et al., 2005: 34). Since these women were classified by wartime Japanese prime ministers (such as Tojo Hideki) as a military asset (Xie, 2005: 407), it is not surprising that the status of such females was extremely low. It was even lower than that of military horses, for these animals were looked after carefully all the time. Their downtrodden position naturally made the soldiers' violent/sadistic behaviors (slapping, hair pulling, cigarette burning, abdomen punching, whipping, just to name a few) a routine part of daily life for comfort women. As one Filipina former comfort woman states: every day there were incidents of violence and humiliation (Henson, 1999: 40). Due to the fact that comfort stations were "playgrounds" or "amusement parks" in which aggressive acts by Japanese soldiers were epidemic, the social environment of these military brothels was essentially the same as concentration camps, where violence was rampant and excessive.[18]

Comfort women were people designated to function as "sex outlets" or "public restrooms" (Jiang, 1998: 150) for Japanese military men: in the eyes of their customers, they were simply public facilities (from the feminist standpoint, even the title sex worker is not suitable for these young women, for genuine sex workers sometimes enjoy basic human rights). This low-grade identity not only made comfort women unable to set their own business hours and work schedule but they were deprived of all civil rights, especially the right to resign (i.e., they were not considered independent beings). Lacking the chance to resign, each comfort woman was forced to service more than ten men per day (some nice-looking comfort women might have to attend to as many as forty to fifty men each day).[19] All of these suggest that comfort women were subjugated people at high risk of getting infected with sexually transmitted diseases (particularly syphilis and hepatitis), and essentially analogous to the untouchables of India.

The great majority of comfort women barely enjoyed human rights. There was hardly a respite for [them] (Tanaka, 2001: 51), and they had to endure seemingly endless violence due to their status as military materiel or sex instruments. Obviously, then, unwanted pregnancy would be another nightmare for comfort women.[20] Comfort women who became pregnant usually would face the following destinies:

The first possibility (which appeared to be the most common one) is that they would be given a shot called "606 injection." Then, whenever the vagina started to bleed, an abortion would be performed (Chen & Su, 2005: 32). Numerous comfort women experienced this surgery three or more times and became barren (Chen & Su, 2005: 32). Some women even lost their womb after such surgery (Lai et al., 2005: 87–89).

The second probable outcome (which seemed unusual, if not rare) is that some pregnant comfort women were allowed to have their baby. As soon as the baby was born, it would be separated immediately from the mother. The mother, however, must continue to undertake her duty as sex provider even though she had not yet recovered from the exhausting process of childbirth (Chen & Su, 2005: 32). This inhumane treatment, predictably, caused certain comfort women death. Furthermore, some comfort women lost their lives because of difficult labor or miscarriage. Not all of these mysterious incidents of death, regrettably, were systematically documented. Since no book, article, or official document gives a detailed account of these deaths, it is very difficult for modern researchers to determine the magnitude of this problem.

The third outcome is undoubtedly the most hideous and malicious. Some pregnant comfort women did not have abortions but were kept as "sex toys" for Japanese servicemen (most of these women were former members of anti–Japan guerrillas or Chinese intelligence agents, betrayed by people who collaborated with Japan or were captured by Japanese troops). When one of these women became too frail to tolerate sexual abuse, she would be tied to a tree or a wooden post. Then she would serve as a living target for newly recruited Japanese soldiers to practice bayonet thrusts (Chen, 2006: 209).[21] After the training, the bodies (both mothers and unborn infants) would be buried onsite. These unspeakable scenarios took place almost everywhere in Japan-controlled districts (specifically in rural areas) during the years of the Sino-Japanese War (1937–1945). Unfortunately, no record shows how many comfort women were murdered due to this atrocity.

Simply speaking, comfort stations were living hells. Some courageous comfort women did attempt to escape. Making an effort to run away was, however, extremely dangerous because if an escape got caught, she would be beaten ruthlessly and tortured. Many comfort women died from this harsh punishment.[22] As with the women who were slain during so-called living-target training, no document reveals how many comfort women who fled and were captured were beaten to death in comfort stations.

Japanese Troops and Indiscriminate Sex Assaults

Once the comfort woman system became institutionalized in 1932, comfort stations functioned all the time as maximum-security prisons: not only were comfort women not permitted to choose customers, determine their work schedule, or quit, but their movements were supervised closely by madams and security guards. Given that comfort stations were brothels directed by the Imperial Japanese Army (in other words, these stations were official institutions), it was obligatory for comfort women to entertain their customers. Those who did not perform their jobs adequately or even refused to serve would be disciplined. The punishments could be "light," such as slapping and face punching; or serious, like water boarding, dog biting, or even cutting off ears, limbs, or breasts.

Comfort women, as sex slaves, confronted an uncertain and miserable life every day. In sharp contrast, Japanese servicemen, despite the fact that they were required to observe various rules in comfort stations (after all, such stations were official establishments), could take full pleasure in these respites from the battlefield. One of the main factors that allowed Japanese soldiers to have a good time in comfort stations was that comfort women were prohibited from leaving their affiliated units. As a result of this zero-absence regulation, comfort women virtually became hidden and entirely inaccessible populations for their relatives. That gave both soldiers and military officers (especially abusive ones) opportunities to engage in phys-ical and sexual assaults without having to worry about being investigated and penalized. In other words, comfort stations were hideouts where violent behaviors, including homicidal acts, could be neutralized or justified easily. All of these freedoms and entitlements to dominate comfort women let comfort stations function like flesh markets (Hicks, 1995: 45), Satan's dens (Glatt, 2002: 54), or men's heavens.

In addition to enjoying various legal opportunities to commit violent acts in comfort stations, another incentive for soldiers of the Imperial Japa-nese Army to visit these places was that they were considered to be hygienic. The chief practice that gave comfort stations the reputation of quality con-trol was that comfort women, as mentioned earlier, had routine physical examinations. With this system, authorized people who went to military brothels, at least in theory, did not have to worry about getting infected with sexually transmitted diseases. Given that comfort women, compared to street prostitutes, were believed to be much cleaner, it is not surprising that the quantity of comfort stations kept increasing during the heyday of the Japanese Empire (approximately 1938 to 1943).

While numerous comfort stations, including the mobile railway com-fort stations utilized in Manchuria (Hicks, 1995: 75), were created right after Japanese troops seized a territory, it appeared that comfort women were still in short supply. The ratio set by the Japanese military of comfort women and servicemen was not 1 to 5 or 1 to 10 but 1 to around 30.[23] This percentage would certainly be much higher for soldiers dispatched to difficult spots such as jungles, isolated islands, mountain areas, out-of-the-way rural villages, or secluded strongholds, because in these gray zones or districts outside the law (i.e., areas where neither Japanese troops nor anti–Japan forces could be wholly controlled), it was virtually impossible for the Japanese military to recruit comfort women. Because it is very unlikely that comfort women could be obtained through official channels, soldiers in war-torn places normally acquired their "prey" by force.[24] In other words, from the perspective of Hirschi ([1969] 2001) and other control theorists, Japanese fighting men garrisoned in hinterlands, small rural towns, or depopulated coastal areas in Asia (particularly in China, Korea, and Southeast Asian countries) in the 1930s and 1940s were largely unsupervised and unattached (Ishida & Uchida, 2008: 147). Since their behavior was largely not regulated by military discipline, these personnel had plentiful opportunities to get involved in the so-called Four Evils — looting, raping, arson, and enslaving males, be they civilians or POWs, young adults or old men (Ishida & Uchida, 2008: 160).

In terms of using raids and other violent means to search for targets of rape, there are many horrible and staggering stories about how innocent females were attacked sexually. For example, according to reports (Cai & Li, 2006; Chang, 1997; Chen, 2006; Chen & Su, 2005; Hata, 1999; Henson, 1999; Hsieh, 1995; Ishida & Uchida, 2008; Jiang, 1998; Suzuki, 1992; Xie, 2005), Japanese soldiers dispatched to China in the 1930s and 1940s would try to seize females from occupied towns (although teenage girls and women in their twenties/thirties were the major targets, some women in their seventies or eighties or even toddlers were also seized). To achieve this goal, Japanese troops, under the direction of officers, would either hunt for females themselves or ask collaborators to deliver a certain number of pretty girls as gifts of appreciation. Under the menace of machine guns, grenades, bayonets, and other weapons, numerous females who happened to be in the wrong place at the wrong time were captured by Japanese soldiers.

Before the end of World War II, almost all females (whether married or unmarried, pregnant or not) caught by Japanese fighting men were assaulted sexually.[25] These women, according to records (Ishida & Uchida, 2008; Xie, 2005), experienced one or some of the following ordeals:

- raped in front of family members and/or relatives
- raped together with other family members or unfamiliar women
- forced to commit incest to "entertain" their captors
- ordered to have sex with animals
- raped after fingers or ears were cut off[26]
- raped right after interrogation (which always involved torture)
- coerced to have sex with unknown male refugees while Japanese soldiers were watching
- tied naked to a tree and served as sexual slaves
- required to become involved in promiscuous sex
- raped continuously for eight or more hours

Since all of these patterns of rape, to a varying extent, involved multiple perpetrators, it was very common that victims, after sexual assault, were killed at the crime scene. This phenomenon of collective sexual violence, from the viewpoint of Sykes and Matza (1957), can be attributed to the fact that Japanese soldiers were indoctrinated systematically to believe that Japanese are the "superior race" while the Chinese and Koreans were the "inferior race" (Suzuki, 1992: 57). Under the support of racist ideology, violent acts were neutralized when the Japanese soldier was trained to be not simply hardened for battle in China ... [but] hardened for the task of murdering ... combatants and noncombatants alike (Chang, 1997: 55).[27] With such a mindset, it is not difficult to explain why hundreds of thousands of sex-connected homicide cases took place in Nanjing (Nanking) and in many other cities of Southeast Asia in the late 1930s and 1940s.[28]

Besides arbitrary killings,[29] numerous young women and teenage girls caught by Japanese soldiers after 1931 were forced to become comfort women. Some of these sex prisoners were lucky in that they were sent to military headquarters or big cities, where living conditions seemed to be better than in rural areas; most, however, were assigned to troops posted on or near the front lines. Women serving in or near combat zones constantly risked death for several reasons.

First, these women were always would be sent to Manchuria/North China or South China/Southeast Asia. As a result, they frequently "were lodged in humble huts or makeshift barracks on the edge of tropical jungle, or surrounded by the bleak loess of northern China" (Hicks, 1995: 72–73). This substandard living environment inevitably constituted a threat to comfort women because if they became critically ill or suffered a serious injury, it was not unusual for their masters to desert them (after all, it was important to reserve the limited medical resources for injured soldiers, not for comfort women). The following description demonstrates the lack of regard for comfort women:

> It is clear that acute abuses [committed by Japanese servicemen] were widespread ... when comfort women ... died in the Manchurian winter, the ground would be too hard to dig, so bodies were left in the graveyard until the thaw. This usually meant abandoning them to the wolves [Hicks, 1995: 72].

In addition to malicious desertion, tens of thousands of innocent comfort women disappeared on the high seas after the Pearl Harbor incident when the ships that transported them were sunk by American fighter planes or bombers (Hsieh, 1995: 96–98). These incidents became more and more frequent in late 1943 and 1944 as numerous regions of the Japanese Empire came under intensive attack from the U.S.

Another factor that put comfort women in great danger was that in the final months of the Pacific war, hundreds of thousands of Japanese soldiers were killed in action in China or Southeast Asia. Although the remnants of Japanese troops no longer had the ability to change the course of war (particularly stop the Japanese Empire from collapsing), they still controlled many strongholds and underground tunnels in China (especially South China), Southeast Asia, and the South Pacific. In the last weeks of the war, lots of the soldiers who defended these fortifications, bastions, and secret tunnels became suicidal because they were faced with inevitable defeat ... [and decided to] follow the tradition of *gyokusai*[30] — either fighting to the death or committing mass suicide as an alternative to surrender (Hicks, 1995: 153). With the troops' determination to sacrifice for the Japanese emperor, certain comfort women were executed by retreating Japanese soldiers or ordered to commit suicide as their captors preferred that their women shared in such a death (Hicks, 1995: 153).

Conditions That Turned Chinese Comfort Women into Missing Persons

Based on the statements above, it should be clear that comfort women were sex slaves who worked under extremely exploitative circumstances: they were not allowed to enjoy any autonomy and could be slain if they failed to satisfy their captors. Since these females were objectified (that is, they were regarded as disposable military goods), it was typical that they were beyond the protection of law (put differently, they suffered repeated instances of physical and sexual abuse as if they were lifeless sex dolls). All of these episodes of "institutionalized gendered social injustice" (Soh, 2008: 139) reveal that the social position of comfort women was exceptionally low. This slave-like status, under many circumstances, made these young females especially vulnerable to officially unexplained death.

While it is not likely that researchers of sex slavery can ascertain the total number of comfort women murdered by Japanese soldiers before and during World War II,[31] it is possible to list the situations (such as secret execution, desertion, and sexual violence) in which comfort women could become missing persons is possible. These situations, as mentioned previously, include (but are not limited to) the following contextual characteristics.

In the first place, comfort stations per se were black boxes or bird cages (that is, they were safeguarded by armed personnel like military police, and unauthorized people were absolutely prohibited from visiting). Therefore, it was hardly possible for comfort women to get help when they were attacked sexually. Since these places were rape camps endorsed by the Japanese government, almost everything done to comfort women inside those houses was legal. In such an environment, comfort women (whether they were recruited through cajolery or compulsory conscription) had no option but to show unconditional submission. If they failed or even declined to follow the commands of their subjugators, then such women always would be beaten and tortured (one common torture was to funnel water down into stomach and let the water run out of the mouth, nostrils, and anus). These cruel punishments naturally generated numerous missing women (who may be assumed to have died, but their deaths cannot be confirmed). No funeral services or memorial ceremonies, of course, were held after women were beaten and tortured to death.[32]

A certain number of comfort women (including pregnant ones) committed suicide because they could no longer cope with enslavement or tolerate the abuse. (It was not unusual for comfort women to sexually serve fifty to sixty unfamiliar men per day.) In addition to physical suffering, it was virtually impossible for comfort women to run away from the heavily guarded comfort stations. Living in these men's heavens and facing seemingly endless persecutions, some comfort women chose to terminate their life by, for example, hanging themselves or drinking disinfectants. Often, women who did not commit suicide, became seriously ill. These abused women eventually would die as well for lack of medical treatment. Regrettably, estimating the total of these comfort women who passed away of non-natural causes is effectively impossible because so few records exist.

For females serving in professional or certified comfort stations where routine medical inspections were performed, the threat of death perhaps was not immediate: as long as they obeyed, they still had a chance of survival. In contrast, a comfort woman who worked in a provisional or unlicensed *ianjo* (that is, fortress-affiliated *ianjo*), always risked accidental death. This is because the great majority of makeshift *ianjo* were located in the countryside, sparsely populated districts, or war-torn areas. In these economically backward and highly dangerous regions, it was impossible for comfort women to obtain careful treatments once they got sick (let alone routine medical examinations). Furthermore, given that such zones were far beyond the direction of state managers, they became excellent places for Japanese soldiers to cover up their heinous behavior (such as turning arrested Chinese women into living targets for bayonet practice; see previous section).[33]

Another milieu that could lead to "secret vanishing" of comfort women was that many company- or platoon-sized Japanese detachments stationed in Southeast Asia or the South Pacific could no longer defend themselves against their opponents (chiefly the U.S. and the Chinese armed forces) in late 1944 and 1945. Knowing that death might descend at any time, soldiers of these weakened units became disturbed and frantic. There was also a concern that comfort women might demonize the Imperial Japanese Army if they told outsiders their miserable stories, so tens of thousands of comfort women who belonged to these dying corps were slain in places like underground tunnels, mountain caves, and the jungle. Estimating the quantity and geographic distribution of these *gyokusai*-related deaths, again, is very challenging because no official data are available.

Concluding Remarks

The military prostitution system created by the imperial Japanese state is matchless in the war history of the twentieth century. Under this system, hundreds of thousands of Asian and European women were forced to become military prostitutes. Although these prostitutes, just like migrant domestic workers of the twenty-first century, traveled from one country or region to another from time to time, such females, unlike migrant housekeepers, could not negotiate multiple identity performances across spatial settings (Lan, 2006: 197). Put more specifically, migrant domestic laborers (almost all of whom are females) will play the role of maidservant

> in front of [their] employers [during weekdays].... On Sundays ... they [are] able to take off the deferential apron and put on the self-proclaimed image. In front of their families and relatives, migrant workers perform the role of national heroes by showcasing their material gains and overseas adventures [Lan, 2006: 197].

This suggests that in spite of serving as contracted laborers supervised closely by employers, migrant domestic employees are free because they still enjoy a certain degree of autonomy and normally work in a nonviolent atmosphere.

Unlike migrant workers, comfort women were completely enslaved. Since comfort women were a controlled population whose status was reduced to absolute servitude, their destiny was largely at the mercy of their owners. This means only the strongest (both mentally and physically) and the luckiest could survive. The weaker or the less fortunate, in one way or another, would lose their life in comfort stations or places which functioned as *se di yu* or hell of lust (Kim, 1997: 152).

In short, aside from those rare circumstances under which some comfort women might have had a few good (caring or less aggressive) customers, almost all comfort women had to endure a variety of physical and spiritual hardships. These adversities prevented lots of Chinese comfort women from returning to their native land after the Second World War. Regardless of the experiences of such survivors after returning to their homeland (getting married, adopting children, establishing legitimate careers, and so forth), most did not want to publicize their heartbreaking stories, due largely to the shame culture of Confucianism and/or the fear of facing prejudice, stigmatization, and social ostracism. This attitude, together with the equivocal stance taken by the postwar Japanese government on the issue of military prostitution system, made comfort women a forgotten subject for decades. Not until the early 1990s when a few seemingly ordinary grandmas in China and Korea brought their sad stories to light did sex crimes systematically perpetrated by the Japanese forces in the 1930s and '40s attract public attention in China, Korea, Taiwan, and the Southeast Asian countries and areas once occupied by Japan.

Although extant historical data (including testimonies of survivors) in the past twenty years allow scholars of different areas of expertise to explore the sex slavery directed by the Japanese government in the 1930s and '40s, it is unlikely that many details will ever be known. This is chiefly because numerous documents were systematically destroyed. Extremist right-wing groups of Japan, unsurprisingly, enjoy plenty of opportunities to obscure or deny the history of Japan's involving in forcing Asian and European women to serve as military prostitutes before and during World War II. Furthermore, given that the Japanese government adopts the Three No's policy (no acknowledgment, no apology, and no compensation) in dealing with the historical issue of sex slavery after 1945, the Pacific war is probably not over for former comfort women and their relatives.

CHAPTER 6

Trafficked Women and Girls[1]

Like the practice of ghost marriage addressed in Chapter 4, the business of selling and buying women/girls has a long history in China and nearby regions. For example, as early as the Qin dynasty (221–206 B.C.), innocent women (whether unmarried or married) could be sold to troops as military prostitutes or banished to barren or disease-ridden districts as slaves if a male member of their clan was proclaimed a traitor or felon (Ma, 1999: 168–169). This cruel punishment was not abolished until the Manchurian regime was overthrown in 1911.[2]

Although modern-day Chinese women are no longer held responsible for any serious offense committed by a male member of their family, trafficking in women and girls is still a grave problem (Altman, 2001; Chin, 1999, 2001; Daye, 1996: 167–170; Gu, 2008: 55–66; He & Wang, 1993: 133–158; King, 2004: 138–141; Kristof & WuDunn, 1994: 210–241; Kwong, 2001; Li, 1999; Liang & Ye, 2001; Shelley, 2007: 123–125; Yi, 2005: 705–720; Zhang, 2007). Several factors play a critical role in sustaining this social pathology.

First, in spite of the fact that China is still a politically authoritarian country, it has experienced vigorous economic growth since the 1990s. Beginning as early as 2000, China has developed into one of the major economies in the world (it became the second largest in 2010).

Second, given that China's export-oriented economy (which includes innumerable labor-intensive industries) is still growing, numerous factories located in the coastal provinces and big cities of inland provinces must keep recruiting workers in order to meet immense market demands. This attracts rural people to participate in the labor markets. Under the stimulus of this structural transformation, each year tens of millions of peasants, especially those from the impoverished inland provinces, head

Guangzhou Railway Station: A hot spot of woman kidnapping and trafficking.

for cities and try to become a part of the manufacturing industry (a typical locale for such population movements can be seen in the photograph above).

As domestic migration becomes more and more pervasive, modern Chinese females, compared to women of earlier generations, also have more chances to get a stable (or even high-paying) job to support their family. This job prospect motivates millions of rural women to travel to metropolitan areas or the newly developed industrial parks of East and South China in the 1990s and 2000s. In addition to heading for economically booming cities or commercial towns, some ambitious women smuggle overseas (particularly to America, Japan, Hong Kong, and Taiwan) to get rich quickly (Li, 1999: 181).[3] These courageous women, according to studies (Chin, 1999, 2001; Smith, 1997; Zhang, 2007), have few chances to get fast money abroad. On the contrary, most are in a predicament: few, if any, can work legally in the host country, and nearly all of them must find ways to pay back tremendous smuggling fees.[4] Since few smuggled females have the financial resources to work out this dilemma within a short period of time, it is not unusual that trafficked women end up the sex industry (including escort services, nightclubs, pubs, and unlicensed brothels). Working in the sex industry, in turn, prevents smuggled women from adjusting their undocumented identity because these women, as they are heavily in debt, can be easily manipulated and exploited by their employer. All of these aspects eventually form a vicious cycle, which not only makes numerous *da lu mei* (young female Chinese mainlanders) fall prey to organized crime figures, but also turns these "private properties" into "reliable" sex workers or employees of sweatshops.

Although getting rid of the fetters of human smugglers is not easy, some smuggled or trafficked persons/women, after years of struggle, do make it.[5] Their remarkable stories make them role models. Inspired by the accounts (normally in the contexts of gossip) that human smugglers represent a shortcut for poverty-stricken people in attaining the goal of financial success, many peasants and unskilled workers from inland provinces travel to Southeast China or go abroad to improve their socioeconomic status. Under the influence of this social culture/ethos, innumerable Chinese look forward to finding the right person who can take them out of their hometown. With these fortune seekers as a demand market, human smugglers have multifarious opportunities to run their scams in the form of a travel agency, investment corporation, or employment bureau. This demand-and-supply chain ultimately turns female trafficking into a highly lucrative and hard-to-suppress business.

Another factor that makes female trafficking a severe problem in China in the twenty-first century is that some corrupt law enforcement agents participate in this offense on a regular basis (He & Wang, 1993: 144–146). Accordingly, owners of massage parlors, nightclubs, hotels, and restaurants can acquire official patronages and transform their business into a legal enterprise. [The *tu huang di* (literally "indigenous emperor," meaning local cadres or leaders) cases discussed in the subsequent pages offer typical examples for this phenomenon.] All of these friendships, partnerships, comradeships, or political criminal nexuses (Glenny, 2008: 362) not only lay a firm foundation for antiestablishment components (particularly organized gangs) to take part in the crime of abducting and selling young women, they also provide human traffickers with legal protection to engage in human trade in impoverished provinces, among them Gansu, Inner Mongolia, Qinghai, Tibet, and Xinjiang. Given that woman trafficking has permeated nearly every province and is no longer a behavior committed solely by civilians (as opposed to law enforcement or politicians), it is very likely that this problem will keep threatening the safety of many young women in the next decade when China's economic growth is expected to remain rapid.

In this chapter, the following two big questions will be explored:

- the socioeconomic factors that turn women/girls into commodities
- the social problems brought about by woman trafficking and smuggling

After these questions have been addressed, some common techniques employed by human traffickers in greater China to abduct young women or girls will be summarized.

Factors Leading to Trafficking in Women

As mentioned, trading women/girls has a long history in China. Three environmental and socioeconomic factors, among others, seem to play an extremely important role in generating and sustaining this social pathology.

I. Natural Disaster

China, just like most places in the world, is sometimes stricken by natural disasters. Whenever and wherever these catastrophes strike, it is all but certain that people will die or go missing. In addition to violent events like tsunami and earthquakes that kill people directly, natural disasters like drought, famine or flood can be indirectly catastrophic, especially to those who depend on the weather to make a living (such as farmers, handicraft artists, and street peddlers). For such people, pleasant weather is usually synonymous with stable income or anticipated wealth. Accordingly, if the weather was favorable, it would be possible to pay taxes and rents. (This task seemed an endless nightmare for most peasants and manual workers because they had to pay local and central governments miscellaneous duties which, according to modern standards, were extremely unreasonable and unjust.) In contrast, if the weather did not show mercy, then destructive outcomes would, sooner or later, befall those who did not have the money to pay for their dues.[6] It was such desperate situations that motivated bankrupt fishermen, peasants, laborers, and petty merchants to sell their wives and/or children to strangers to pay off taxes and rents and avoid legal troubles.

From the angle of sociology, the above social tragedy can be represented by a proposition: the longer the duration of weather anomaly, the higher the possibility that working-class persons will face serious financial trouble and be forced to engage in the activity of human trafficking. This proposition can be well exemplified by the development of Yangzhou, one of the most important human flesh markets in China before the 1940s.[7]

Situated in western Jiangsu and now renowned for its historic buildings and cultural activities, Yangzhou was merely a small village during the Han dynasty (202 B.C.–A.D. 220). This seemingly insignificant place, however, did not remain trivial. On the contrary, its status, step by step, became more and more noteworthy. One of the most crucial factors that turned this area into a commercial, transportation, and amusement hub was that during the Sui dynasty (581–618), the Grand Canal was constructed. Since Yangzhou was located alongside the Canal, its position was geographically and economically pivotal. Thus this rural community, starting in the seventh century, began to draw great numbers of construction workers, drifters, petty traders, sailors, seasonal laborers, and sojourners. The little settlement kept expanding in the next three centuries as more and more outsiders became permanent residents. In the end, Yangzhou grew to be a big city during the Tang dynasty (618–907).

After Yangzhou became a hub of commerce and transportation, it was widely viewed by economic refugees as a safe haven: for these dislocated people, Yangzhou was an ideal place to make a living because it had job opportunities and, technically speaking, could provide homeless persons with food. Based on this impression, scores of displaced persons swarmed into Yangzhou to hunt for employment, shelter, and economic relief whenever a large-scale natural disaster occurred.

While a few refugees were fortunate enough to acquire a job or to rebuild their career in Yangzhou, it was not unusual that refugees could not find any employment and sanctuary. For refugees, it was a feat to obtain a job in an alien town even the economic condition of that place was good; that struggle would be gargantuan if the local economy was in a bad shape. This disappointing and discouraging situation inevitably forced some refugees (especially single young males) to join well-structured beggar gangs (as well as other delinquent groups) or turned physically weak refugees into beggars themselves. In addition to becoming desperados or beggars, a few refugees decided to sell their maidservants or even wife/daughter(s) for taels (before their homeland was ruined by natural disasters, such refugees could be middle-class landholders or property owners). Two sorts of business owners appeared especially enthusiastic in getting involved in this transaction.

The first kind, needless to say, was bosses of brothels: for these persons, the most important thing concerning their business was to keep it prosperous. To achieve this objective, they must keep recruiting new faces so that the passion of the customers (who, more often than not, loved the new and disregarded the old) could be sustained: in other words, (older) prostitutes would be resold if their physical appearance had started to wither; sex workers who were no longer attractive usually could do nothing but search for menial jobs (such as selling themselves as maidservants) to survive. (This might explain why traditional China always had a sizable marginalized populations.)

The second type was owners of tea houses, restaurants, and/or hostels, especially formal and large ones. These businesspersons wanted to purchase women and girls because the latter could be trained as singers, dancers, or actresses. If their performance could fascinate the audience, they would function as live money machines. They could continually provide their master with wealth; to use the Chinese phrase, such performers would become *jin mu ji* (the hen that lays golden eggs).[8]

In any event, due to all of these different channels and networks of human transactions, Yangzhou eventually became an entertainment and commercial center in the Song dynasty (960–1279). Artists and literati (painters, philosophers, poets, and their ilk) headed to Yangzhou to look for inspiration. This intellectual movement was chauvinist and, to a considerable extent, endorsed gender hierarchy; so woman trafficking, as early as the tenth century, had already grown to be a tradition of Chinese society in general and of Yangzhou in particular.[9]

The tragedy that women and young girls from natural disaster areas were systematically trafficked and sold by human traders persisted into the twentieth century. One typical example took place in the 1920s and the 1930s when North China was hit by a drought that caused famine (Snow, 1968: 216). During the Great Famine, hundreds of thousands (or even more) of females were put up for sale by dealers in humans. In local communities, these females were considered "surplus." Since the supply of displaced females was ample and human traders could obtain their merchandise easily, numerous women and girls were sold to Yangzhou, commercially prosperous cities of Central China (Nanjing, Shanghai, Suzhou, and Wuxi), or even Southeast Asian countries as sex workers, laborers, or child brides. These deals not only played a crucial role in promoting the sex and tourist industries of China and Southeast Asian countries (particularly Singapore), they also turned countless Chinese females into hidden populations.

II. War

The practice of selling and buying women or young girls usually would develop into a social movement in China whenever China (particularly rural districts) was stricken by an enduring natural disaster. By the same token, war (whether civil or international) also had the effect of transforming young females into commodities.

China has experienced war (whether national or regional) many times since the Opium War of 1840. Whenever a war occurred, people (especially criminals) of war-affected areas could enjoy "moral holidays" and "legal Sabbaths." Because of these moral and legal vacuums, not only could armed personnel sexually assault females without fearing that such behaviors would be sanctioned (see Chapter 5), but woman trafficking (as well as other antisocial behaviors) would inch by inch become pervasive before social order was restored.

In terms of opportunity structure, war in China produced at least two advantageous conditions for human brokers. The first was that war by definition motivates fighting parties to annihilate their opponents. Based on this goal, contending blocs, more often than not, would use methods that could lead to mass destruction to conquer the enemy and win the war. This phenomenon can be well exemplified by the Sino-Japanese War (1937–1945).

In July 1937, a skirmish took place between Japanese and Chinese troops in North China. This clash could have been solved peacefully if the Japanese military, as the stronger side that could determine the courses of development of this event, had chosen a conciliatory policy to handle the issue. Instead of adopting a peace-making approach to deal with this conflict, the Japanese military decided to launch a formal war against China. Facing this unexpected challenge and catastrophe, the Nanjing government decided to engage in a total-attrition war, despite the fact that Chinese troops were, on the whole, ill-equipped, poorly trained, and lacking in a unified leadership system.

During the first year of the Sino-Japanese War, the Nationalist government, as expected, lost almost all of its best-equipped and best-trained troops while resisting the Japanese aggression. Accordingly, the Nanjing authorities could only resort to extraordinary methods to stop the Japanese armies from advancing westward and southward. One such desperate action was to blow up the dikes of the Yellow River to drown Japanese troops. According to the reports, the result of this "strategic" military action was unbelievably miserable:

> An agonizing death has overtaken approximately 900,000 Chinese who lived in the treacherous river valleys of Central China. Twelve million homes have been destroyed and 55,000,000 people are affected [Snow, 1983: 42].

It took seven years for those irregular and volatile streams of the Yellow River to converge. Before the Yellow River stabilized and followed its new channel in 1945, deaths continued: many people died from epidemics (especially cholera) and malnutrition. Numerous people, stuck in a quagmire of three nos (no shelter, no job, no social salvation), were forced to sell their children, especially daughters, to pay off debts to landlords or to raise cash (Snow, 1983: 45). This appalling condition can be represented by a photo provided by Snow (1983: 48). The caption is "A woman in a rural marketplace with two children for sale."

In any event, hundreds of thousands of women as well as teenagers and little girls were sold during the Sino-Japanese War. Largely because of the emergence of these transferable populations, components of the recreation industry (such as bars, brothels, nightclubs, tea houses, and restaurants) and employment bureaus or match-making agencies installed by criminal elements as hubs for human trafficking thrived in wartime China. This incredible phenomenon was seen in all major cities (including Chungking, the wartime capital) located in the western and southwestern provinces that were controlled by the Nationalist government. As a result, numerous trafficked women (whether married or unmarried) and girls became "permanent assets" of organized crime associations in cities or bandit cliques in rural areas. These females rarely were found; one important reason for this was that Chungking law enforcement was too corrupt to handle this issue. Only a handful of trafficked females were fortunate enough to be ransomed by their family members or rescued by religious groups (like the Christian church).

Like many other wars in the modern world, the Sino-Japanese War did not simply lead to displaced populations. Another serious social problem was that many young girls became orphans: regardless of age, the destiny of these parentless girls was essentially the same as that of contemporary Natashas (teenage girls who were sold as sex slaves during and after the civil war of the former Yugoslavia; see Malarek, 2004: 14–15). More specifically, female orphans of wartime China, whether they lived in cities or rural towns, have several features in common. First, they usually were deemed by mainstream society as economic and social burdens. So even though these orphans could be adopted by their relatives, many (or most) of them were sent to poorly equipped orphanages. (Some facilities were better equipped if they were managed by a philanthropic organization; such facilities, however, were few.) Second, after such unwanted children were transported to a dilapidated and dull orphanage, they normally had to stay in that place for a few years. At many orphanages, there was insufficient food, few caretakers, and little proper medical treatment. Accordingly, some orphans died of disease, malnutrition, and/or physical injury.

Another noteworthy problem was that most older orphans had to take care of themselves. Therefore, they must invest most of their time every day on unskilled, unclean or even unsafe activities, such as scavenging for food, gathering twigs as fuel, drawing water from a river, and collecting valuables from the battlefield, to support themselves. With such a "busy schedule," it is no surprise that few female orphans could get any formal education or training. As a result, lots of them became exchangeable merchandise: whenever they "graduated" from an orphanage (at the age of sixteen, seventeen, or eighteen), few possessed any professional skill or expertise. Like modern-day teenage runaways who cannot get a decent job because of their lack of education (see Flowers, 2001; Reid, 1999; Shoemaker, 2009), these "graduates" could not enter the regular job market and become economically independent. These "blemishes of individual character" (Goffman, 1986:4), together with the fact that almost no orphans had legal guardians, pushed a large amount of "social freshmen" to the streets. That gave brothel owners, pimps, and other exploiters opportunities to play street politics: by claiming that they could provide shelter or offer a job, such human traders played diverse confidence games with the unwanted population of youths roaming on the streets. Since the traffickers' persuasion was hard for street kids to resist, it is certain that tens of thousands of homeless orphans and girls were seized by woman traffickers and other "street hyenas."

All of the predatory behaviors mentioned above were by-products of the Sino-Japanese War. Seeing that female trading was a booming business in Nationalist China in the late 1930s and the 1940s, the relationship between war and woman trafficking can be summarized by following paragraph:

> Wars ... as well as the many national disasters that took place in many regions of the world ... created many orphans and orphanages.... These orphans and orphanages brought about adoption hysteria and consequently, some child predators found the orphanages and other orphan concentration areas to contain readily available populations for trafficking in children. In Southeast Asia [for example], there are so many orphans that the orphanages could not handle them all.... Some of these orphans roam the streets and are easy prey to the traffickers and sex tourists who flood Southeast Asia for the sole purpose of sexually abusing these minors [Ebbe, 2008:35].

III. Poverty

When the above-noted factors, natural disaster and war, are used to explain the etiology and dynamics of woman trafficking, it may give the public an impression that human/woman trafficking was merely a short-term or provincial issue in China: after all, neither natural disaster nor war are long-lasting events (usually). So if these two factors did not occur, were absent, one might reason, then woman abducting should not be a noteworthy problem either.

As a matter of fact, woman trafficking was not a short-lived or regional problem in Nationalist China. On the contrary, this offense, despite being suppressed by the communist government in the early 1950s, remains an underground mechanism of population adjustment in present-day China. It therefore is foreseeable that females will keep disappearing in the future, like those who were lost in the human flesh markets in the past one hundred years. There is an invisible hand that can methodically manipulate young female populations, and detecting or eradicating criminal acts associated with women kidnapping is difficult for law enforcement authorities. This is because such actions are, as a rule, structured and carefully planned (even worse, some are ignored by corrupt law enforcement agents). That enables woman-hunters to place innumerable traps to obtain more women.

In terms of the social factor that encourages some persons to choose woman trafficking as their occupation, it seems reasonable to conclude that the emergence of this profession is, at least in the past century, indivisible from the structural problem of poverty. As in modern Somalia where nationwide impoverishment motivates certain coastal people to become pirates (see Cawthorne, 2009: 43, 51), poverty also inspires some in China to become involved in a venture that does not require capital or investment. As the emergence of this "social movement" is for the most part caused by economic hardship, it is necessary to transform the concept of poverty into a variable so that a causal model can be established.

From the perspective of methodology, choosing a suitable variable to measure the notion of poverty always involves the process of intra-societal and inter-societal comparison. For example, compared to typical middle-class workers (whether white-collar or blue-collar), married people who live in a small house (1,200 square feet or less) with their children normally are considered to be poor in America in the twenty-first century (even if the house has amenities like air conditioning, cable TV, Internet, and so on). The same persons, however, would be considered rich if their assets (real and movable) are contrasted with those owned by average people who live in an underdeveloped country.

Given that the sociological meaning of *poverty* is determined largely by the socioeconomic status of a certain country during a specific historical period, this term is defined in this chapter as "a social condition under which certain people have few opportunities to increase personal wealth or to preserve the economic resources they already have." In China, the emergence of this social condition was inseparable from the following structural factors.

1. REPUBLICAN/NATIONALIST CHINA

The first factor, the extremely unreasonable land tenure system, was a core social feature of China during the Republican/Nationalist years. Before 1950, more than 80 percent of China's population comprised farmers or workers of the primary economy (i.e., less than 20 percent of the population belonged to the manufacturing and service industries). This population composition was, at least in theory, not necessarily connected with social inequality, for social injustice could be minimized if farmland was evenly distributed and the tax system was fair. Both circumstances, however, were absent in China prior to the 1950s.

As several studies indicate (Eastman, 1984: 45–88, 1990; Eastman et al., 1991), wealthy landlords of rural districts (who did not live in the so-called Soviet areas and had not experienced the land redistribution program carried out by the communists) in Nationalist China typically controlled far more farmland than other peasants did. (Put another way, landlords were upper-class peasants.) This institutionalized monopolization made it extremely difficult for middle- or working-class farmers (or "petty bourgeois") to obtain additional land and to augment their income. For that reason, peasants of this class typically became poorer and poorer while their family became larger and larger, or "pressed by debts or taxes," they "were forced to sell land to clear their financial obligations (Eastman, 1990: 192). Even worse was that these situations let numerous peasants become purely proletarians because they could not inherit or own any land. As long as such peasants who owned no land kept working as growers of crops, they generally could not do anything but to sell their labor: they could either become a family member of a well-to-do landlord and work as a serf or lease a small piece of land from a petty bourgeois (incredibly, rents usually accounted for at least 50 percent of regular annual yields; renters, by whatever means, still had to pay off the rents even if the crops they planted were destroyed by natural disaster, locust plague, or other unexpected reasons).

The Nationalist state of China was clearly a land of injustice. Another indicator was the tax system: like its counterpart in the United States, the tax system in Nationalist China frequently was criticized for being bureaucratic, inefficient, or even chaotic. The term *merciless* aptly describes this system. Table 6-1 provides a working example.

According to Table 6-1, peasants of Gansu (one of the poorest provinces during the Nationalist rulership) paid forty-four taxes every year. Of these items, many of them did not have precise definitions and clear-cut rates; examples include soldier reward tax, military-aid tax, miscellaneous expenses tax, and temporary expenses. Due to this extremely perplexing tax system, together with the fact that the great majority of peasants relied on primitive production methods in generating income, taxation actually became a state-endorsed extortion engaged in by government officials and military commanders in Gansu before 1950. The same or worse situation could also be found in other provinces. One dramatic example is provided by Dai (1990: 676). According to Dai, peasants in Sichuan, just like their counterparts in Gansu, had to pay more than forty taxes each year. In addition to this obligation, most county governments "pre-collected" taxes that were scheduled to be collected in the future. For instance, in 1933, the government of Chengdu county pre-collected taxes which were not to be paid by peasants until 1979. The government of Guangyuan county did the same in 1933, but it was far more efficient: it pre-collected taxes which farmers did not have the obligation to pay until 2011.

TABLE 6-1. REGULAR TAXES PAID BY CHINESE PEASANTS
DURING THE NATIONALIST ERA, GANSU AS AN EXAMPLE

acreage tax	land tax
penalty tax	military-aid tax
purification of countryside tax	hemp shoe tax
skin overcoat tax	military clothing tax
wheat bran tax	circulation (of money) tax
army mule tax	miscellaneous expenses tax
stocking tax	troop movement tax
soldier reward tax	merchants loan
uniform-alteration tax	cereal-price tax
military expenses tax	house tax
kettle tax	copper tax
change of defense expenses	repair of weapons expenses
repair of defense expenses	hog tax
trestle work tax	public debt
special loan item	temporary expenses
wealthy-house tax	communications tax
kindling-wood tax	flour-shop tax
bedding tax	soldier-enlistment tax
general headquarters loan	extraordinary tax
purchase of equipment tax	road-building expenses
water-mill tax	horse-fodder tax
investigation expenses	additional goods duty

SOURCE: Clubb (1978: 187).

Facing such an enormous tax burden, which few self-employed peasants could afford, some farmers sold all of their farmland to get the money for taxes; some deserted their homeland and escaped to remote places; some became slave laborers; some committed suicide. All of these misfortunes probably were not sufficient conditions for revolution (see hypotheses proposed by Selden, 1995: 28–29). But they did lay a firm foundation for woman trafficking. Investigative reports (see Dai, 1990: 677; Snow, 1983: 95) indicate that if peasants were so poor that even their wives, daughters, and sisters did not have clothes to wear, then what other options were there than to sell them? In other words, this necessary evil at least gave utterly destitute rural populations a chance to survive.

2. COMMUNIST CHINA

After 1950, the structural problems examined above had essentially disappeared. This momentous transformation mainly came from the radical land policy carried out by the communists. After the communist regime was established formally in Beijing in October 1949, the Mao government initiated the Land Reform Movement in 1950. During the frantic years of that extreme left-wing movement, millions of landlords and rich persons (whether such individuals truly belonged to the so-called exploitative class or not) were put to death (see Chapter 2). Due to these deliberate and large-scale executions, people who otherwise would be graded by left-wing-extremists as class enemies or anti-revolutionaries had essentially vanished in China. The disappearance of these bad elements then paved the way for the Beijing authorities to establish an egalitarian or classless state: starting from the early 1950s, all farmland (located in the liberated districts) was nationalized and redistributed. That allowed lower-class peasants to enjoy at least two things. First, such laborers no longer had to worry about the problem of making a living, for this necessity was guaranteed by the people's government. Second, given that the privileged class had been wiped out and no villagers could continue customs of the Nationalist rulership (that is, accumulating individual wealth and/or generating economic benefits by land privatization), peasants, just like the black American slaves emancipated after the Civil War, no longer had to pay appalling taxes. Under this righteous environment, peasants essentially did not have to (and were not allowed to) compete with one another for land ownership or engage in the zero-sum game that would give power to the strongest or fittest persons to annex the land.

Present-day Chinese peasants seem to have broken away from the economic predicaments that dogged them during the first half of the twentieth century, yet it is estimated that at least one hundred million of them are still not able to get out of poverty and realize their "Chinese dream" (especially those younger than 35). This potential crisis, according to Wu's (2009) study, is closely related to uneven development of industrialization and commercialization.

As mentioned previously, the economy of modern China is export-oriented. This official policy defines economic progress as the first priority of national development. Together with China's seemingly inexhaustible supply of labors, it took this "communist" country just twenty years (late 1970 to late 1990s) to become the "world's factory" and one of the most important markets on earth in the twenty-first century. By all economic standards, these achievements are without doubt dazzling because in the past two decades, no country could reach (or maintain) economic growth rates as high as those enjoyed by China. On the other hand, as these accomplishments are realized through an asymmetrical economic framework, it looks very likely that in the next ten years, China will keep functioning as a "paradise" of human trafficking.

Before examining the connection between unbalanced economic structure and woman trafficking, I will summarize how economic wealth is unequally distributed in China.

Disproportionate allocation of economic wealth is not new in China: as early as the late seventeenth/early eighteenth century, this phenomenon was already a tradition in China (see Naquin & Rawski, 1987: 138–216). No matter how this socioeconomic tendency is scrutinized and explicated by historians, the distribution of economic wealth in current China can be broadly divided into five subsequent tiers.

The highest one (where national wealth concentrates) is composed of Shanghai, Dalian, Fuzhou, Guangzhou, Hangzhou, Qingdao, Shenzhen, Xiamen, and other industrial/commercial centers of North, Central, and South China. Compared to cities of inland provinces (especially those located in northwestern and western provinces), these coastal cities are a magnet for college graduates and *nong min gong* (peasant workers). This is because these cities have more jobs available to native and foreign populations than other places. Accordingly, they attract millions of job seekers (as well as human traffickers) from all over the country each year.[10]

The second tier is composed of provincial capitals (or other large cities) of inland provinces (such as Chengdu, Chongqing, Kaifeng, Kunming, Wuhan, Xian, and Zhengzhou). Compared with local towns surrounding them, these regional centers have better public facilities, medical services, and other infrastructures. As a result of these advantageous conditions, such cities, like those first-rank hubs of commerce, manufacturing, and industry, can draw low-income people from neighboring cities or provinces as well. Similarly, these provincial commercial/industrial centers can attract human traffickers, too, although these criminals are more likely to be provincial residents, than foreigners. Nevertheless, these cities appear less attractive than the "dream cities" of coastal provinces because of geographic or ecological problems (for example, far from ports, polluted, or subject to natural disaster). These problems are barriers to expanding job markets in second-tier cities.

Cities of the third tier include medium-sized towns of inner provinces with populations between 100,000 and 500,000. These places, to an extent, function like those of the first and second ranks. However, the job markets they can supply are much smaller, partially due to incomplete or backward infrastructures or geographic seclusion. Thus these cities serve as purely regional centers. Such cities usually will operate as transit stations or rest areas for trafficking rings (that is, few human dealers will choose these places as their final destination). Females of these areas are more likely to be impoverished than their counterparts in larger cities, so the former tend to face higher risk of being recruited by human traders than the latter — after all, professional, skilled, or well-paid jobs are fewer in these less developed cities.

The fourth tier contains small rural cities with populations of less than 100,000. These cities, despite being located in rural districts where most residents are peasants, have a few light industries, such as enterprises that manufacture bicycles, fireworks, food processing, garments, and textiles, toys and souvenirs. There may be heavy industries (agricultural machinery or auto parts) run by local people, foreign investors, or national enterprises. Thanks to these industries, local residents enjoy certain job opportunities when they have "spare time." For example, during wintertime, the majority of peasants in North China will not farm because of the severity of the weather. To increase income, many peasants and their family members enter factories and become full-time or part-time workers. The same situation can also be found in Central and South China, where peasants also enjoy "leisure time" during certain months or weeks (although this vacation is mostly caused by non-weather factors, such as the preparation interval of post-harvest).

The final tier consists of those rural towns/villages where no manufacturing industries exist and cultivable farmland is in short supply. Demographically, these rural communities are quite small (fewer than 10,000 residents); geographically, such settlements are located in "wasteland" such as desert, mountainous areas, or islands in southern, western, and northwestern provinces; and economically, the great majority of local people acquire their income from agriculture only (that is, these populations constantly face the threat of absolute poverty if agrarian jobs become unavailable because of the situations mentioned above). This underdevelopment makes it very hard for residents to realize the goal of *fan shen* (literally to turn over; meaning to get out of poverty completely, see Hinton, 1966).

Based on the typologies of city development summarized above, it is apparent that the final category of rural communities is most likely to export surplus populations (although cities of the other tiers will export surplus women as well, these exportations seem less frequent). In these least developed areas, almost every household is struggling for survival. Therefore, like their counterparts of the Nationalist era, most peasants have to seek ways to increase income when jobs of the primary economy are unavailable or scarce in the bitter cold winter or during a natural disaster. One way to deal with the seemingly hopeless circumstance is to sell girls (or, to a lesser extent, boys) to human traffickers, even though the price offered is minimal.

Unsurprisingly, if peasants have to sell teenage girls (or younger ones) to make a living, then this way of life, to an extent, will evolve into a culture of poverty. Understandably, numerous young women from the poorest provinces want to leave their hometown, go to a big city, and find a stable job. As a consequence, tens of thousands of such females accept the assistance of their friend or their friend's friend and join the rank of migrant populations. Some of these female drifters become hidden populations in coastal cities or provincial centers, while some go abroad and immigrate illegally to other countries (see the third section). No matter where these women ultimately stay, their leaving inevitably brings the serious social problem of imbalanced sex ratios to their homeland.[11] Because of this problem, an unknown number of households of peripheral provinces or economically backward regions are forced to buy a wife or daughter-in-law from coastal or more developed provinces (see Wang, 2007). Even worse is that this act is often supported by local officials (He & Wang, 1993: 145–146) or "normalized" (that is, widely tolerated) by local residents (Wang, 2007: 161). That makes the investigation, let alone the suppression, of human trafficking a lengthy, costly, or even futile task in present-day China.

Major Social Problems Produced by Trafficking in Women

Whenever women are trafficked in China, it is certain that they will be poorly treated, experiencing sexual assault (especially gang rape) and other violent conducts (He & Wang, 1993: 146). As a result, trafficked women always have to face the fact that they have been reduced to merchandise. As merchandise, their price will be determined by quality: good quality entails high price (as well as lower possibility to be resold) while poor quality leads to low price (as well as higher probability to be resold). This economic law, at least in the past twenty years, produces serious social problems in China.

I. Domestic Abuse and Suicide

The first one is that people who want to buy a woman or girl (as wife/concubine, maidservant, or prostitute) always have to take some preventive measures to keep the product they procure from escaping. One extensively used measure is home confinement, in which a room in a residential building is turned into a detention center. There, trafficked women and girls must stay in that room twenty-four hours a day, seven days a week. In addition to losing their freedom of movement, kidnapped women and girls usually will be intimidated and physically tortured during this period of "training" or "orientation" — for instance, not allowed to eat anything or to wear any clothes — if they refuse to concede to the demands of their "boss." Believing that they can do nothing to change the status quo, most confined women and girls stop resisting after they are locked up for a while.

Although trafficked women and girls will, sooner or later, become a part of their "husband's house" or "adopted family,"[12] it is not unusual for them to keep experiencing physical violence (Yi, 2005: 720): after all, the possibility that these females will escape always exists. So, just like the Chinese film *Ju Dou* exemplifies, domestic violence, or what Kurst-Swanger and Petcosky (2003: 124) called hidden violence, appears common in those families (including pseudo-families) that include trafficked or purchased persons. Unfortunately, this situation usually is disregarded by street bureaucrats (including law enforcement agents) because the oppressive relationship between a "husband" (who might be a nice person in the eye of his neighbors and friends) and his "wife" could be explained away easily by their "marital bond."

If domestic violence is still considered an inconsequential, negligible, or trivial problem by public security officials in New China (in Nationalist China, this problem was not simply minor; it was not considered a problem at all), then it is bound to happen that certain women commit suicide because they can no longer endure the extremely abusive environment of their "family."[13] More precisely, this type of suicide is a fatalistic suicide, "deriving from excessive regulation, that of persons with futures pitilessly blocked and passions violently choked by oppressive discipline" (Durkheim, 1966: 276). Since this self-destructive behavior tends to occur in exceptionally violent or dysfunctional families (particularly those located in secluded villages or geographically isolated towns), investigating and recording this category of suicidal acts is, more often than not, unfeasible.

II. Forced Marriage and the Creation of Broken Families

In one of the most comprehensive studies concerning the issue of woman trafficking, Wang (2007: 161) points out that many rural communities in current China confront the grave problem of excessively skewed sex ratios caused by large-scale emigration of female populations (see above) or girl infanticide (see Chapter 3). As a result of this asymmetrical population structure, tens of millions of males have to rely on human traffickers to get a wife. To help these males keep their spouse and to avoid the potential problems caused by the escaping of this purchased woman, some cadres in the above-noted fourth-ranked towns utilize two strategies to prevent the women from running away.

The first tactic, normalization, refers to the process of constructing or endorsing a unique social custom (which, from the angle of criminology, is a delinquent subculture). Once this norm is generated or becomes manifest, local people can use it to justify and to legitimize the criminal behavior of paying money for females. In addition to serving as a subculture of neutralization, this local custom enables community residents to create a "social security" network: such an interpersonal web not only allows local dwellers to set up and to share a system of supervision, one which will place the movements of the purchased bride under total control, it also authorizes local people to take collective action to seize the woman if she is trying to flee.

The second approach, stabilization, refers to the practice of providing the imported bride with generous economic benefits (in the eyes of local people) and necessary legal aides if she marries a low-income and/or physically disabled peasant — for instance, offering salvage money, distributing farmland, or furnishing loans. Through these social welfare measures, the bride can obtain lawful documents (which will give her legal residential identity) within a short period of time, but she also will find that her registered permanent residency will stop her from leaving the town.[14]

Undoubtedly, both the normalization and stabilization strategies did help many single males (who otherwise would remain bachelors) find a spouse in the 1990s and 2000s. Nevertheless, these practices totally undermine the marriage prospect of countless females. For unmarried trafficked women, arranged or coerced marriage is not too different from servitude, for domestic chores and enormous economic pressure seem endless. So unless such women are treated compassionately by their buyer-cum-spouse (a situation that seems infrequent, if not rare), it appears very common that these women always view their husband as a stranger. (Since this apathetic attitude, in one way or another, can trigger domestic violence, young mothers, due to whatever psychological reasons, generally exhibit deep emotional attachment to their child; see Wang, 2007: 163.)

Compared to single women who might find a caring husband and/or have a child even if they are pressed to establish a family with an unfamiliar male, married women seldom can return to their normal life if they are kidnapped and forced to remarry. For these wives/mothers, it is rare that their second or even third marriage turns out to be a happy ending because not only must they deal with various problems of their new home, they also have to overcome intense anxiety and tremendous psychological pressure caused by separating from their original home (this may explain why some of these women commit infanticide if they have another baby; see Chapter 3). No matter how these women handle their stresses or psychological traumas, forced marriage of this kind always devastates the victim's family. One destructive outcome is that such families, virtually without exception, become broken homes: as wife or mother is missing, the household obviously will be headed by husband or father only. Facing this crisis, these unlucky men (who have no hope of recovering their wife) naturally have to develop coping strategies.[15] These strategies, as modern strain theorists suggest (see Agnew, 1992: 57–58), can be characterized by the following three items[16]:

- retrieving the lost stimuli;
- obtaining substitute stimuli; and
- using prohibited drugs.

The first strategy, retrieving, probably is the best solution for a married male who unexpectedly lost his wife (or, to use modern strain theorists' terms, a positively valued thing in life). That is, by means of culturally and legally accepted methods, the husband/father remarries and recreates a seemingly healthy family for himself and for his child (if he has one). Through this practice, an abnormal family may possibly go back to normal.

The second alternative, obtaining a substitute, includes two possibilities. The first one is that the husband/father reorganizes his family via remarriage, but he does not obtain his second wife through socially acceptable channels. Instead, he finds his new spouse by way of human traders. Partially because of this act, the human flesh market of modern-day China is supported. The other option is that the man can frequent underground brothels, massage parlors that provide sex services, nightclubs, or similar places to get substitute wives. No matter how many wives this person eventually can get, this practice, to an extent, also contributes to the expansion of the sex industry in contemporary China.

The third choice, using illegal drugs, refers to withdrawing from mainstream society. Broadly speaking, this behavior involves not only drug abuse but alcoholism as well because its underlying intention is to delete unwanted memories and/or smother guilt. No matter which stimulants or depressants are chosen to realize these goals, the abandoned husband/father who decides to keep a safe distance from the outside world by resorting to drugs or alcohol will always turn his broken home into a dysfunctional family.

Whichever approach listed above is selected by a male deserted by his wife to normalize his life, families affected by woman trafficking are ideal places for producing juvenile delinquents, as social disorganization theorists indicate (see Shoemaker, 2010: 117–118). The internal structure of these families is, to an extent, analogous to criminogenic environments. One indicator of this feature is that children of such households generally are improperly supervised. Since these children may have what Tittle (1995: 180) called control surplus (that is, insufficient social control or excessive personal freedom) or suffer control deficit (lacking personal freedom because of too much family control; see Tittle, 1995: 177), they engage in delinquent acts or delinquent subcultures (which might center on the techniques of neutralization, see Sykes & Matza, 1957; or aim at the focal concerns, see Shoemaker, 2010: 163–164) much more frequently than average youngsters. Furthermore, given that these under-controlled or over-controlled children seem to be more likely to run away from home (due to intrafamilial problems or personal factors like peer pressure), it is no surprise that such children often end up as drifters in big cities. As wanderers, they are regarded as social burdens or "urban parasites." That leaves them few options to survive in an alien city but relying on antisocial behavior, especially property offenses (see Rebellious Girls in Chapter 7).

III. Repeat Victimization

Another aspect of human trafficking is that some trafficked females are repeatedly manipulated by human dealers. Thanks to this experience of repeat victimization (Felson and Boba, 2010: 130–131), a good number of completely objectified young women are sold to the most underprivileged areas or are driven to join the sex industry. In addition to these destructive outcomes, certain victims, with their first-hand knowledge of the techniques of kidnapping and selling people, are motivated to engage in the very crime that ruins their life (that is, they can work for professional human smuggling rings or act alone). That makes the industry of woman trading in modern China more and more professional and harder and harder to prevent. These two questions will be examined separately. The first question, about the dynamics of repeat victimization, will be explored in this section. Second, I will explain why and how trafficked women decide to get involved in the offense that was nightmarish to them.

From the angle of crime typology, the act of trafficking women can be defined as a white-collar crime. This is because white-collar crime includes virtually any non-violent act committed for financial gain, regardless of one's social status (Brightman & Howard, 2009: 3). So if woman traffickers simply utilize nonviolent methods (such as confidence games) to control and sell their "products," then it should be reasonable to view this offense as a specialized-access crime (which is a special pattern of white-collar crime).

According to Felson and Boba (2010: 122), the chances that people will commit a specialized-access crime (for example, a sadistic person physically abuses his/her cohabitant or a prison guard sexually assaults a female inmate) are determined by the following three variables:

- the extent to which offender and victim have activity space in common;
- the extent to which offender and victim share personal ties; or
- the extent to which offender assumes a specialized work role.

Building upon these elements, not only do people of high social position enjoy better opportunities than average people in perpetrating certain types of misconducts (which can be economic, moral, or political offenses), working/lower-class people can also take advantage of these three factors to acquire illegal economic benefits or to engage in aggressive behaviors.

Inspired by the idea of specialized-access crime, factors that make certain Chinese females repeatedly victimized are recapitulated as follows.

When women are trafficked and sent to a place far from their hometown (for instance, minority females of Yunnan, Guizhou, or Xinjiang sold to coastal cities or provinces, or young females of Fujian, Guangdong, and Zhejiang transferred to inland provinces or Inner Mongolia), they always become totally isolated. The reason is obvious: almost all of them lose their original interpersonal networks/social identities and are strangers to local people, just like English-speaking fugitives who hide in a non–English-speaking country. Their isolation then turns trafficked women into "transparent" persons who can be held readily as prisoners. That is, these women possess distinctive identities (such as accent, clothing style, dialect, physical appearance, and so on) that can be recognized easily by organized, professional human trafficking rings as well as by informants hired by woman buyers to locate suitable candidates. So even if such women run away, their helpless/marginalized position is still visible to women dealers. This exceedingly vulnerable status, coupled with the condition that women who run away from their "guardians" must find a job as soon as possible (for these women, finding a job is undoubtedly the most urgent problem), gives human traffickers a variety of opportunities to play specialized roles: the latter can serve as a tour guide, a "social worker," a "philanthropist," or even a plain-clothes "law enforcement agent." All of these guises enable human dealers to assume the role of *gui ren* (literally, "valuable man" in Chinese; meaning a person who can provide help at a critical moment) or *gong an* (policeman) and to get access to their victims.

Even if trafficked women (whether they were sold as brides or sex workers) do find an opportunity to escape, they may enjoy freedom only briefly. Many again fall into the trap set by human brokers. The interaction between these two parties generally contains the following scenarios.

One common development is that some of these women and girls (who perhaps desperately need help and believe that their captor is trustworthy) are sold to the poorest districts. These are the districts where the problem of superfluous male populations and the problem of poverty are most serious in China nationwide. Therefore, local young adult males constantly face enforced singlehood.[17] Since young female populations are scarce, it is evident that these areas are excellent spots to undertake human transactions (from the perspective of economics, these trades are determined completely by the law of demand and supply). Simply speaking, in economically unpromising regions, single women in their twenties or thirties generally are deemed as "scarce resources" or "precious articles." So whenever women are shipped to those economic badlands, human traffickers can always find potential customers. On the other hand, buying a woman (as a wife) is by no means simple for local males because the price, compared to the income of local residents, is rather high. That means males who want to purchase a woman usually cannot afford it. They must ask their relatives or friends for a loan to be able to buy the woman they desire. Since this expense mainly comes from community members, which normally will cost buyers a few months (or even several years) to pay off, it is typical that trafficked women are monitored not only by their "husband"/"master" but by local inhabitants as well.[18] This normalization practice (see the prior section) usually is sufficient to lead to permanent ownership of trafficked females, no matter whether the measure of stabilization is adopted or not. In other words, victims of forced marriage that takes place in the fourth-level villages, or, to a lesser extent, third-grade cities, might be rescued by law enforcement agents; this possibility basically is nonexistent in the most impoverished rural sectors.

Unlike the above situation in which trafficked females are kept by their buyer as personal property, some kidnapped women undergo multiple ownerships because they are sold to underground figures who have intricate socioeconomic relationships (including connections with corrupt police officers). Under the jurisdiction of these "big brothers" (sometimes "big sisters"), such defenseless women are merely "gifts," "awards," "token money," or "merchandise" for the former always have a variety of "obligations" to fulfill, such as bribing crooked officials, maintaining a brotherhood with other delinquents, or clearing financial debts caused by illegal gambling. Accordingly, when the right time comes, kidnapped women could be conferred on a crooked official as a present, given to a brother of big brother as a reward/souvenir, transferred to a owner of gambling house as payment, or sold to an underground brothel (normally fronting as a barber shop, beauty salon, foot spa, or massage parlor) as an employee. Due to these commercial or contractual behaviors (all of which were legal in China before 1950), an unknown number of women are forced to "live in thick darkness" (Qiu, 2001). Staying in a purely black environment means that these females eventually will become elements of permanent underclass because they are largely poorly educated and do not have the skills "that would allow them to become profitably integrated into the [national] economy" (Flanagan, 2010: 293). As components of a permanent underclass, such women can be abandoned randomly in the street, like trash dumped on the road, and auctioned repeatedly. All of these can turn these females into serial missing populations.

IV. From Victim to Perpetrator

In victimology, an emergent area of study is the subject of the Van Dijk chain reaction (Felson & Boba, 2010: 131). According to this concept, victimization can be a source of crime because the unpleasant experience of suffering economic or financial loss can stimulate a victim to compensate for the property he/she lost. Based on the theory that a crime victim may turn out to be a crime perpetrator, modern criminologists (especially rational-choice theorists) have published numerous papers and books concerning the issue of how and when one crime leads to another (Felson & Boba, 2010: 129).

In terms of the phenomenon that one crime may push the victim to commit the very crime he/she underwent, the industry of woman trafficking in contemporary China does contain the feature of Van Dijk chain reaction. This quality, from the angle of criminological theory, can be explained by Sutherland's differential-association theory (which is a learning theory; see Sutherland et al., 1992: 88–90).

According to Sutherland (as well as other learning theorists), all human behaviors, whether socially endorsed or antisocial, come from the process of learning. The products of learning generally are determined by the variables of duration and frequency: the former denotes the period during which someone keeps learning a given behavior while the latter refers to the amount of time someone spends on learning a certain behavior. By using the copying of delinquent acts as an example, Sutherland proposes the following two propositions to demonstrate the effects of duration and frequency:

- the longer the period of interaction with a chronic offender/professional criminal, the higher the probability that a law-abiding person will become a lawbreaker
- the more frequent the interaction with a chronic offender/professional criminal, the higher the possibility that someone will commit a delinquent act.

If these two propositions are used to answer the question examined in this section, then the learning contexts under which certain trafficked women in China acquire necessary trainings and are motivated to take part in the activities of human trafficking should incorporate three factors: circumstance, actor, and course of action. The directions/variations of the interplay among these elements can be hypothesized as follows:

- the longer the period during which a kidnapped woman is kept in the circle of trafficking, the higher the probability that this person will deviate from the protection of social security networks and lose contact with her original family

- the longer the period during which a kidnapped woman remains in the circle of trafficking, the higher the possibility that this individual will be "forgotten" by her original family and the lower the possibility that this woman will be able to return to her initial life
- the longer the period during which a kidnapped woman stays in the circle of trafficking, the higher the possibility that the victim will accept her "new family," alter her self-image, and adopt a new lifestyle
- the more frequent the interaction between a kidnapped woman and a human smuggler/trafficker, the higher the probability that the boundary between these two parties will become less and less rigid (or the social distance between these two parties will become shorter and shorter)
- the less rigid the boundary (or the shorter the social distance) between a kidnapped woman and a human trafficker, the higher the possibility that the former will be deemed by the latter as a friend or social equal (that is, the previous hierarchical/exploitative relationship between these two parties will be replaced gradually by an equal one)
- the more equal the relationship between a kidnapped woman and her ex-captor, the higher the probability that the former will be viewed by the latter as a business partner or teammate
- the greater the extent to which a kidnapped woman is perceived by her ex-captor as a colleague, the higher the possibility that the former will enjoy the opportunity to perpetrate the crime of human trafficking and the higher the probability that the former will acquire pecuniary rewards if the crime is committed successfully
- the more the occasions in which a former trafficked woman is able to participate in human trafficking, the higher the probability that this person will become an active or full-time member of an organized trafficking ring
- the stronger the connection between a kidnapped woman-turned-human trafficker and a structured human trafficking circle, the higher the probability that the former will master the techniques effective in catching prey and the higher the likelihood that this woman, if she becomes an independent human trafficker, can establish social networks necessary to sell her victims.

Taken together, it seems appropriate to conclude that human kidnapping and woman trafficking, as a ghastly retail business for numerous parents and married males (who fear that their daughter or wife might be kidnapped), is still prevalent in China in the 21st century. One chief factor that keeps this industry flourishing is rapid social change, especially unprecedented urbanization and economic liberalization. Since traffickers, whether amateur or professional, still enjoy a variety of opportunities in buying and selling naive females, it is sociologically/criminologically important to list the modi operandi that human traffickers frequently use to acquire their supplies.

Techniques Commonly Employed by Human Traffickers to Abduct Young Females

Generally speaking, when human traffickers in China try to catch their prey, they usually will start with evaluation, which includes the assessment of relationship with a potential victim and the appraisal of latent risks and economic benefits. Then, based on this evaluation, traffickers will designate appropriate strategies to manipulate a certain victim. That is, if traffickers and victims are acquaintances (whether they know each other very well or they simply have friends in common), then the former normally will use nonviolent methods (such as deception) to control the latter. On the other hand, if traffickers and victims are strangers, then the former, to a considerable extent, will employ aggressive behavior to have the latter submit. Each of these two approaches includes several characteristics (Yi, 2005: 705–720).

I. Trafficker and Victim Are Acquaintances

The first approach (that is, nonviolent or diplomatic means; see specialized-access crime above) typically will be adopted if trafficker and victim share a social bond. With this bond, woman traffickers, more often than not, can conceal their true identity or plots. Such a personal tie also makes certain women (particularly those in low-income regions) exceptionally vulnerable to human trade.

Typologically, woman trafficking can be differentiated into two versions if perpetrator and victim know each other. The first one is that the trafficker or traffickers and the victim are residents of the same village located in an economically underdeveloped area. Due to this residential linkage, the trafficker can invite the victim to go to a big city to find a stable job. Once the victim accepts this proposal and follows her "friend" to an unfamiliar city to apply for a position, the victim unknowingly falls into the prearranged trap and is sold to organized human trafficking rings.[19]

The second pattern also involves the scenario of job-searching: the victim is asked to go to an economically booming city to get a permanent or better-paid job. Shortly after the victim arrives at her destination, she is transferred (unwittingly) to gangsters specializing in trafficking. Because of this transfer, the victim is reduced to an object that will be handed over to any purchaser who can pay the right price. Victims of the second situation are far more likely to suffer severe psychological traumas than their counterparts of the previous case because in the second condition, the trafficker and the victim are not merely ordinary friends but lovers (or even husband and wife): just like the traditional process of mate selection, the trafficker can establish an intimate or marital relationship with his victim, which can make the latter believe that this association is sincere. After this truthful relationship is constructed, the victim will be sold to wholesale women buyers at the right time (if the trafficker and the victim have a child, the child, depending on age and gender, might be abandoned or slain).

II. Trafficker and Victim Are Strangers

Compared to cautious woman traffickers who take a steady but time-consuming approach to manipulating their commodities, many women brokers (in both Old and New China) prefer to seize their targets as soon as possible. This choice obviously is based on the assumption that a fast approach is more efficient and productive than a slow approach because it may enable human traffickers to get a sufficient amount of merchandise and thus generate enormous economic benefits within a short period of time.

While the "quick combat, swift withdrawal" strategy is potentially more rewarding, it is clear that this method entails higher risk of failure, for many factors are uncertain and unpredictable (such as weather, traffic, the potential threat of the police, possible intervention of witnesses, victim's response, and the like). That means traffickers can get into serious trouble if they try to snatch an unfamiliar woman or girl from a public (or even private) place. With this in mind, human dealers normally will use dependable methods to help them achieve the desired ends.

The first alternative, which probably is safest and easiest, is that traffickers go to an underprivileged town where the practice of selling young females is tolerated (or even endorsed by street bureaucrats). They then find a good household, negotiate the price with victim's guardian(s), and take the girl or woman away.[20]

The second method is pure violence or, in other words, a blitz attack. In this case, woman traffickers must prepare the following three things before taking action:

The first one is weapons, possibly an ax, meat chopper, handgun, knife, or even stun gun. With these menacing arms, woman traders, if they choose the right place and the right time, usually capture their victims swiftly.

The second one is a vehicle. This vehicle, which usually is a commercial van or SUV, can assist traffickers to transport the victim and to escape from the crime scene as soon as possible without drawing the attention of the police.

The third one is restraint kits (duct tape, handcuff, rope, eye mask, and the like). These tools enable human dealers to monitor their victims closely, to punish them if they resist, and to remove all potential opportunities for the victim to escape.

When all of these components are ready, women sellers can either kidnap their targets randomly — for example, forcing a single young woman who walks in an empty street during late night hours to enter a minivan for a joy ride — or stalk a preferred victim for a period of time and take this person as a prisoner when she is totally unprepared and unaccompanied.

Another way to get fast money is "framing." The following is an example of this ploy (see Yi, 2005: 707):

From time to time, traffickers will find that their target is escorted by an adult male. If this discovery occurs in a public spot (especially a tumultuous one like a railway or subway station, a crowded bus, or a night market), then it is clear that traffickers must devise ways to separate the woman from her guardian. One alternative is to wrongly accuse the man: traffickers can create a mêlée situation in which the man is charged with abducting the woman. After this chaotic situation is initiated, the woman's escort (who could be the target's relative, friend, or even husband) will be intercepted and interrogated by human traffickers for the "crime" he has committed (it is not unusual for this man to be seriously injured by the thugs to prevent him from counterattacking; certain enthusiastic passersby may also join this operation of apprehension).

The woman will be pulled away immediately by associates of woman traders and transported to a prearranged location. Since this woman essentially has no opportunity to explain or to cry out for help (after all, no one will pay close attention to what she is trying to say on "opportunity" to suppress a crime), human traffickers, if their actions are not stopped by witnesses or suspicious bystanders, usually can seize the female. This ownership will become permanent if law enforcement agents do not show up and intervene. (Even if the police get involved in the case, the criminals who keep victim's male companion in check still can get away successfully; for example, the gangsters can claim that the whole thing is a misunderstanding and insist that they do not know the persons who took away the woman.)

Concluding Remarks

From the perspective of social history, woman trafficking was a structuralized part of the Chinese society before 1912: not only could wealthy families and brothels legally purchase young females as maidservants, concubines, or sex workers, but trafficked women would be punished by the authorities if they ran away (or attempted to run away) from their owner. Although this slave system no longer exists in present-day China (including Hong Kong and Taiwan), woman trading is still a major social problem in the China proper in the 1990s and 2000s. Facing the issues brought about by this problem, the Beijing government launched several large-scale anti-trafficking movements in the past two decades. As a result, tens of thousands of human dealers, woman brokers, and corrupt officials were arrested and sent to jail. Some of them were even put to death shortly after they were found guilty.

While the Beijing government did demonstrate its determination to eradicate the problem of human trafficking, what functionalists called social pathology or social disease still can be found in every province of contemporary China. Due to the existence of this underground world, millions of families suffer the loss of a loving wife, mother, or daughter.

Based on the descriptions above, it seems appropriate to conclude that the evolution of woman trafficking in China in the 20th and 21st centuries proceeds along two trajectories. One track, the classic or domestic path, involves those females who were auctioned in the human flesh markets of Greater China in the past one-hundred-plus years. Three environmental factors tend to predestine these individuals to the lot of public sale: natural disaster, war, and extreme poverty. Since an unknown number of these marginalized women and girls could not break away from forced marriage or the sex industry, it is inevitable that numerous females, as they were kept in the dark corners of big cities or rural districts, eventually become "unnamed," "unidentified," or even "unheard of."

Besides the classic line, the international trajectory (that is, smuggling women out of China) also plays a critical role in dehumanizing females and in manufacturing missing females. In this regard, the human smuggling movement in China (as well as in "victim countries") tends to exhibit the subsequent traits:

First, this movement is "young": before the mid–1970s, human smuggling seemed to be a minor issue in China. This situation changed dramatically in the late 1970s/early 1980s when the Chinese communist government, under the leadership of Deng Xiao-ping, took steps to liberalize the economy and loosen travel restrictions (Chin, 1999: 15). As more and more opportunities became available to the public to travel overseas, human smuggling also became a collective behavior or "fashion" in China (especially Guangdong and Fujian) in the 1990s (Chin, 1999: 9–16). Despite the facts that the communist government punished those who traveled abroad without official documents and that China's economy has boomed in the past twenty years, the allure of going to America, Canada, or Europe to earn quick money still inspires a certain number of legally and professionally unqualified young Chinese women to go to the West.[21]

For Chinese women who arrive in Western societies through unlawful means, finding a stable job (let alone a well-paid job) is not easy. This is due to the fact that smuggled persons (no matter which country they are from) do not enjoy legal employment status (or if they do, this status normally is brief). Hence, they usually will not be hired by regular businesses. In the meantime, they also face the risks of arrest, detention, and deportation. In addition to the difficulty in getting a real job, the employment prospect for smuggled women appears to be even less promising than that of their male counterparts. This job discrimination can be seen in the following aspects.

In the first place, due to physical limitations, illegal Chinese female immigrants generally will not get jobs that require great physical strength, such as construction worker, fisherman, porter, truck driver, and so on. So even though many physically demanding occupations are low-paid, smuggled Chinese men, compared to their female counterparts, enjoy more opportunities to become employed and have better chances to change their "illegal" status.

Second, given that most jobs that call for physical strength are dominated by men, female Chinese smugglers, on the whole, can find jobs only in the underground clothing factories known as sweatshops that are mostly located in large cities (Esbenshade, 2004); in certain Chinese-owned carry-out/fast food restaurants, cafés, or tea houses, which from time to time will hire illegal immigrants to minimize costs or to evade taxes (Huston, 1995: 166); or in business like beauty salons, foot massage parlors, skin care centers, gambling houses, and travel agencies, controlled by Chinese or Asian gangs (Chin, 1999).

No matter which industry female Chinese smugglers eventually enter, such women always face two harsh challenges. The first one is that very few of them can get jobs offered by legitimate (American) companies (Kwong, 1997: 120–124). As a consequence, the majority of female smugglers are beyond protection of the law. Second, almost all smuggled Chinese women are "assisted" by loan sharks to leave China. Therefore, it is not uncommon for smuggled Chinese women (as well as men) to be charged smuggling fees ranging from U.S. $40,000 to $60,000 (Chin, 1999: 124–125). In this respect, most smuggled Chinese women have to spend many years working as bonded seamstresses or sex laborers to pay off debts. Essentially prisoners, these women usually can do nothing but provide free or underpaid labor to their debtors in order to pay off smuggling fees.

In a nutshell, many women from coastal provinces (including some from Hong Kong and Taiwan) went abroad illegally in the past three decades. Since these smuggled women usually can find only unskilled and low-paid jobs in the gray sections of mainstream society (i.e., segments not fully regulated by the law), they more often than not have to work long hours to repay loans. During this period, they are especially vulnerable to economic exploitation, physical violence, and/or sexual assault. Accordingly, smuggled Chinese women, as they live in milieus not fully or effectively supervised by the law, tend to confront far greater risks in becoming missing than do mainstream women.

CHAPTER 7

Runaways/Thrownaways

After describing several types of missing females in Chapters 2 to 6, it appears valid to claim that the disappearance of those categories of women and girls is connected closely with certain structural arrangements (particularly ideology and public policy; see Table 7-1). Such a direct connection (or definite causal relationship) probably is less likely to be observed when other sorts of missing females (for example, women with mental or cognitive issues, teenage runaways, and ostracized leprosy sufferers) are investigated.

In this chapter, female runaways and thrownaways are inspected. In the course of inspecting these two categories of lost women and girls, two questions will be posed:

- What are the socioeconomic and demographic features of female runaways and thrownaways in Greater China?
- In addition to all-encompassing forces operating at the macro/national rank (such as an official policy and collective norms), how are the life experiences of certain missing females influenced by contextual causes working at the micro/local level (for instance, physical attributes and family background)? In other words, how are the life experiences of (senile) females with dementia, teenage girls who run away from home or school, and female lepers affected (or even determined) by individual traits, such as mental ability and physical appearance, or personal memberships, such as emotional attachments to family and school?

After these two subjects have been explored, the philosophical paradigms followed by the authorities of Greater China in enacting and implementing social policies will be evaluated.

TABLE 7-1. PLAUSIBLE CAUSAL RELATIONSHIP BETWEEN STRUCTURAL
ARRANGEMENTS AND THE DISAPPEARANCE OF FEMALES

Cause: Structural Arrangements	*Effect:* Typologies of Disappearing Females
1. Extreme Anticommunist Ideology 2. The Purge Policy of Eliminating the Communists (i.e., the White Terror) 3. Extreme Socialist or Collectivist Ideology 4. The Purge Policy of Suppressing anti–Marxists/Maoists (i.e., the Red Terror)	Exemplar: Female Political Prisoners
1. Patriarchal Thought 2. The Dowry Culture 3. One-Child-Per-Household Policy	Exemplar: Aborted/Slain Baby Girls
1. The Custom of Patrilineal Descent 2. The Faith of Afterlife 3. The Belief of Otherworld	Exemplar: Ghost Bride
1. The Military Prostitution System 2. Sexist and Racist Population Policy Implemented by the Japanese Colonial Authorities Before August 1945	Exemplar: Comfort Women
1. Massive Population Migration Created by Economic Liberalization 2. Distorted Distribution of Male and Female Populations 3. Legal Loopholes Caused by Massive Population Migration	Exemplar: Trafficked Women

Female Runaways: Unaware vs. Aware

In sociology, the term *runaway* usually is defined as "a person under the age of eighteen who voluntarily leaves home or another residence, and thereby the custody and control of parents or guardians" (Flowers, 2001: 3). Based on this definition, the issue of running away from home typically is analyzed by sociologists/criminologists within the paradigm of juvenile delinquency.

While I adopt this approach in this book (see the section on Rebellious Girls, below), I also argue that people younger than eighteen (including teenagers and boys and girls younger than twelve) are not the only actors who will escape from their home. Instead, people with Alzheimer's disease (AD) may also run away from their residence without leaving any clues or messages behind. It is these types of missing persons that will be looked at in the subsequent section.

I. Women with Alzheimer's Disease

For sociologists, the academic responsibility of researching and reporting the dilemmas confronted by people who have Alzheimer's disease undoubtedly belongs to those sociologists specializing in themes related to public health — epidemiology, history of medicine, spreading of deadly diseases, and so on. Given this academic division of labor and role assignment, medical sociologists usually are expected to provide the sociology community (as well as the health authorities and general public) with all possible information on a certain disease, including its etiology, prevalence, possibility of contagion, diagnosis, and social impacts.

Alzheimer's disease is, needless to say, one of the topics that must be explored by medical sociologists. In this regard, it might be controversial to conclude that AD is the most often studied topic in the area of sociology of medicine. Except for this debatable issue and no matter which aspects medical sociologists concentrate on when they address dementia, the generally accepted symptoms or core features are as follows:

> People suffering from dementia get around just fine, but they are often moody, imagine things, hallucinate, and the like. Sufferers often leave home and then can't find their way back. They hide things, forget they've already taken their medicines and then grouse at family members for not bringing the meds, or take medicines on the sly and end up overdosing. Eating can be a problem, too, because they may have trouble using chopsticks (or forks/spoons), or forget to chew before swallowing. They have to be watched 24 hours a day [Teng, 2010: 81].

All of these signs clearly indicate that, when caretakers are absent, aged people with dementia are at high risk of becoming missing. This quality can be elaborated as follows:

First, despite the fact that biosociologists, genetic specialists, and researchers of human health are still arguing about the root cause of AD (that is, whether there is a causal relationship with "geneticization" or if negative social and ecological factors also play a part in shaping this cause; see Lock, et al., 2006), it seems undeniable that this presymptomatic illness (Lock, 2006: 127) is, to an extent, biologically programmed: compared to people whose genetic makeup tends to be more resistant to memory decline, some people (regardless of their body shape, gender, intelligence, personality, social class, education level, occupation, race, marital status, religious affiliation, lifestyle, and special talents) appear more likely to undergo the problem of memory worsening. An example may be found in the Gao Kun case. (While this example is probably not representative or typical, it is informative.)

In 2009 Professor Gao (1933–) was awarded the Nobel Prize in physics. He was known as the "father of optical fibers." Professor Gao's brain, in terms of resisting brain aging, should be far better-equipped than an average person's. This is because his brain must be very active. Therefore, his brain, constantly in the ready to think status, was very unlikely to be influenced by the disease(s) caused by the rusting process of a less active/inertial brain. However, Dr. Gao began to show signs of Alzheimer's disease in the early 2000s. He was eventually diagnosed to have AD in the late 2000s. Now, Professor Gao is, by all measures, no longer one of the intellectual elites. He can recollect very little, if any, information about his specialty, the science of optical fiber. His current mental status is essentially the same as that of a psychologically disabled person.

The Gao case suggests that, possibly due to different combinations of genetic composition, certain persons (including the most talented or intelligent) tend to have a stronger propensity to experience Alzheimer's disease. In addition to this "biological determinism," dementia has several sociological attributes. One is that, according to statistics, most AD sufferers in greater China are 65 or older (Hong Kong Alzheimer's Disease Association). This age-concentration phenomenon probably is not sufficient enough to verify the theory that normal aging, pathological decline of the body, dementia/brain disease are synonyms because some senile persons still have the ability (both mental and physical) to engage in highly risky activities (for instance, parachute jumping). However, the association between the variables of aging and the frequency of dementia seems pretty strong, for when people have passed a certain age threshold, their brain tends to become less and less resistant to pathological processes (see Kaufman, 2006: 25–27).

Another sociologically important quality of dementia is that this disease is a "mind-losing illness" (DeBaggio, 2003). Therefore, people with such a disease will, to a varying degree, "experience disorientation towards time, place, and person" ("About Dementia," Hong Kong Alzheimer's Disease Association). That is, AD patients will undergo "some failure in brain function" (Sabat, 2001: 4). As a consequence, such sufferers will, step by step, show limited ability (or inability) to distinguish between authentic and imaginary worlds (Taylor, 2006). This process of deterioration will progressively confine sufferers within their own inner sanctuary. That makes it harder and harder for these cognitively impaired people to communicate with the outside world.

If people slowly but surely lose the mental ability to interact with others, then from the perspectives of criminology and victimology, they (especially those who have become less and less responsive) will in due course become totally defenseless. The only option for these elders to handle daily affairs is to rely on the assistance of caregivers. Hiring competent and caring caregivers to provide services to seniors with dementia, however, is not easy in Greater China because on the one hand, lots of caregivers in China are unqualified (they might be inexperienced students, untrained peasant workers, or part-time medical staff); on the other hand, it is procedurally complicated for an elder who truly needs help to hire an eligible caregiver (who usually is a foreign worker) in Taiwan (Teng, 2010: 80–81). As a result of these problems, an unknown number of sufferers of Alzheimer's disease are not supervised adequately.

The mental ability of these patients might still allow them to act normally. Nevertheless, as their ability to recognize things and people is slowly but continually deteriorating, such seemingly normal sufferers do face a risk of getting lost if they take a trip alone. This mode of running away from home, depending on the severity of memory loss, tends to exhibit the following features.

First, at the slightest level (or level I), AD sufferers are not completely helpless: during this stage, they still can remember the features of acquaintances (name, face, relationship, and so forth) and know how to make contact with their relatives when they are lost (including places with which they used to be familiar). By way of this ability to report their whereabouts, such individuals with amnesia still may return home safely.

Unlike those AD patients who still can make clear statements, AD sufferers who belong to the medium level (or level II) have great difficulty remembering their identities or roles: during this period, not only have patients of dementia exhibited a very limited ability to retain information in the brain, they also have revealed that they can no longer travel without help. If this trait does not cause sufficient attention among a patients significant others or even is disregarded, then it is very likely that AD sufferers will go missing if they do make a journey by themselves. These lost persons (especially those who can supply a little bit of personal information to local residents or law enforcement agents), however, may still be able to go home if they do not travel far.

Finally, at the most serious level (or level III), AD sufferers have essentially lost the entire ability to memorize or recall things.[1] Because of this mental disability, such innocent individuals always have to be accompanied by a caregiver if they take a walk or make a journey. That means these aged persons are extremely likely to become missing if they go someplace alone. This vulnerability can be illustrated by the following two propositions:

- the longer the distance of a trip engaged in by type III AD patients, the higher the probability that they will become stray populations
- the longer the distance traveled by type III AD patients, the higher the probability that they will be lost permanently to their family because they lack the psychological ability to give social workers or law enforcement agents the information necessary to return them home.

At any rate, these propositions suggest that if type III AD sufferers go out alone, then the potential of returning home generally is determined by two factors. One is traveling distance: the shorter the distance, the higher the possibility that women or men with severe dementia will be found and sent back home. The other is setting: if women or men with serious dementia live in a *gemeinschaft* (a small or closed community where interpersonal interactions appear intimate); then they, compared to their counterparts who live in a *gesellschaft*, or big city where interpersonal interactions seem aloof, if not unfriendly, tend to have far more chances to be intercepted by community members if they roam in the street. This may explain why women with type III dementia usually are not gone very long (probably one to two days or just a few hours) if they get lost in a small city or rural town (Liberty Times, 2005; Taitung County Government, 2005).

Based on the descriptions above, it appears appropriate to draw the subsequent conclusions: in terms of the predicaments commonly encountered by missing populations (for example, getting involved in extremely exploitative jobs and/or inability to stay with family members), females with Alzheimer's disease obviously are luckier than the disappearing women and girls listed in Table 7-1. This is because the former normally will not become victims of human trafficking, indeterminate sentence, sex predation, slave labor, or cultural murder, while the latter will, in one way or another, be victimized by violent crimes.[2] Furthermore, as aged persons whose mind has become dormant appear more likely to trigger societal reactions if they walk aimlessly in the street, the duration of their absence is generally not long. (Whether they can return home is another issue; see distance and setting above.)

II. Rebellious Girls[3]

Like the "old runaways" portrayed above, young runaways in Greater China also can display the dynamics of missing populations. Before considering this problem, it is necessary to enumerate the defining characteristics of teenage runaways in China, Hong Kong, and Taiwan so that these features can function as conceptual frameworks.

The first characteristic is that before the Beijing authorities started to relax economic control in the late 1970s, running away from home, as an antisocial behavior, seemed to be a minor social problem in this totalitarian and ideology-directed country. (The same situation, to a lesser extent, could also be observed in Taiwan in the 1950s, '60s, and '70s, when this island was governed by the authoritarian Chiang Kai-shek/Chiang Ching-kuo regime.) Two reasons appeared crucial in keeping this social pathology minimal.

The first one was that during those highly suppressive years, almost all residential areas (including embassy districts and gated communities), public buildings (especially airports, museums, rail stations, theaters, and universities), tourist facilities (hotels, small inns, and parks), government offices, factories, and plazas (including Tiananmen Square) were closely supervised by the armed police, the militias, patrol officers and other security agents. Even graveyards and public restrooms were monitored regularly. Under this tremendously secure environment, it was extremely difficult, if not impossible, for teenagers to find a shelter after sunset if they left their home without permission or escaped from school. Even if such young rebels could find a place to stay, it was virtually impossible for them to stay there for several days, let alone weeks, without being discovered.

Besides the seemingly omnipresent public security agents who made it exceptionally difficult for runaways or homeless persons to enter an empty building and to enjoy asylum, another (institutionalized) cause that discouraged teenagers from running away from home or school was that the Beijing (and to an extent, the Taipei) authorities used the criminal justice approach to punish teenage runaways and their parents. That is, if teenagers ran away from school or home, they would be treated like criminals after they were caught by the police or school administrators. (The punishments varied, but they always involved shaming, public humiliation, and degradation ceremonies.) In addition, their parents could be investigated or even detained by the security units. Given that the act of running away from home or school (which, for law enforcement authorities of modern America, is merely a status offense) was criminalized, most young people of China and Taiwan were controlled firmly by their parents or the other family members before the 1980s.

The social mechanisms which enabled parents or capable guardians to keep minors docile/submissive began to lose their social control power in the early 1980s when economic liberalization policies and political liberalization policies were carried out respectively in China and Taiwan (see Chapters 2 and 6). Due to these structural transformations and reforms, educational problems increasingly were not handled by the criminal justice, juvenile justice, and law enforcement authorities. Under this new environment of decriminalization, teenagers on both sides of the Taiwan Strait, starting in the late 1980s or early 1990s, enjoyed more and more individual freedom (including the freedom of running away from school, because the outcomes were no longer as serious as they used to be). That enabled parents to pay less attention to the prospect that their children might bring them legal troubles because of skipping school or poor academic performance.

All of these big social and policy changes were examples of new social trends (or mega-movements) that occurred in Greater China in the past twenty years. They allow modern researchers and educators to explain why the behavior of breaking away from home or school is no longer a social taboo in present-day Greater China. On the other hand, such developments (as they were too all-embracing to show the variations and idiosyncrasies of individual behaviors) cannot help social scientists answer a key question; namely, why some youths are more likely to become runaways or school truants than others. To answer this question, it is methodologically necessary to examine factors functioning at the personal and group (whether primary or secondary) level to see how and why the operation of those forces (especially disadvantageous and dysfunctional ones) causes certain teenagers to take the desperate action of abandoning their family and friends and seeking asylum in the street.

Criminologically, identifying the root causes of the act of running away from home is a pretty intricate task. This is because this work requires investigators to create a research boundary: was the act committed by a married woman who, as a mail bride, was physically attacked by her American husband? Was the act committed by a minor who felt he/she was mistreated? Investigators also must assess the possible impacts of risk factors at both individual and ecological levels — that is, whether the behavior of escaping from home is influenced or directed by personality disorders, by environmental pressures, or by both. Finally, it calls for criminologists and sociologists to propose a causal model (or even a theory) to explain why and how the "disturbing world" (Hare, 1998) that teenagers face can motivate the latter to deny a crucial social establishment. All of these investigations, in one way or another, have been explored by professionals specializing in juvenile delinquency of American and other English-speaking societies (among them Chesney-Lind & Pasko, 2003; Flowers, 2001; Laser & Nicotera, 2011; Shoemaker, 2009).

The same situation can also be found in Greater China. In the past twenty years, innumerable articles and books on delinquent behavior perpetrated by teenagers have been published. While many of these publications are very important, Ju's (2008) comprehensive and systematic report probably is the most noteworthy.

Like their counterparts in the West, Ju and his colleagues argue that the behavior of running away from home or school (in China) does not involve a single factor only. Instead, this act is, more often than not, caused by the multiple but intertwined reasons (Ju, 2008: 20). Such reasons, for the purpose of analysis, can be classified into several underlying variables. The first (and perhaps the most remarkable) one is family background.

According to Ju (2008), (female) runaways normally come from families overwhelmed by one or some of the subsequent problems:

- extreme poverty: in one example, a child in an impoverished village of Yunnan ran away from home because the father could not (or did not want to) pay the six-dollar (approximately one U.S. dollar) school tuition, forcing the child to quit school (Ju, 2008: 13)
- single parenthood: compared to a family with both parents present, children are more likely to leave their home if it is headed by a single parent. Factors that could lead to this unfavorable situation include separation, divorce, imprisonment (one of the parents is incarcerated), death, desertion (one of the parents forsakes the family), and human trafficking (mother is a victim of woman trafficking; see Chapter 6)
- absent parenthood: in this situation, the child runs away because both parents of the child have died or because the child is abused by one or more members of his/her foster family
- totally inadequate parenting: some teenagers abandon their family because their parents are critically ill or have severe physical/psychological problems
- intense relationship between parent(s) and the runaway child: in some superficially healthy families, the relationship between a parent (or

both parents) and the runaway child is terribly conflicting (for instance, the child is scolded or physically punished frequently by her mother, father, or both), a situation that makes a youth feel safer on the street
- incompatible/irreconcilable relationship between parents: in certain families, the couple act like a cobra and a mongoose — that is, not only do they frequently quarrel with each other, even over trivial matters, they also physically fight habitually; frequently witnessing these altercations motivates the runaway child to escape from a terrible situation
- lack of parental supervision: in some working-class families, both parents have to spend most of their time at work. On the one hand, this can force the neglected youth to assume the household responsibilities. On the other hand, it gives the runaway child abundant opportunities to leave home hoping to find an exciting life in the street
- authoritarianism: some parents overemphasize the values of obedience, discipline, and coercion; this highly suppressive education philosophy gives the over-controlled child few spaces to enjoy privacy or become independent. Facing nonnegotiable rules imposed by strict parents, the youth is motivated to leave his/her environment to avoid seemingly never-ending pressure of being a good student or well-behaved child.

In addition to these domestic problems, a seemingly less common family crisis is underground romantic relationships. In one instance provided by Qiu (2001:151–152), a teenage girl reported that she ran away from home because she was trying to retaliate against her father, who allegedly maintained a sexual relationship with her sister-in-law (that is, her brother's wife).

Resembling the damaging or devastating effects caused by dysfunctional families, rapid and massive population shift also plays a critical role in stimulating teenagers or younger kids to reject their linkages to family. As indicated in Chapter 6, communist China, as early as the 1990s, had already become a de facto capitalist country. This "placid revolution," however, did not take place all over China. Instead, it occurred in a couple of provinces of East and South China only. As the impacts of this development are skewed in structural distribution, it is predestined that the economy, infrastructure, and social resources of coastal provinces and cities are far more thriving, advanced, and abundant than those of inland regions.

While it is unclear whether the new economic programs implemented by the Beijing authorities in Southwest and West China at the present time will improve the life quality of people in this economically underdeveloped territory before 2030, it is clear that hundreds of millions of peasants and laborers in less developed provinces are trying to settle down in Shanghai and other populous coastal cities in the 2010s. This "collective will" inevitably constitutes a thorny problem for the Beijing and local governments because Shanghai and other metropolitan cities, among others, do not have enough living space to hold so many illegal immigrants. Accordingly, it is extremely difficult, if not totally impossible, for rural residents who have already immigrated to an economically booming city to change their nonresident identity.

Given that it is very challenging for rural populations (many of whom are farmers) to become permanent residents of a "dream city,"[4] it is unsurprising that they cannot get a permanent job. Sooner or later, this tenuous status transforms such marginalized populations (as well as their relatives, if any) into a permanent underclass (who may turn out to be "city scavengers," like professional beggars; or "urban frontiersmen" like nomadic temporary workers). As these social groups are least likely to enjoy city services and social welfare, all of them, regardless of their age and gender, face the following problems:

- unstable living environment: rural persons who unlawfully migrate to a city normally cannot settle in a neighborhood because these people are, as mentioned above, not qualified to apply for permanent jobs; as a result of this limitation, it becomes necessary for such persons to travel in order to find a temporary job[5]
- involvement in highly exploitative labor: despite the punishment that rural people who reside in a city must recurrently change their domicile so that they can find provisional work, the jobs they can acquire are, more often than not, manual and unskilled; since such low-paid jobs alone are far from sufficient to support peasant families in a city, it is not unusual that all family members must get a job (no matter how dangerous, tedious, or poorly paid it is) in order to sustain a minimal living level.

Under the enormous pressure of the law of survival, only the luckiest (and the most diligent) children of *hei hu* (literally, "black households"; meaning unregistered households of a city) can go to elementary and middle schools (or even university), get diplomas, find a technical job, and eventually obtain city residency. With the exception of this small, elite group, millions of children can go to school only briefly, from a few weeks to a few years. Deprivation of schooling usually is closely related to two factors. One is that, as indicated, a good number of undocumented parents (who will be among the poorest of the poor if they are critically ill or physically handicapped) are too poor to afford education-related expenses in a city. Therefore, their children, after a period of formal education, can receive home schooling only. The other cause is that many rural youths are deemed to be problem students in an urban school if they have difficulty handling schoolwork, cannot get along with classmates and/or teachers, are not interested in learning, and/or argue with school administrators (Ju, 2008: 19–20). So, regardless of their intelligence and aptitude, these maladjusted children, after a while, have to drop out of school as well.

No matter how long children and teenagers of *hei hu* stay in a school, they typically have to work as child laborers after quitting school. For these apprentices and teenage manual workers, life is usually limited to toil and moil. This pressure can easily prompt some youngsters to escape from an unendurable workplace.[6] In addition to escaping from work, such minors may run away from home as well if they believe that they will be punished sternly by their parents because of quitting a precious job without permission.

Finally, even if young persons of highly disadvantaged families do not formally flee from home in the short run, it is still possible that such good boys and well-behaved girls will officially become runaways in the long run. One crucial factor that can turn this prospect into a reality is that minors who do not follow a mainstream lifestyle (that is, those who do not attend school but spend their time hanging around in the street or in shopping malls and Internet bars) are far more likely than average youths to become habitual school truants or join professional beggar rings, juvenile gangs led by adults, or even human traffickers (because these parties share the same activity space; see Chapter 6). If the interaction between these two parties (that is, would-be runaways and career delinquents) does happen, then the former may become what Flowers (2001: 5) called "policy-focal runaways"[7] if they keep receiving financial support and other assistance from the latter (generally speaking, the more frequent and the stronger the support, whether financial/material or emotional/nonmaterial that nonmainstream societies or criminal associations can furnish, the higher the probability that children who neither go to school nor have a job will leave their home).

In Greater China, policy-focal runaways, as chronic street wanderers, tend to display the subsequent demographic and socioeconomic characteristics (Ju, 2008: 10–33):

• in terms of demographic background, approximately 70 percent are between eleven and fifteen years old; around 70 percent to 80 percent are boys, 20 percent to 30 percent are girls; over 80 percent are from

underdeveloped rural areas; over 50 percent belong to the Han ethnic group (if they are racial minorities, most of them are Uighurs of Xinjiang); and over half of them do not finish primary school (that is, over half of them are primary school dropouts)
- in terms of family background, the great majority are from malfunctioning or dysfunctional families (see the previous pages for the attributes of such families)
- in terms of frequency of running away from home, over 50 percent have the experience of escaping from home at least twice
- in terms of duration of leaving home, at least 40 percent have left their biological family and supposedly stay with "pseudo-family-members" (such as other drifting children) for one year or longer.[8]

Besides these general traits, almost all girls and boys who flee their home will face one simple but extraordinarily urgent problem: how to make a living on the street. To overcome this formidable challenge, the life of street boys usually is full of violence and law-breaking behaviors. In Ju's (2008: 27–28) study, around 40 percent of such boys depended on burglary, shoplifting, forced begging, intimidation, physical assault, robbery, or even murder to survive in the urban jungle.[9]

As for street girls, their life, more often than not, involves prostitution or commercialized sex (Fu, 1994; Qiu, 2001; Tai, 1993). This feature has some social policy implications. One is that female policy-focal runaways usually are far less visible on the street than their male counterparts because the former, as the main sources of supply for the sex industry, can be absorbed easily and quickly by escort companies, massage parlors, nightclubs, pubs, and other recreation firms (that is, by providing board and lodging, sex-related businesses can function as "asylums" for runaway girls). As these "men's heavens" can operate as "safe houses" for escaped teenage girls, who otherwise are very unlikely to become employed in the mainstream society, it seems to have become a rule that only after dark from approximately 8:00 P.M. to 6:00 A.M., will such girls start to emerge from their "hideouts" and become active.

Working for sex businesses, on the other hand, does not imply that this profession is composed of sex and parties. On the contrary, this occupation encompasses four Ds: directives, discrimination, drugs, and diseases.

The first D refers to the practice that in Greater China, almost all owners of sex businesses adopt the business philosophy of military management to control their young ladies: not only are the latter ordered to stay in their room during non-business hours (essentially house arrest, because the buildings are always monitored by enforcers); it is mandatory that these young girls must fulfill the minimal requirements of their jobs — providing sexual services to a certain number of men within a designated period — and have to be "on duty" punctually, no matter whether they have recovered from bodily discomfort caused by, for example, binge drinking or menstruation.[10] Under these regulations, it is not unusual that female sex workers are beaten and lose all of their wages because of "substandard performance" or inability to fulfill "obligations."

The second D means that whenever teenage girls become sex workers, their position, to a considerable extent, will be determined by their utility: those who can keep helping their boss accumulate wealth might gradually enjoy certain privileges (for example, pay raise and sick leave). In contrast, those who cannot fulfill the quota of sexual services usually will be punished, sometimes by deprivation of meals, solitary confinement, or even sexual sadism. Based on this discriminatory reward system, child prostitutes usually can be easily manipulated and firmly controlled. In other words, from the angle of behaviorism, this system can function as a differential reinforcement structure, which can motivate teenage prostitutes to work hard and make the girls believe that they can eventually reach the status of "superstar."

The third D denotes that when girls join the sex industry, they have to adjust their biological clock and get used to miscellaneous irregularities such as working and resting according to a nocturnal (abnormal) schedule or providing sexual services to those customers who have odd personalities or hobbies. This suggests that girl prostitutes, to a considerable extent, must rely on drugs (whether soft or hard, stimulants or depressants) to help them remain energetic and/or to overcome negative feelings (anger, anxiety, disappointment, melancholy, and so on). Given that using drugs has become an indivisible part of the sex industry in China (Zheng, 2009), it is not uncommon that teenage girls become drug addicts after they act as sex workers for a period of time.

Finally, teenage girls are extremely likely to become infected with hepatitis, venereal diseases, or AIDS if their sex life is promiscuous (Qiu, 2001: 181).

Female Thrownaways: Female Leprosy Patients

Before the twentieth century, numerous diseases in the Western and Southern Hemispheres were endemic (gonorrhea, malaria, pneumonia, smallpox, syphilis, among others). Of these infectious diseases, leprosy (now known as Hansen's disease) perhaps was the most feared because it causes facial and limb deformities and is incurable. In hopes of hiding horrible signs of leprosy, many European and Latin American governments constructed leprosariums and other segregation facilities to separate people with leprosy from mainstream society.

As in Latin America and Europe, where people were terrified of leprosy, lots of people in the Eastern and Northern Hemispheres were frightened of this illness. Even worse is that leprosy victims in Greater China (as well as in other Asian countries) were commonly regarded as deviants or potential offenders (partially because of the grotesque appearance of lepers; see Leung, 2009). Accordingly, in Asia to this day it is not unusual for lepers to be locked up in maximum-security penitentiaries, detention centers, hospitals surrounded by barbed wire, and other institutions, as if such patients had committed crimes.[11] Some lepers even become targets of beatings, sexual harassment, or even homicide because from the perspective of somatology or physiognomy, they are viewed as aberrant, threatening, and extremely dangerous.[12]

Based on the statements above, it should not be hard to explain why lepers in China, Hong Kong, and Taiwan are segregated.

Believed to be the most effective way to limit or terminate the proliferation of leprosy, segregation can bring at least two negative outcomes to (female) leprosy patients.

The first result is that most (female) leprosy sufferers must stay for decades in leper colonies, which can be buildings inaccessible to the public, secluded sanatoria, "gated communities," or remote villages, on the grounds that leprosy is incurable. Leprosy patients usually are treated like felons or "demons." In this regard, the following statement about how segregated lepers were treated in Carville, Louisiana, before the 1990s also reflects the circumstances endured by (female) sufferers of leprosy in Greater China:

> Patients were often involuntarily admitted to the barbed wire enclosed facility and were told to assume new names to protect their families. Their mail and money were sterilized, they were denied the right to vote and to marry, children they bore were taken from them, and they were imprisoned without trial for escaping [Frantz and Sato, 2005: 162].

As for (female) sufferers of leprosy in China, they usually have to tolerate worse situations:

> In China ... victims of the disease were routinely cast out of towns and villages and herded into walled enclaves that were so squalid that some preferred to take their own lives rather than enter one. They were also subject to periodic massacres[13] [Gould, 2005: 8–9].

Long-term segregation, however, is not the only challenge that (female) lepers must overcome. Another hardship is that leprosy victims are what Goffman (1986) called stigmatized individuals.[14] As a result, it is rather difficult, if not impossible, for such abnormal persons to be reaccepted by mainstream society and even their relatives. Put differently, most (female) lepers in Greater China are banished. So unless someone can prove she has totally recovered from leprosy (which appears quite difficult), she will still be prohibited or at least strongly discouraged from contact with the outside world. This strongly implies that female lepers will be deprived of social status, cut off from family ties, and become ostracized.[15]

Being viewed as the best solution to leprosy, segregation, like political imprisonment, girl infanticide, and the "comfort" system, also creates a group of deserted females. Although no data show that (female) patients of leprosariums or sanatoriums in China, Hong Kong, and Taiwan are forced to participate in slave labor, such a humanitarian treatment does not mean that the civil rights of such victims are not violated. As a matter of fact, the segregation measure has become a killer policy (Wang, 2005: 4) because leprosy sufferers, almost without exception, have been turned into "untouchables." Since these untouchables are broadly treated by average people as symbols of wickedness (just like the witches of medieval Europe were labeled as agents of demons), it is not unusual that many of these disgraceful persons can barely maintain familial linkages.

Concluding Remarks

Three types of missing females are described in this chapter: women with Alzheimer's disease, female policy-focal runaways, and female lepers. From the viewpoint of demography, finding those lost women with type II or III dementia is a task of pure luck. This is due to the fact that such females do not have the mental capacity to store information. Therefore, the disappearance of this population normally involves accidental events or oblivious behaviors (both of which seem to function like sabotage waged by hidden terrorists without warnings). All of these casual or spontaneous occasions make it difficult for social workers, law enforcement agents, or medical staff to take precautionary measures to prevent the loss of such females. With this in mind, relatives of these disappearing women can only count on fortune to bring back their loved one.

In a sharp contrast to missing women with severe Alzheimer's disease, the street life of runaway girls usually is not formless or untraceable.

Instead, this life is closely connected with the sex industry: as indicated previously, the great majority of runaway girls in Greater China are from families in crisis. Many of these girls are primary or middle school dropouts. Quitting school, in turn, means that such girls do not have the knowledge or skills to get a good job. As an alternative, these young girls must sell their bodies in sex-related businesses in red-light districts (which are highly abusive and manipulative workplaces) so that they can become economically independent. Since this life trajectory seems to have become the common destiny for escaped girls who try to survive on the street, it is clear that before the social problem of child prostitution can be solved, family disasters (especially family disorganization/disintegration) must be dealt with in the first place.

Unlike runaway teenage girls and women who get lost because of Alzheimer's disease, female lepers, as missing females, probably are easiest to find. The reason is quite simple: these females become missing not because of their individual act but because of institutionalized segregation. Subsequently, their whereabouts is, at least in theory, fixed (they can be found in leper settlements). On the other hand, these abnormal women are very likely to remain missing because before the collective fear toward leprosy is minimized or removed, they still have to stay in "poor, mountainous regions, where the disease ... is still prevalent" (Leung, 2009: 208).

No matter whether the missing females portrayed in this chapter can attract more attention from the authorities of Asian nations in the future, the present social policies carried out by the Beijing, Hong Kong, and Taipei governments in handling/helping these hidden populations appear inadequate. This inadequacy seems to come from two social control philosophies upon which these policies are based. One is that all of these policies, to an extent, endorse, or at least inescapably involve, red tape (which includes the elements of slow reaction or even inaction). Accordingly, certain women cannot acquire the assistance they truly need and ultimately become missing. This situation can be characterized by Taiwanese women who, firstly, are experiencing deteriorating memory, and, secondly, are denied the right to hire skilled foreign workers as caretakers because their Alzheimer's disease is not considered serious enough.

Besides sophisticated bureaucratic procedure, the ideology of containment is equally noteworthy: for policy makers in these Asian countries, missing populations (except for institutionalized or confined lepers) are potentially disorderly. To prevent them from undermining social stability, karaoke pubs, motels, nightclubs, and other places of entertainment defined by law enforcement authorities as hot spots of crime normally will be inspected periodically. This security measure, in terms of eliminating criminogenic environments, does allow the police to find certain missing girls and women or even illegal immigrants. However, such a policy is totally ineffective in solving the problem of missing females because it fails to get to the essence of the issue (for example, family crisis [runaway youth] and excessive segregation [lepers]).

To sum up, the social policies currently in force tend to overemphasize administrative rules and social order. Accordingly, they may be too rigid to reflect social varieties. Since these policies seem inflexible or even unrealistic, it is apparent that such policies must be modified before the root causes can be addressed which lead to missing females as depicted in this chapter.

Conclusion

In this book, several typologies of missing females are presented, conceptualized, and examined. (See Table C-1.) This nomenclature will provide social scientists with a conceptual tool to distinguish between groups of lost women and young girls in Greater China. It can also give demographers an auxiliary device to examine missing males in the East as well as missing populations in the West.

In addition to these advantages, the classification system suggested in this book can assist gender researchers, feminist writers, and law enforcement officials to theorize or hypothesize the following features of missing females.

First, this system shows that with the exception of comfort women, none of the categories is entirely a historical phenomenon. This means that there will always be some females who will join the ranks of lost populations because certain factors that support institutionalized violence against women are still functioning. For example, despite official prohibitions, the custom of infanticide is still popular in some parts of India (Sen, 2002). This custom makes numerous young males unable to find spouses. As a result of the distorted gender structure, an unknown number of destitute rural girls (from India as well as from Bangladesh, Myanmar, Nepal, and Thailand) are sold to brothels patronized largely by working- or lower-class males (Mark, [1981] 2005; Thapa, 2008). Since the great majority of these prostitutes lose familial ties and eventually are abandoned, they are normally unknown to law enforcement authorities and social control agencies in charge of population statistics.

Second, according to the suggested typological system, some disappearing females seem to be concentrated in concealed places (for example, political prisons), isolated neighborhoods (such as leprosy communities), and hot spots of commercialized sex (specifically unlicensed hotels/motels,

TABLE C-1. A COMPARISON OF DIFFERENT TYPES OF MISSING FEMALES IN GREATER CHINA

	FIU type	FNU Type	FIL type	FNL type	VIU type	VNU type	VIL type	VNL type
Exemplar	Female Political Prisoners	Slain Baby Girls	Comfort Women	Abandoned Females: Female Leprosy Sufferers	Trafficked Females	Kidnapped Women Murdered for Ghost Marriage	Runaway Teenage Girls	Aged Women with Alzheimer's Disease
To Whom Are They Missing?	Family members & Human/Women's Rights Advocates	Family Members & Local Authorities	Family Members & Human/Women's Rights Advocates	Family Members & Human/Women's Rights Advocates	Family Members & Local Authorities	Family Members & Local Authorities	Family Members	Family Members
A Purely Historical Phenomenon?	No	No	Yes	No	No	No	No	No
Truly or Nominally Missing?	Can be both	Truly	Can be both	Nominally	Nominally	Truly	Nominally	Nominally
Primary Aid/Rescue Targets for Civil/Women's Rights Societies in Hong Kong and Taiwan?	Yes	No	Yes	No	Yes	No	No	No
Active or Passive Role in Shaping Collective Memory of?	Active	Passive	Active	Active	Active	Passive	Passive	Passive

massage parlors, and nightclubs). This characteristic strongly implies that, if certain measures are taken, many lost girls and women can actually be recovered. In other words, compared to aborted or drowned baby girls and murdered ghost brides, female political prisoners, neglected female leprosy sufferers, runaway teenage girls, and women with Alzheimer's disease have better chances of reemerging. That means that if the Chinese communist government can relax political restrictions and if the authorities of China, Hong Kong, and Taiwan take more active steps to alter the irrational and prejudiced attitude held by the public toward leprosy patients, to suppress human/woman trafficking, and to shelter teenage girls who desert their family, then tracing those women and girls who are just nominally missing (Jiang et al., 2005: 3) should become an achievable task.

Third, some lost women (such as female political prisoners, former comfort women, and trafficked young women) are viewed by most human/women's rights associations in contemporary Hong Kong and Taiwan as showcase examples of structuralized violence, which can be political persecution, gender hierarchy, male chauvinism, or one-child policy. For that reason, these disappearing women and girls are regarded as the principal victims of social injustice. Since such missing females are deemed to be classic/typical instances of political suppression and infringement of human rights, it is natural that feminist groups in Hong Kong and Taiwan concentrate their efforts on providing help or rescue to these populations.

Finally, given that certain lost females are, by any measure, tangible proof of institutionalized inequality/gender discrimination, such females tend to become the spokeswomen of all mistreated wives and daughters. Put differently, numerous events of human history are framed by the mechanism of collective memory (Gedi & Elam, 1996: 40). Under the influence of this shared mentality, the stories (which always contain appalling and atypical scenarios) provided by severely suppressed women appear much more liable to attract attention from social historians and investigators than tales (which may seem tedious, for they largely involve familiar accounts) offered by average abused women. With this in mind, women (e.g., female political prisoners, former comfort women, trafficked young women, and isolated and helpless female lepers) who can and want to make their awful experiences of victimization known tend to play a more active role in shaping women's history (including that of Greater China) than do women and girls who have not undergone terrible experiences. In other words, "normal" and well-behaved women are less likely to make history.

Notes

Introduction

1. Even in demography, the study of missing populations seems unpopular. For example, in a recent paper about the possible number of lost females in China, Jiang and his colleagues (2005) cited no more than ten articles that are directly linked to "missing girls," "missing females," or "missing women." Of these articles, none is a typological paper about lost females.

2. Although statistics on missing women/girls are available, these statistics tend to concentrate on certain time intervals only. One of the best examples is provided by Hudson and den Boer (2004: 159–163).

Chapter 1

1. Snow and Benford (1992: 136) call this process *framing*.
2. This concept comes from Kalberg (1994: 29).

Chapter 2

1. This may explain partially why governments of economically developed and politically democratic countries, where incidents of political murder and mass killing appear to be few after the Second World War, also rely on the practice of PI to govern. For example, despite the fact that the U.S. federal government, during World War II, detained nearly 120,000 Japanese and Japanese Americans in "relocation camps" in Arizona, Arkansas, California, Colorado, Idaho, Utah, and Wyoming (Daniels, 1993); incarcerated more than 25,000 Germans, German Americans, and German–Latin Americans in "enemy alien camps" (Krammer, 1997), and tightly regulated the acts of hundreds of thousands of Italians living in the "prohibited" and "restricted" areas of California (Fox, 1990), the U.S., compared with Latin American countries such as Nicaragua, El Salvador, and Columbia, does not have many assassination or massacre cases in the twentieth century. Nevertheless, the Federal Bureau of Investigation still makes various containment efforts (e.g., the COINTELPRO Program) to spy on and to disrupt the communist and other left-wing political movements (Theoharis, 1996).

2. This does not mean that imperial China did not have a secret police apparatus. As a matter of fact, as early as the Ming dynasty (1368–1644), the eunuchs directed the *Dong Chang* (the Eastern Depot) and the *Jin Yi Wei* (the embroidered-uniform guard) to spy on literati-bureaucrats, military commanders, landlords, leaders of secret religions, and potential organizers of rebellion (Tsai, 1996).

3. Chen Guo-fu was Chen Li-fu's elder brother. Their uncle, Chen Qi-mei, was Chiang Kai-shek's mentor when Chiang went to Japan to study military science in 1906. Chen Qi-mei himself was one of the confidants of Sun Yat-sen. He helped Chiang to meet Sun in 1913 when Sun had become the revolutionary and political leader of South China (North China was controlled by Yuan Shi-kai and his Bei Yang government). That meeting paved the way for Chiang to get access to the power core of the Nationalist Party in 1914 when the Nationalists launched the so-called Second Revolution, attempting to overthrow the rulership of Yuan Shi-kai. In 1916, Chen Qi-mei was assassinated by order of President Yuan Shi-kai. Chiang was then in a position to claim that he would replace Chen Qi-mei as the "legitimate inheritor" of Sun's revolutionary career. This enabled Chiang to dominate the Kuomintang after Sun died in 1925. Since Chiang's rising to power came mainly from Chen Qi-mei's assistance and patronage, Chen's nephews, Chen Guo-fu and Chen Li-fu, enjoyed the political power and privileges reserved for them by Chiang (Wang & Li, 1995: 58–63).

4. Xu En-zeng, one of the confidants of the Chen brothers, was appointed as the supervisor of the ISPAKMT. Xu remained as the director of the ISPAKMT, the investigation department of the party affairs of the Kuomintang (IDPAKMT), and IDPAKMT's successor, the Central Executive Committee's Bureau of Investigation and Statistics (CECBIS) until 1945.

5. Before the Chen brothers helped Chiang Kai-shek to suppress the communist movement and to clean up the "radical" elements in the Nationalist Party, at least 1,000 people who survived the slaughter by the KMT forces had already been either sent to military prisons or to introspection institutes/reformatories (Lin, 1997: 362).

6. In addition to incarceration, about 100,000 communists and communist supporters were killed by the KMT troops during the three-year purge.

7. One possible reason that the ISPAKMT grew in 1929 was that, during that year, Chiang Kai-shek initiated the first post–Northern Expedition civil war to fight against the Guangxi forces led by Li Zong-ren and Bai Chong-xi. Attempting to defeat the Guangxi armies from within, Chiang sent secret agents to the Guangxi camp to bribe Guangxi generals and to break the secret codes of the Guangxi troops. That tactic, to a considerable extent, undermined the leadership of the Guangxi forces and contribute to the victory of Chiang's troops (Wang & Li, 1995: 251–254, 284–285). With such an impressive performance, Chiang, from the early 1930s, actively sponsored the development of a nationwide secret service network in China.

8. The Blue Shirt Society was a Chinese version of the National Socialist Party of Nazi Germany (Chang, 1985: 21; see note 11 for the origin of this organization). Four possible reasons may explain why the fame and political influence of the IDPAKMT was surpassed by that of the BSS after the early 1930s. First, as early as the spring of 1932, when the BSS was officially created, the secret service department of the BSS had already become involved in assassinating political dissidents and liberals. That made the BSS notorious shortly after it was organized. Second, despite the bad reputation of the BSS, the political murder cases associated with the BSS during the mid–1930s and the Military Commission's Bureau of Investigation and Statistics (MCBIS, the successor to the BSS) during the era of the Sino-Japanese War assisted Chiang Kai-shek to alleviate public criticisms that the Nationalist regime did not take actions to resist the Japanese invasion. With that "contribution," the political importance of the BSS and its succeeding organizations was, to a significant extent, promoted. Third, before the Japanese navy initiated its air raid on Pearl Harbor on December 7, 1941, the U.S. military authorities had already received relevant intelligence and warnings from the MCBIS (Shen, 1994: 207–208). Since the American officials did not take those warnings seriously, nearly 2,500 American sailors were killed. Despite the heavy casualties suffered by the U.S., the intelligence "achievement" of the MCBIS did allow it to gain an international reputation. Finally, given that the personal relationship between Chiang Kai-shek and Dai Li, head of the MCBIS, were much closer than that of Chiang and Xu En-zeng, head of the previously noted CECBIS (Liu & Wu, 1994: 82–83), it is not surprising to learn that Chiang Kai-shek trusted the MCBIS more than the CECBIS (Tang [Su], 1997: 5).

9. During the period of public demonstrations of 1931, more than 1,000 protesters (most of them appeared to be students) were arrested or even killed by the IDPAKMT and the

IDPAKMT-commanded Nationalist troops (Huang, 1949: 17–18). Few people know what happened to the female students who were sent to jail and not bailed out.

10. According to the official explanation of the Nationalist government, China was not strong enough to fight against Japan in the Nanking Decade. Therefore, to avoid China being completely conquered by the Japanese, it was necessary for China to take a low-profile stance to handle the territorial controversies between China and Japan.

11. Before Chiang left office, a tiny group (roughly 30) of "theorists" of the KMT (such as Liu Jian-qun) and graduates of the Huang-pu Military Academy (among them Dai Li, Deng Weng-yi, Feng Ti, Gan Guo-xun, He Chong-han, Kang Ze, Qiu Kai-ji, and Teng Jie) had suggested Chiang imitate the Black Shirts in Italy and the Brown Shirts in Germany to establish a highly disciplined elite corps in China. The goals of that elite corps were to transform China into a powerful nation and, by consolidating the leadership of Chiang, to turn the Nationalist Party into a highly disciplined organization. Chiang Kai-shek, who probably was inspired by the absolutist doctrine of European Fascism and Nazism, permitted these loyalists to set up a "clandestine" organization to have younger Nationalist members swear absolute allegiance to the KMT in general and to Chiang himself in particular. With the ratification by Chiang, the so-called Blue Shirt Society (BSS) was established formally in Nanking on March 1, 1932. Dai Li was appointed as the director of the secret service department of the BSS.

12. From then on, the secret service agencies of Nationalist China were split into two major systems: one controlled by the Chen brothers as mentioned previously; the other commanded by Dai Li, who later was viewed by many people as "China's Himmler" (Eastman, 1990: 75).

13. Candidates for the society had to be recommended by at least two members of the Blue Shirts and "had to undergo an extraordinarily thorough background investigation" (Eastman, 1990: 56).

14. Chang (1985: 4) estimates that, by 1938 when the Blue Shirts was dissolved because of merging with other organizations to handle the Sino-Japanese War, it had at least 100,000 members.

15. The division of labor between the IDPAKMT and the SSD of the Blue Shirt Society did not become institutionalized until 1938 when Chiang Kai-shek ordered the Central Executive Committee's Bureau of Investigation and Statistics (successor to the IDPAKMT) to focus on the investigation of party, political, cultural, educational, and economic affairs while the Military Commission's Bureau of Investigation and Statistics concentrated on the collection of military intelligence, the militarization of secret agents, and the cleansing of traitors (Zhao, 1988: 217). Before 1938, the boundary between the missions assigned to the IDPAKMT and to the SSD/MCBIS was perplexing, if not indistinguishable.

16. After successfully taking over the PA and the SSLA, the secret service department of the Blue Shirts, under the command of Dai Li, established many "special training classes" to recruit new secret agents. These "educational measures" swiftly expanded the size of the SSD in 1933 and 1934 (Zhang, 1992: 286–290).

17. These offices were the outposts for the Nanking regime to gather intelligence about the communist and anti–Chiang movements. Since these offices could provide first-hand information about the communists and anti–Chiang political figures, it is not difficult to understand why, based on their political considerations (such as the prospect of getting a promotion), Xu En-zeng and Dai Li wanted to monopolize those offices (Liu & Wu, 1994: 87–88).

18. Theoretically speaking, these unlucky agents could be released after completing the political courses (which, according to stipulations, normally lasted six months) at reformatories. But in reality, few incarcerated agents were set free after the six-month-long course. Many were still held in reformatories until their political allegiance was confirmed fully. For agents who were released, the nightmare of "re-education" was far from being over. All of them still had to go regularly to local secret service offices to participate in political instruction classes and to report their daily activities (generally speaking, this control measure would last three years). Those who were in charge of the local secret service offices, on the other hand, had the discretionary power to re-imprison someone who was judged to be violating the rules of "repentance" (Zhang, 1988: 31–33). As for agents who were locked up in

military prisons, the length of detention usually was indefinite. It was not unusual for innocent agents (or even civilians) to be detained for several years without getting any public trial.

19. This phenomenon derived mainly from the fact that Dai Li opposed Chen Li-fu's being appointed as the head of the MCBIS. Chen was the former superintendent of the IDPAKMT, so it was very likely that Chen would protect and expand the advantages of the first division of the MCBIS by sacrificing the interests of the second division. To counter Chen's favoritism, Dai, in one way or another, avoided taking orders from Chen (Zhang, 1992: 298).

20. Before the Sino-Japanese War started in July 1937, one of the major tasks performed by Nationalist secret agents was to suppress anti–Japan rallies and demonstrations, which were often seen as equivalents of anti-Chiang movements because of Chiang Kai-shek's nonconfrontation policy toward Japan. Students and political dissenters usually became the targets of arrest because they initiated and participated in almost all of these public protests. Although students and political liberals were active in the anti–Japan (or anti–Chiang/anti-fascism) movements in the 1930s, the figures about how many political demonstrators were imprisoned by the secret service and law enforcement authorities of the KMT are sketchy and speculative. In any event, based on the reports of Huang (1949: 17–19), Zhang (1988), and Zhang (1996), at least several thousand students and political activists were arrested in the years after the Japanese Guan Dong army occupied Manchuria in September 1931.

21. These "achievements" included, but were not limited to, bribing the generals of the Guangxi army to stop the civil war between the Guangxi and the Chiang troops in 1929 (see note 7); bribing the political leaders and military commanders of the 19th Route Army to make sure that the People's Government of Fujian, installed by these chief officers during the fifth anticommunist campaign in November 1933, would not ally with the nearly defeated Communist forces (Yang, 1994: 88–95); and bribing the pilots of the Guangdong air force to thwart the power of Chen Ji-tang (the so-called Heavenly King of South China), an act which ended the semi-autonomous status of Guangdong province in the summer of 1936 (Yang, 1994: 138–145).

22. This incident took place in December 1936 as Chiang was "arrested" by the commanders of the Northwest Army. These commanding officers asked Chiang to cooperate with the communists and to change his "inactive" policy toward Japanese invaders.

23. The fifth "communist bandit" suppression campaign of 1934 forced the communists to escape, first to the southwest and then to the northwest. Only several hundred Red Army soldiers survived in the Long March. It took Mao Tse-tung and other communist leaders several years to reestablish the Red Army and to set up new "red regimes" in remote, isolated, and destitute mountainous sections of northwest China.

24. This was the second time that the KMT and the CCP established the United Front. The first United Front was created in 1924. It collapsed in April 1927 because of the Shanghai White Terror.

25. The first and the only battle fought by both the KMT troops and the Red Army during the Sino-Japanese War was the battle of Ping Xing Guan of 1939. More than 1,000 Japanese soldiers were killed during that battle.

26. Eastman (1986: 571) reports that over 500,000 Chinese armed personnel (including former Kuomintang secret agents) surrendered to the Japanese in the early years of the Sino-Japanese War. After joining the Japanese camp, a certain number of ex–KMT secret agents still worked for the Chungking authority. Some (or probably most) of these "two-faced spies" (including female double agents) were arrested, incarcerated, or even executed on the grounds of miscellaneous factors. Unfortunately, statistics about these invisible cases are not available.

27. Another organizational reform of the MCBIS took place in August and September 1937, when the Japanese forces attacked Shanghai. During those months, Dai Li stayed in that city to militarize the organized crime elements (chiefly the Green Gang controlled by Du Yue-sheng). Although this criminal gang-turned-troop (Zhong Yi Jiu Guo Jun, or the Rescue Army of Loyalty and Justice) was defeated quickly by the Japanese marines, it continued to engage in guerrilla activities in the greater Shanghai area during the entire period of the Sino-Japanese War.

28. The living condition of military prisons was equally inferior. See Huang (1993).

29. The main reason that *fan xing yuan* and *gan hua yuan* were moved to Northwest China is that, shortly after the Sino-Japanese War evolved into a total confrontation in late 1937, many students and refugees escaped from the Japanese-occupied or -dominated districts and attempted to enter Yanan and neighboring communist bases to join the Red Army led by Mao Tse-tung. In the 1930s and 1940s, Mao was seen by numerous Chinese as the genuine leader of China because, unlike Chiang Kai-shek who did little, if anything, to improve the lives of destitute peasants and to resist the invasion of Japan, Mao did help tenants living in the red areas to obtain land. By working closely with his Red Army generals, Mao also defeated the Japanese forces in several battles. In order to prevent the communists from getting international recognition and the support of politically influential social elites, the Chungking regime sent troops to blockade the main routes to the communist bases. Thousands of students and communist backers (some of them women) were caught at the checkpoints established by the Kuomintang soldiers. These unlucky students and pro-communist actors were then sent to the so-called youth camps or labor corps for "reform." (Jiang, 1994: 178).

30. The construction of these camps was proposed by Jiang Ding-wen, one of the confidants of Chiang Kai-shek, in a special meeting held in Sian (Zhang, 1995: 126–130).

31. During the Sino-Japanese War, Chinese people living in the Nationalist areas in general and those in the city of Chungking in particular could be easily charged with collaborating with the enemy. Jiang's (1994: 154–155) book recounts an incident which shows how human rights in "Free China" could be violated randomly by secret agents. In 1938 or 1939, a couple with a child escaped from the Japanese-occupied region in South China and managed to travel to Chungking. One day when the Japanese air force bombed Chungking unexpectedly, the family sought shelter hurriedly in a nearby graveyard. During the process of finding shelter, this couple unintentionally broke their thermos bottle. Unfortunately, the reflection of the shattered thermos bottle was seen by nearby secret agents while at the same time Japanese bombers chanced to hit a nearby arsenal guarded by Nationalist troops. This couple was arrested immediately. They were charged with the crime of collaboration and executed a few days later.

32. Because of inheriting the tradition of a power struggle between the Investigation Department of Party Affairs of the Kuomintang and the Secret Service Department of the Blue Shirt Society, the Central Executive Committee's Bureau of Investigation & Statistics (Zhong Tong) and the Military Commission's Bureau of Investigation & Statistics (Jun Tong) still treated each other as rivals rather than comrades during the war years. This interagency hostility, in one way or another, resulted in the imprisonment of numerous agents, particularly lower-ranking ones. One instance offered by Zhao (1988: 220) shows how easily "undisciplined" agents would be punished. In 1940, one individual was hired by Zhong Tong. This man, after working for Zhong Tong for a period of time, decided to enroll in the foreign language school set up by Jun Tong in hopes of being sent to a ROC embassy overseas. This man did not know the unwritten rule that agents (as well as former agents) of both organizations were strictly prohibited from assuming a position in (or being trained by) the other organization. Shortly after he enrolled in the Jun Tong–directed foreign language school, he was detained by Jun Tong. After being locked up for four years, he escaped. Without this stroke of good luck, he would most likely have remained in prison indefinitely and would have been executed before the communists took over China in October 1949.

33. After the Kuomintang government was forced to retreat from Nanking in late 1937, the great majority of political prisoners confined in *fan xing yuan* or *gan hua yuan* were sent to Northwest or Southwest China (Jiang, 1994: 166). These "senior" prisoners, just like the other inmates, were ordered to do tough jobs like constructing roads, building airports, and maintaining drill grounds in the jungle (Lin, 1991: 128).

34. After the Nanking regime retreated to Sichuan, the Chiang Kai-shek government began to receive some financial and military aid from the United States. A certain portion of this aid was used by Jun Tong and Zhong Tong to construct concentration camps.

35. Some of the frequently utilized tortures included pulling out finger- and toenails, pouring pepper water or urine into the nose, burning with hot iron, burning the bottom of the feet with a candle, high-voltage electric shock, beating with a club studded with needles or nails, breaking bones with bricks, pouring alcohol or saltwater on wounds, and so

on. In addition to these tortures, female prisoners were also subject to other tortures, such as having their breasts stung with needles, their genitals whipped, and gang rape (Meng, 1996: 9–10).

36. Oddly enough, the secret agents and Nationalist soldiers who carried out these tortures seemed to be as exhausted as the detainees. This may be because most Kuomintang secret agents had to scream at and harangue prisoners for hours to get the information they needed. These actions naturally would bring tremendous pressures on those in charge of obtaining "confessions" (Meng, 1996: 11).

37. Some books published in China in the 1990s and early 2000s do contain information about how females were treated in concentration camps during the Sino-Japanese War. These books, however, are not serious academic publications, being sensationalistic and fabricated. None of them are fact-based. Instead, they describe in great detail the sadistic sexual behaviors (such as animal sex) that took place in the prisons of wartime China. These books are not quoted in this chapter.

38. One possible reason that the Chiang government punished only certain collaborationists was that an unknown number of state managers of the Chungking regime secretly contacted high-level officials of the puppet regimes during the Sino-Japanese War for diplomatic, political, economic, or even military issues (Jiang, 1994: 275–298). Any legal action taken to punish all collaborators would definitely have disclosed some shocking inside stories and seriously undermined the legitimacy of the postwar Nanking government.

39. According to the official explanation of the Kuomintang regime, the main reason to carry out this policy was that former puppet students were not trained properly because they had long received "slave" education. As a consequence, it was highly dubious whether these diplomas could serve as legitimate certificates of academic performance.

40. Before the anti–civil war movement rose again in 1947, there were two noteworthy public demonstrations in the second half of 1946. The first one was the anti–Chiang demonstration triggered by the murders of Wen Yi-duo and Li Gong-pu. Both Wen and Li were professors and human rights activists. They were assassinated by secret agents in July 1946 because they delivered anti–Kuomintang/anti–Chiang speeches on several occasions. Wen's and Li's deaths precipitated memorial meetings in almost every big city. Many of these meetings were turned into anti–KMT rallies. The second "milestone" public struggle was the anti–American demonstrations provoked by the rape case of Shen Chong. Shen was a student at Beijing University. She was raped, allegedly by two American soldiers, on Christmas Eve in 1946. This incident soon caused widespread public indignation because, before the Shen event, the Americans had already been deemed responsible for more than 3,800 personal assaults in China between August 1945 and November 1946 (Zhang, 1996: 157). At any rate, when the Nanking government decided to drop the Shen case and release the rape suspects, student activists formed an anti-assault committee (*kang bao hui*), boycotted classes, and staged protest marches (Wasserstrom, 1991: 261–263).

41. The decline of the Chinese dollar is illustrated vividly in a political cartoon offered by Ebrey (1996: 290). This caricature demonstrates that in 1937, one hundred Chinese dollars could buy two oxen. The same amount of money allowed people to buy one pig in 1939, one sack of flour in 1941, one hen in 1943, two eggs in 1945, one piece of coal in 1947, and one sheet of paper in 1949. Zhang (1996: 186) also reports that in 1947, among other cases, the total loans borrowed by eighty professors of Beijing University alone reached 400,000,000 Chinese dollars.

42. Wasserstrom (1991: 267) reports that in Shanghai alone, "at least several hundred and perhaps as many as several thousand students" were arrested.

43. This number does not include those Taiwanese who were arrested by security agents of the Nationalist authorities because of their alleged link with the February 28 uprising of 1947. The February 28 incident was primarily a civil reaction against the rampant corruption of the Nationalists in Taiwan in late 1945 and 1946 (shortly after World War II, Taiwan, a former colony of Japan, was unified with its motherland and became a province of Nationalist China). Instead of treating this event as a public protest, Chiang and his security heads viewed it as a conspiracy plotted by the communists in Taiwan to disrupt the KMT's rulership. That led to tens of thousands of innocent Taiwanese men and women being arrested in the late 1940s, 1950s, and even 1960s (Lai, et al., 1991).

44. In addition to political and military reorganizations and reforms, the land-to-the-tiller program implemented by the Kuomintang in rural Taiwan from 1949 to 1953 was equally important in the defeated Chinese Nationalists' efforts to install an emergent regime. As Fei et al.'s (1979: 38–46) research shows, the land reform projects significantly reduced farm rents and redistributed farmlands among landlords and destitute farmers. That paved the way for the KMT to consolidate its power in Formosa because Taiwan's peasants, unlike their counterparts in mainland China, were no longer a proletarian class. Accordingly, they could not be mobilized easily by the communists. Income redistribution and the lack of peasant strikes, in turn, contributed to Taiwan's impressive economic growth in the 1960s and 1970s and to the legitimacy and stability of the Chiang administration.

45. Before Chiang died in 1975, few people in Taiwan dared to call the president "Chiang Kai-shek" (Jiang Jie-shi) in public. Instead, they usually called him by his alias, Chiang Chung-cheng (Jiang Zhong-zheng). According to Dai (1998:73), a former political prisoner in Taiwan, this political "custom" (no matter how ridiculous it may sound) derived from the fact that the Chinese communists seldom, if ever, referred to Chiang Kai-shek as Jiang Zhong-zheng. Therefore, if people in Taiwan called him Jiang Jie-shi, they would be identified as communist suspects and be arrested.

46. The chief difference between the Constitution of the Republic of China and that of the United States is that the former is based upon a five-branch instead of a three-branch system of government. China's has the executive, legislative, judicial, and two other politically important but functionally insignificant branches — examination and supervision.

47. As a matter of fact, the constitution of the ROC was hardly carried out in mainland China. It was promulgated in January 1947 and implemented formally in December 1947. The Chiang regime, before it withdrew from China in 1949, had just one year (1948) to realize the regulations of the constitution. Since 1948 was the year the Nationalist forces suffered fatal military failure, the constitution of the ROC was essentially lip service for Chinese mainlanders.

48. Because of these prohibitive practices, the Taipei authorities were able to censor all sorts of information (including scientific knowledge), to create an educational environment dominated by an extreme right-wing political ideology, and to indoctrinate the public about the "infallible" leadership of the Nationalist regime. Such measures also prepared the foundation for the Chiang regime to establish a national data bank and a surveillance system in Taiwan in the 1950s when Chiang Ching-kuo served as the de facto head of security apparatuses (Taylor, 2000).

49. The first head of Bao Mi Ju was Zheng Jie-min (July 1946–November 1947). He was succeeded by Mao Ren-feng (December 1947–1955) See Shen (1994: 388–389).

50. In his memoir, Fariello (1995) describes how certain Americans — some of the most prominent scientists, professors, artists, musicians, Hollywood stars, and social movement activists — were investigated or purged by the U.S. government (particularly the FBI) during the Cold War era. These stories, to a varying extent, involved malicious tricks like putting someone's name on the blacklist; publicizing someone's private activities (many of these revelations appeared to be fabricated); forcing people to perjure themselves; and forging documents to undermine careers. All of this right-wing hysteria made the 1950s one of the darkest periods of American civil rights history.

51. Of the five national security authorities and secret service agencies, the DGCOPP was definitely the most noteworthy because Chiang Ching-kuo, the eldest son of President Chiang Kai-shek, was appointed as the head of the DGCOPP in 1950. With the full support of Chiang Kai-shek, Chiang Ching-kuo soon became the actual (although not the highest) decision maker for the secret service and intelligence communities of Taiwan. Numerous political cases (particularly those involving commercial, cultural, and political elites) were thus adjudicated by "prince" Chiang.

52. Friedrich and Brzezinski's (1966: 129–147) study of totalitarian regimes also reveals that the construction of a national data bank (which always involves the process of centralizing all types of mass communications) is critical for an autocratic state to consolidate its authority.

53. The *mei li dao* parade was the first large-scale march that occurred in a metropolitan city in Taiwan before 1987. As a milestone, the significance of this parade in the democra-

tization history of Taiwan is analogous to that of the Civil Rights movement in black American history.

54. The term *defensive suppression* refers to oppressive actions taken by the authorities to prevent all possible political dissident movements from taking shape.

55. During the period of Land Reform, landlords and well-to-do peasants were not the only persons who had experienced ruthless suppression. A great number of city dwellers categorized politically as "counterrevolutionaries" (e.g., persons who had once condemned the Communist Party or its leaders in public or people accused of being "Nationalist spies") were also the targets of what Martin (2009: 123) called "social cleansing."

56. Mao declared that the Soviet Union, under the leadership of Khrushchev, had given up the ideal of international communist revolution (see MacFarquhar, 1997: 349–377). So only the Chinese communist leaders can be considered the "legitimate heirs" of Leninism/Marxism.

57. In addition to the fact that political imprisonment had become a routine part of daily life, it was not unusual that political prisoners were recharged and rearrested by contending clans of the Red Guards. That meant political prisoners rarely were released once they were taken into custody.

58. According to a retired military surgeon, at least 120,000 *Fa Lun Gong* members are detained in Heilongjiang, Jilin, and Liaoning. Some of these "felons" inadvertently become suppliers of human organs after they die in prison. See *Ta Ji Yuan Shi Bao* (The Epoch Times, http://www.daijiyuan.com), May 2006, 2e.

59. The term *offensive suppression* refers to oppressive actions taken by the authorities to quell political dissident movements that have become organized or active.

60. One possible reason for this is that certain Tibetans in exile did not or do not have formal nationality or permanent residency.

61. According to Harff and Gurr (2003: 27), ethnoclasses "occupy distinct social strata and have specialized economic roles in the societies in which they now live." In the case of Xinjiang, Islamic minorities, unlike the Chinese entrepreneurs and factory owners who enjoy an economically advantageous status in Southeast Asia, inhabit "occupations at or near the bottom of the economic and social hierarchy" (Harff & Gurr, 2003: 27).

Chapter 3

1. Under this social ethos, infant girls born with physical deformities faced an even greater risk of being deserted or slain.

2. While not all midwives were baby killers (some of them might even stop the practice of girl infanticide), this homicidal behavior usually was perpetrated by the nursing staff.

3. Again, this murderous act usually was committed by midwives.

4. In this case, mother tended to be the chief perpetrator.

5. In well-to-do families, this crime usually was perpetrated by male servants or maidservants.

6. This crime could be committed by any member of the murdered girl's family. No matter which person actually carried out this offense, this wicked act, compared to drowning (whether it was performed indoors or outdoors), choking with ashes, and starving to death, was more visible because it entailed "public exposure" (Mungello, 2008: 10).

7. That means the Chinese authorities do not welcome any researchers (regardless of their nationality and research field) to investigate the girl infanticide problem in contemporary China. The Mosher case provides a typical example (see Mungello, 2008: 119–120).

8. According to a news report, induced abortions in China amount to at least thirteen million cases per year. That means nearly one-fourth of all artificial abortions in the modern world take place in China. See http://www.worldjournal.com/view/full_china/10118502/article.

9. Since the information supplied by ultrasound scanner operator could be inaccurate, it is possible that even normal babies are aborted.

10. What should be noted is that the one-child policy may encourage some married people who have a "wrong" child to commit girl infanticide; however, using this policy to

explain why unmarried young people/females abort their baby might be oversimplified. In other words, non-instrumental reasons (e.g., anger, depression, fear, ignorance) appear more prominent than instrumental ones in the latter case.

11. In an interview conducted by the author of the book in Tainan, Taiwan, in July 2010, a obstetrician-gynecologist mentioned these features.

12. During the period of Mongolian rulership, people in China proper were classified into four principal categories. The highest one, needless to say, comprised Mongolians, especially aristocrats and monks. The second tier comprised people of Central Asia, including Xinjiang and Tibet. People of North China constituted the third rank while the fourth and lowest level was made up of residents of South China.

13. In terms of ethnocentrism, this ideology was precisely the same as the Christian Identity philosophy advocated by white supremacists (see Perry, 2001: 143–178).

14. A similar situation can also be observed in Hong Kong and Taiwan, although to a lesser extent.

15. In greater China, the color *huang* (yellow) represents obscenity. The literal meaning of the term *huang liu* is "yellow streams." It implies waves of obscene behavior.

16. *San pei* (three accompaniments) means *pei ho* (accompanying drinking), *pei chang* (accompanying singing), and *pei wu* (accompanying dancing). All of these involved commercialized sex.

17. In addition to cheap labor, another important factor that attracted Taiwanese businessmen to invest in China was that people of China and Taiwan use the same language.

Chapter 4

1. While *ying hun* is still practiced in modern China and Taiwan, this custom seems more visible in Southeast Asia, especially among Chinese communities in Singapore and Malaysia. One possible reason for this phenomenon is that in Singapore and Malaysia, people of diverse religious background are expected to respect one another because of national traditions and/or legal requirements. As a result, people who belong to various religious groups (whether "orthodox" or "heterodox") typically enjoy freedom to express their beliefs. Unlike people of Singapore and Malaysia who seldom, if ever, impose a "label" on specific religious denominations (particularly small ones), people of China and Taiwan are more likely to denounce or reject certain "unorthodox" or "delinquent" religious practices. Partially due to this social ethos (which, compared to that of Singapore and Malaysia, can be characterized by a lower degree of religious tolerance or a higher degree of religious prejudice), people in China and Taiwan, whether they are mainstream Buddhists/Taoists or members of unorthodox sects/cults, who want to engage in non-mainstream ceremonies (such as celebrating posthumous marriage) usually have to keep their actions quiet and invisible.

2. From the standpoint of cultural anthropology, *ming hun* is not a system which can be found solely in Chinese communities. As a matter of fact, this custom can also be observed in other societies (both ancient and contemporary). For example, in certain tribal enclaves, priests or shamans can help living people and supernatural beings to "get married" (Lehmann & Myers, 2000: 98–99).

3. Of course, it is love and reminiscence that motivate some parents to find a "spouse" for their deceased child. Apart from this, it is beyond the scope of this chapter to examine whether such behavior is ludicrous or unscientific.

4. Generally speaking, two factors will precipitate some parents to hold a ghost marriage for their dead child. The first one, which appears to be far more common than the other, is the child's *ming sui* (theoretical age): when he/she is near or around twenty years old, his/her parents will hold a "wedding" without the request from the child. The second factor may sound odd and unbelievable: the deceased boy or girl (who, in terms of *ming sui*, might still be a teenager or has become an adult, whether in his/her twenties, thirties, or forties) will appear in dreams of the parents and/or in-laws. In that dream, the child will request to get married as well as supply directions or clues (such as the buildings the parents will see or a certain household located in a specific neighborhood that the parents will come

across) to help find the "right person." Facing this unexplainable/paranormal phenomenon, most parents will view it as a heavenly mandate and will do whatever the dream has instructed them to do.

5. Although ghost marriage may be arranged by families of all social classes, well-to-do families tend to engage in this practice much more often than impoverished households.

6. Before choosing a bride or bridegroom for their ghost son or daughter, most parents will have a fortune-teller or medium determine whether the horoscope (birthdate, birth time, birthplace, and the like) of their prospective daughter- or son-in-law is compatible with that of their dead son or daughter. A wedding will be held only if the horoscopes are found to be well matched.

7. In terms of function, the main task of *yin miao* (literally "gloomy" or "dark" temples) is to serve the beings of the netherworld (e.g., assisting wandering souls to deliver messages to their family members/friends, and vice versa). One such temple is the Eighteen Lords located in northern Taiwan (see Weller, 1994: 124–128). Unlike *yin miao* which allegedly specialize in serving homeless spirits and roaming ghosts, the core mission of *yang miao* (literally "sunny" or "bright" temples) is to help living persons make decisions and/or to offer advice to people who face thorny problems in life. In addition to the psychological counseling, *yang miao* can also arrange matters for people who want to give offerings to certain deities or hold misfortune-eliminating ceremonies.

8. One of the key parts of these rituals involves shamans' chanting incantations (which are very difficult for outsiders to comprehend) and burning spells in front of a big altar covered with idols, which can be as big as real persons or as small as dolls (and which to non–Buddhists usually look grotesque). In addition, shamans with burning joss sticks in hand must say grace before the idols. The main purpose of this phase of the ritual is to please the king of the Sheol and to acquire marriage approval from him.

9. Depending on family status and wealth, dowries sent to the otherworld vary: if both bride and groom are from impoverished families, they may get merely several packs of *ming zhi* as living expenses. On the contrary, if the couple are from well-to-do families, they usually will receive handsome dowries and gifts (e.g., paper furniture, paper house, paper vehicle, and so on) from their parents and relatives.

10. Although this imaginary or hypothetical wedding has only symbolic implications, its functions include, among others, helping parents and grandparents eliminate or reduce anxiety caused by the singlehood of their child or grandchild and consolidating traditional monogamy.

11. One exception is that in China and Taiwan (mostly in rural areas), some families, particularly affluent ones, will find a dead adult female to be wife or concubine for a deceased adult male in the clan (e.g., brother, uncle, or cousin), the chief reason being to preserve or multiply the bloodline of that male. Simply speaking, when such a wedding is held, bride and groom usually are strangers because when they were alive, no interaction between them had taken place.

12. It seems that parents are especially likely to take such actions when the wedding date prearranged for the couple (whether or not they were already engaged) was just a few days hence, or when the lovers used to play a critical or unforgettable role in the in-law family.

13. Of course, no one knows for sure whether or not the date picked is really "propitious."

14. Sometimes, the effigies are about three feet tall. They are used at weddings where surrogates of the bride and groom (who will hold up the effigies) are appointed.

15. This phenomenon can provide a superb example for the notion of "dramaturgical loyalty" (see Goffman, 1959: 212).

16. For detailed information about why and how people may alienate when they are engaged in interpersonal interaction, see Goffman ([1967] 1982: 113–136).

17. In Singapore and Malaysia, *ming hun* is easier to observe than its counterpart in China and Taiwan: unlike the latter, which usually takes place at night or just before dawn, the former usually is held in daytime or at early morning. This variation might be caused by differing degrees of religious tolerance (see Chapter 4, note 1).

18. Holding an assembly like this was hardly possible in China before the 1980s when civil society was still under absolute control of the government. One chief reason that pre-

cipitated the Beijing government to suppress this custom before the 1980s was that people who dared to meet after dark were considered to be treacherous. If they assembled in the name of attending a midnight supper, the security authorities identified it as an anti-government gathering like that waged by revolutionary groups and rebellious secret societies in imperial China. Such control seems to have become less rigid after the 1980s when a series of economic liberalization policies were implemented.

19. In ancient China, the titles for ghost grooms (especially for those from wealthy or royal families) can be *gong zi* (Young Gentleman), *shao zhu* (Little Lord/Prince), *shao ye* (Young Master), or *xiao wang ye* (Young Marquis); for ghost brides, the designations, among others, can be *fu ren* (Madame), *gong zhu* (Princess), *qian jin* (literally "a thousand pieces of gold," but idiomatically meaning Very Precious Daughter), *gu nian* (Young Lady), or simply her surname.

20. In theory, he will become a fixed member of his wife's family. But in reality, few single males who marry a spirit wife remain solitary. Almost all of them will marry a real woman some time after their ghost wedding.

21. One interesting case of this special arrangement was provided by a concubine who appeared on a Taiwanese TV show. Without informing her husband, she opened the door of the master bedroom on the second day of the three-day "honeymoon" period to see what was going on. The bedroom was vacant, but she smelled a female fragrance which totally differed from hers. Since no other females had been in the house or the master bedroom on the previous night, the source of this aroma remains unexplained.

22. Due to insufficient literature, it is hard to assert whether ghost marriage of the fourth variety ever appeared in Taiwan. If it did, then its features should be the same as those of its Chinese counterpart: after all, Taiwan, just like China, was an authoritarian patriarchal society before the twentieth century.

23. It is beyond the scope of this chapter to analyze whether or not the personality traits or lifestyles of these kidnappers-cum-killers are the same as those identified by Strong (2008: 33–34).

Chapter 5

1. In Japanese, the term *ianfu* means "comfort women." It is translated in general as "military prostitutes" in English. The author of this book believes that defining *ianfu* as military prostitutes is inadequate for four reasons: First, although *ianfu*, just like ordinary prostitutes, provided sexual services to unfamiliar males, these women, more often than not, could not obtain pecuniary rewards. Second, in addition to providing free sexual services, hundreds of thousands of such women were forced to live with their customers (i.e., comfort women were not merely sex workers; they were caretakers as well). Third, unlike average prostitutes who may enjoy a certain degree of independence/freedom (in terms of choosing customers), comfort women did not select their customers or determine their work schedule or location. In other words, comfort women simply had to obey when told to serve their customers. Finally, given that the human rights of comfort women were not protected by the law, these females were considered as virtually subhuman. Based on the attributes listed above, the term *ianfu* is defined in this book as "sex slaves controlled by the Japanese military."

2. Although *ianfu* came from all regions and countries annexed or occupied by Japan before 1945, most of them were Chinese or Korean. Researchers at the Research Center of the Chinese Comfort Women Issue of Shanghai Normal University estimate that the total number of comfort women at 360,000 to 410,000 (Chen, 2006: 195). This estimation is based on the following three parameters:

- Total Japanese armed personnel in China, 1937–1945: 3,000,000
- Percentage of comfort women to Japanese troops as determined by the Japanese military: 1 to 29 (Kim, [1976]1992: 50)
- Projected turnover rate of comfort women (i.e., the rate of replenishing dead or missing comfort women): 1 to 3.5 or 1 to 4.0 (Chen, 2006: 195).

So $3,000,000/29 \times 3.5 = 362,069$ while $3,000,000/29 \times 4 = 413,793$.

3. Such houses are equivalent to contemporary nightclubs or strip clubs.

4. The "relatively tolerant sexual climate" (Goodwin, 2006: 41) of Nara and Heian Japan might lead directly to this.

5. According to Kim (1997: 14–15), Toyotomi Hideyoshi allowed the construction of two *yūkaku* in the 1580s, one in Osaka, the other in Kyoto. As a result of this, more and more "playgrounds" (amusement districts) were established during the Tokugawa years (1603–1868).

6. As a rule, samurai who left their hometown to participate in a battle or on other official business were not permitted to bring their family with them. Hence, these men were effectively single when they were away from home.

7. In terms of assisting the authorities to keep an eye on possible rebellious movements, owners of *yūkaku* can be regarded as the secret police of early modern Japan.

8. For a detailed history about the emergence of the feminist movement, see Tobias (1997).

9. The phrase *kashizashiki* can be translated literally into "rental apartments." It is an obscure term for brothels because it gives outsiders the impression that women living and working there are simply tenants or apartment staff.

10. According to this policy, people who agreed to go abroad would be financially sponsored by the government (Chen, 2006: 43).

11. For a history of the Atlantic slave trade, see Pope-Hennessy ([1967] 2004), Rediker (2007), and St. Clair (2007).

12. Despite the fact that Japan was the only Asian superpower before the end of the Second World War, some modern historians appear to reject the idea that Japan was a "true" empire. For example, in the volume *Empires That Shook the World* (Taylor, 2008), the Japanese Empire is not listed as one that "shook the world."

13. In terms of etymology, the root word *kara* has different meanings in Japanese. It means "Tang China" here (Hata, 1999: 47). On the other hand, *yuki* means "going to." So together, *karayuki* refers to those people who went to China during the Tang dynasty (A.D. 618–907). In modern Japanese, this word denotes Japanese women who went to Southeast Asia (especially Singapore) to work as prostitutes (see Warren, 2008: 220–283).

14. This relationship is described vividly by Hicks (1995: 28): "Mars and Venus have gone hand in hand throughout [the] military history [of Japan]."

15. Manchuria became a puppet state of Japan in 1932. See Hsu (2000: 545–552).

16. While acquiring records which describe systematically how Japanese troops dealt with comfort women who got infected with venereal disease is very difficult, limited data (e.g., Jiang, 1998) suggest that such women usually would be treated minimally. If symptoms of venereal disease are undetectable (or under control) after treatment, these women would keep providing sexual services. On the contrary, if symptoms become unmanageable, then it is very likely that such "dirty" women were executed secretly.

17. The great majority of these stations were located in civilian residences seized by Japanese troops.

18. For a detailed description of the social environment of concentration camps, see Sofsky (1996).

19. Some comfort women died because of excessive "workloads." If comfort women were fortunate enough to survive, they would, more often than not, become unable to bear children.

20. Ordinary soldiers and lower-ranking military officers were required to wear condoms when they had sex with comfort women. However, this precautionary practice was violated from time to time, inevitably causing certain comfort women to become pregnant.

21. The main purpose of this "training" was to "numb [newly recruited soldiers] to the human instinct against killing people who are not attacking" (Chang, 1997: 55). In addition to the "game" of slaying pregnant comfort women, numerous unarmed Chinese soldiers and unarmed young males were also employed as living targets for bayonet "practice."

22. Xie (2005: 400) reports that two POW-turned-comfort women in a concentration camp in Jinan, Shangdong province, attempted to flee but were captured. As a warning for other imprisoned women not to try escaping, both of them were fastened to a wooden post. Japanese soldiers had military dogs bite their genitals. Then the belly of each woman was cut open. Finally, both women were killed.

23. This ratio is lower in areas where large amount of females were caught by invading Japanese troops. On the other hand, this proportion would be higher when Japanese troops were besieged or under attack. In the latter situation, comfort women were also at greater risk of losing life.

24. One story (see Jiang, 1998: 72–78) may well demonstrate how Japanese soldiers stationed in remote locations or isolated areas used the method of plunder to seize women: A squad of Japanese soldiers was deployed in North China to safeguard a bridge. Since this bridge was located in an unmanned mountain area, it was virtually impossible for these soldiers to meet any females. Then, in May 1938, an officer riding a motorized tricycle with his wife intended to cross this bridge. However, they were forced to walk across because their motor trike broke down. This situation proved to be disastrous to the couple. As the soldiers on the bridge had had no contact with a woman for a period of time and had become restless, they started to harass the officer's wife, first touching her hips and then her private parts. Realizing that the soldiers were sexually assaulting his wife, the officer began to bellow at the soldiers and threatened to execute them. Instead of apologizing, the soldiers bayoneted the officer, then bound him with ropes and tied him to a post. After the officer was restrained, the soldiers began to take turns raping the woman. After seeing his wife being sexually assaulted for four days, the officer died. Te woman was raped for six days and died.

25. In addition to those who were raped by Japanese soldiers, other girls and women were assaulted with objects inserted into the vagina. These included bayonets, chalk, eggs, broken glass bottles, grenades, mud, pointed sticks, roasting iron rods, sharp bamboo, sharpened carrots, and wooden clubs. This ordeal made numerous females die in great pain.

26. This category of rape usually involved drastic resistance on the part of victims.

27. Another plausible explanation is the concept of "risky-shift effect" (see Knox, 2000: 235–236). According to this notion, which is used by gang researchers to describe gang behaviors, people (especially males) tend to feel safe and to have the desire to exhibit "heroism" or "masculinity" when they commit a violent crime as part of a group. Due to this social psychological characteristic generated by mutual support and encouragement, people usually will become much more aggressive when they perpetrate an interpersonal crime in a group context. Victims typically suffer far more serious injury than those who are harmed by only one perpetrator.

28. This is why the Imperial Japanese Army was called the most barbarian troop in the world (Xie, 2005:408).

29. These killings were justified essentially by the so-called *san guang*, or "Three Alls" (i.e., looting all, killing all, and burning all) policy of the Japanese military.

30. In Japanese, *gyokusai* means "jade-breaking." The origin of this term is from a Chinese proverb: *ning wei yu sui, bu wei wa quan* (literally, "even at the expense of smashing a jade, an earthenware is not allowed to remain as a whole piece").
It means "better to die proud than to live in disgrace" in English. See *The Oxford Chinese Dictionary*, 2010: 529).

31. This difficulty is related directly to the factor that lots of records about *ianfu* were deliberately destroyed by the Japanese military on the eve of Japanese surrender in August 1945 (Jiang, 1998: 152). Due to this cover-up, numerous missing comfort women became "undetectable": their relatives or friends did not know where they went, and their fate was unknown. This situation is especially true for comfort women who lost their life in places far from their hometown.

32. No one knows for sure where the bodies of these deceased women went. Some of them probably were dumped into rivers, lakes, the sea, or swamps. The others might be left on wasteland to be devoured by animals.

33. This is partially why the history of comfort women did not draw public attention in countries and regions formerly ruled by Japan until 1991–92, when a small number of former Korean comfort women brought their stories to the media (Yoshimi, 2000: 33) and as human rights investigators in China found and interviewed some elderly rural women who had been enslaved sexually by the Japanese military (Hsieh, 1995: 220–222). Since then, many Western and East Asian scholars and human rights organizations have begun to examine methodically the issue of militarized rape committed by the Japanese Imperial

Army; however, it seems that the topic of comfort women is still highly sensitive, if not taboo, in the educational and political communities of contemporary Japan.

Chapter 6

1. In this chapter, trafficked women and girls are classified into two different but interrelated groups of females. One is composed of those young women who are enticed to leave for an unfamiliar place to get a good-paying job or to "enjoy life." The other consists of teenage and younger girls whose parents or other relatives sell them to brothels as prostitutes or mail-order brides. These two sets of females have some features in common. First, such females will, more often than not, experience verbal threats and violent acts as they proceed to their destination. Then within a very short period of time, they will be transformed into virtual prisoners (i.e., their movements are closely supervised). In addition to losing the freedom of moving around (let alone leaving their confines), these detained women and girls are compelled to do highly exploitative tasks such as providing sexual services without getting pay. This slavery-like life can last years and become normalized unless law enforcement agents intervene. Simply speaking, these features can be summarized by the processes of recruitment and exploitation (see Davidson, 2005: 71). The former, almost without exception, involves deceptive and fraudulent behavior. Due to these behaviors, millions of women and young girls fall prey to these recruiters. The latter is largely examined within the paradigm of slavery. Writers specializing in this paradigm indicate that whenever women or girls are under the control of strangers or outlaws, such females will, as a rule, be driven to engage in extremely unfair and/or highly repressive transactions or activities.

2. More specifically, human trade was lawful in China before 1912. Consequently, the practice of buying and selling females was a routine part of civil life in China before the Republican Revolution. This practice, legally speaking, was illegal after the Republican Revolution, and it was committed extensively by organized gangs and human-trafficking rings. Since law enforcement authorities of the Nationalist government were noted for corruption, few of them made any effort to suppress woman trafficking. This did not change much until the early 1950s when most "godfathers" of structured criminal societies were purged by the communist government. Anyway, according to Ma (1999: 208–210), selling and buying females was a contractual behavior in China before the Republican era. The contract that allowed women purchasers to keep their "movable properties" could be *hong qi* (the red contract) or *bai qi* (the white contract). The only difference between these two agreements was that the former was endorsed by local officials while the latter involved only buyer and seller. Except for this variation, both contracts had the same effect in law.

3. According to Lee (2007: 11), "a discrete categorization of 'trafficking' and 'smuggling' may be artificial and unhelpful." With this in mind, these two terms will be used interchangeably in this chapter.

4. For example, as early as the 1990s, people who wanted to go to America had to pay $30,000 (Chin, 2001: 217). This fee must have increased dramatically after the September 11, 2001, terrorist attacks in the U.S., when entering the United States via illegal means became much harder than it used to be.

5. One typical example is Sister Ping, the "queen" of Chinese smuggling rings. See Zhang (2007: 79–86).

6. These outcomes could be corporal punishments such as caning, incarceration, or torture, and/or tremendous debts usually caused by loan-sharking. The former might lead to permanent injuries (or even death) while the latter always far surpassed someone's ability to pay.

7. The other equally famous "human flesh" markets were Suzhou and Hangzhou. Since both were Grand Canal cities as well, these two cities and Yangzhou have many features in common (e.g., history of urban development and the tradition of woman trafficking).

8. To make sure that these women could keep generating wealth, people who "owned" them usually would coerce such females into undergoing strict, or even inhumane, "training" and to follow a rigid working schedule. Those who failed to meet the requirements would be scolded and disciplined). Under this authoritarian, highly repressive environment, some

women, overwhelmed by their situation, hanged themselves. Few of these suicides were reported to the authorities because such incidents were commonly viewed as "family affairs." Even if law enforcement agents did learn of these events, they still could be disregarded easily: after all, the great majority of local officials of premodern China delivered judgment based not on professional knowledge but on interpersonal relationships (see Yang, 1994). That allowed wealthy families to bribe local bureaucrats and security agents. These connections, as they entailed the elements of nepotism and preferential treatment, then gave certain families an above-the-law status. With this status as a buttress, local gentry (let alone high-ranking government officials) usually could take care of intrafamilial scandals (which could be child abuse, spouse abuse, incest, or even private torture) without difficulty.

9. Instead of paying attention to the historical fact that immeasurable women and girls were sold to Yangzhou as sex workers in the past one-thousand-plus years, most modern Chinese tend to believe that it was pleasant living conditions and superior natural environment that made Yangzhou (as well as Suzhou and Hangzhou) a unique place in producing beautiful women.

10. While numerous professional, semiskilled, and unskilled workers from inland provinces are able to find a job in a coastal city, they cannot stay there permanently unless they become legal residents. That means foreign employees such as interns or seasonal workers must return to their hometown after they have completed their assignments. Despite this limitation of residency, a good number of this migratory workforce does come back to the cities (whether regularly or irregularly) to enjoy the amenities.

11. It was estimated that at least seventy millions of *guang guen* ("bare sticks"; i.e., single males) could not get married in the late 1990s (He & Wang, 1993: 150). This number must have become greater in the late 2000s.

12. This condition generally can be observed in country areas, especially those located in West and Southwest China. Some factors make escape extremely challenging for women and girls sold to geographically isolated regions; these include a lack of transportation, lack of personal income, language barrier, and/or little or no contact with the outside world. Besides these factors, the crime watch programs installed by neighborhood committees seems especially noteworthy: according to Wang (2007: 161–162), the sex ratios of certain villages in modern China are highly distorted. Therefore, young males of those villages usually cannot get married until they buy a trafficked woman as a "wife." To help these married males maintain a "harmonious family," not only will local people closely monitor the actions of that woman, but villagers will collectively "arrest" the woman if she is attempting to escape.

13. In feudal/imperial China, trafficked women and girls could escape only with help. This is because human trade was legal in China before 1912 (see note 2). Therefore, trafficked women, if they ran away, were regarded by the authorities as fugitives and faced the risk of being arrested (in other words, people who bought women and girls could legally ask law enforcement agents to search for and apprehend these females if the latter were believed to have deserted). On the contrary, human trafficking is illegal in modern China. Accordingly, trafficked women can ask the police or relevant agents for assistance if they flee. This transformation, of course, no longer permits modern women procurers to do what their counterparts did during the imperial years. On the other hand, given that woman purchasers are defined by the criminal laws of the People's Republic of China (as well as the Republic of China) as criminals, they dare not report those trafficked females who have gone missing to the authorities. This "inaction" may either make local authorities downplay the work of searching for missing women; or it may lead to an "intelligence vacuum" which, in turn, makes it very difficult for law enforcement agents to look for those females who are believed missing.

14. Technically speaking, these women are still missing persons for mainstream society. This socially detached status will not come to an end until the roles played by such females in their new home and community have become fully "normalized" (i.e., they become active members of their community, reestablish fixed interpersonal relationships, and are no longer subject to limitations in movements).

15. According to Agnew (1992), these strategies can assist stressed people to cope with anger and other negative emotions if they lose "positively valued stimuli."

16. The other two strategies, "preventing the loss of the positive stimuli" and "seeking revenge against those responsible for the loss," are not applicable here because the first measure suggests that historical fact can be altered (i.e., if the victim's husband had taken certain precautionary steps, then his wife would not have been trafficked). The second measure implies that the victim's husband enjoys certain chances to take back his spouse because "those responsible for the loss" of his wife are identified.

17. According to Stein (1981: 10–11), singlehood can be divided into four typologies: voluntary but temporary, voluntary and stable, involuntary and temporary, and involuntary but stable. Forced singlehood refers to the final type (involuntary but stable singlehood).

18. Due to data insufficiency, it is unclear whether the practice of polyandry (i.e., several men "sharing" a woman) is popular in underdeveloped regions of modern China.

19. One typical scenario is that the trafficker reserves a hotel room or condo in the destination city. Once the victim arrive in that city and is taken "hospitably" to the prearranged location, the place becomes a "workshop" where the trafficker can perform his "job" (sexually assaulting and confining the victim, selling the "product" to professional human dealers, etc.).

20. The act of purchasing aboriginal teenage girls in Taiwan during the period of 1960s to 1980s provides an excellent example for this: in late 1949 and early 1950, approximately 600,000 Nationalist troops defeated by the communist armies retreated to that island. Believing that they could go back to mainland China within a short period of time, most Nationalist officers and soldiers did not bring their family members with them to Taiwan. Many people, however, began to lose hope of returning home in the 1960s when it became apparent that the Chiang Kai-shek government, as a refugee regime, could not return to China in the foreseeable future. Partially due to this disenchantment, some single servicemen started to purchase teenage girls from human traffickers (most of whom were aborigines who lived in the least developed mountainous communities) as wife and created their own family in Taiwan. To meet these demands, woman traders must visit aboriginal neighborhoods frequently to get "brides" for their customers.

21. Due to geographic proximity, Japan, Korea, Hong Kong, and Taiwan are also hot spots for female Chinese smugglers. For undocumented Hong Kongese and Taiwanese women who do not plan to go to the West but want to get a "good job" overseas, Japan usually is their final destination. No matter where these females come from (China, Hong Kong, or Taiwan), the great majority of such "less adventurous" smuggled women will be drawn into sex industries if their smuggling actions are successful.

Chapter 7

1. In Taiwan, these sufferers are also called *zhi wu ren*, or "vegetable persons" (meaning they are alive, but they cannot communicate with the outside world).

2. Although females with dementia appear "luckier" than the other typologies of missing women, they perhaps suffer more than their male counterparts because women usually play the role of caretaker. Accordingly, women with Alzheimer's disease may still have to assume dual responsibilities: namely, taking care of themselves and their family members. On the contrary, men with Alzheimer's disease seem to enjoy the "privilege" of full-time care.

3. Another example is runaway foreign spouses in Taiwan. According to Cheng (2007), numerous single adult males in Taiwan cannot get married because their inferior socioeconomic position precludes them from finding girlfriends. Hence, lots of these low-status males can only "order" brides from or find brides in less developed countries and regions, such as Burma (Myanmar), Cambodia, Indonesia, the Philippines, Thailand, Vietnam, and especially China. Some foreign spouses who voluntarily go to Taiwan, however, run away from home because they cannot tolerate social prejudice, overcome the language barrier, or get along with their in-laws. These escaped foreign spouses usually cannot support themselves financially because the labor laws of Taiwan prohibit unauthorized foreigners (including "international brides" who have not obtained permanent residency status in the Republic of China) from getting jobs. So unless these "renegade" wives can acquire long-term assistance from friends (very unlikely), they will normally face financial trouble before long.

Largely because of these negative factors, fled foreign spouses generally return to their home in Taiwan after a cooling-off period. This tends to be especially true if foreign wives are found by their relatives or by social workers.

4. This situation is exactly the same as that of illegal immigrants (no matter where they come from) to the United States who want to obtain permanent residency (i.e., the green card).

5. Some fortunate ones, however, are able to find a permanent residence. On the other hand, this residence is, most of the time, located in a crowded slum where few people enjoy privacy.

6. One example provided by Ju (2008: 68–74) is a teenage girl who once worked in a tinfoil factory. She fled the plant because she could not stand her workload.

7. According to Flowers (2001: 5), runaway children can be divided into three categories: runaway gestures, broad scope runaways, and policy-focal runaways. The first two categories of runaways appear less likely to experience starvation and other problems encountered by homeless persons because they can find safe and sound shelters offered by relatives or friends. In contrast, policy-focal runaways are "endangered due to not having a familiar, safe place to stay" (Flowers, 2001: 5).

8. Such children may sever family ties permanently and become what English (quoted in Flowers, 2001: 4) called "hard-rock freaks."

9. This percentage might be an underestimation of the real situation because the samples (n = 314) appear not large enough.

10. Only in rare circumstances (e.g., critical illness) can these girls (under the supervision of a guard) visit a doctor.

11. According to Leung (2009: 208–209), there were 662 leper villages in China in 2005. Of these communities, 120 were located in Yunnan, 90 in Guangdong, and 80 in Sichuan.

12. That means female lepers are "born criminals" (Lombroso & Ferrero, 2004: 8), who deserve to get punishments.

13. Slaughtered female lepers should be viewed as missing females of the FNU type.

14. According to Goffman (1986: 4), stigma can come from three sources: abominations of body, blemishes of individual character, and tribal identity. Of these sources, the first one is highly visible, the second one is lowly visible, and the third one goes from high visibility (e.g., racial background and gender) to invisibility (e.g., nationality and religious affiliation). Since leprosy belongs to the first category, it is not difficult to understand why leprosy patients always will be the objects of prejudice and discrimination.

15. While both male and female lepers are considered "unclean," the latter may suffer more because according to symbolic interactionists, the female body, regardless of its part, tends to attract more public attention than the male body. Accordingly, physical deformities appear more likely to bring to female lepers "double discrimination" (i.e., discrimination based on gender and abnormal bodily features) or even "triple discrimination" (i.e., discrimination based on gender, ethnicity, and abnormal bodily features).

Bibliography

English Language References

Agnew, Robert. 1992. "Foundation for a General Strain Theory of Crime and Delinquency." *Criminology* 30 (1): 47–87.

Albert, Alexa. 2001. *Brothel: Mustang Ranch and Its Women*. New York: Random House.

Allison, Anne. 1994. *Nightwork: Sexuality, Pleasure, and Corporate Masculinity in a Tokyo Hostess Club*. Chicago: University of Chicago Press.

Altman, Dennis. 2001. *Global Sex*. Chicago: University of Chicago Press.

Altink, Sietske. 1995. *Stolen Lives: Trading Women into Sex and Slavery*. Binghamton, NY: Harrington Park Press.

Amir, Menachem. 1971. *Patterns in Forcible Rape*. Chicago: University of Chicago Press.

Bales, Kevin. 2005. *New Slavery: A Reference Handbook*, 2nd ed. Santa Barbara, CA: ABC-CLIO.

_____, and Ron Soodalter. 2009. *The Slave Next Door: Human Trafficking and Slavery in America Today*. Berkeley and Los Angeles: University of California Press.

Banister, Judith. 2004. "Shortage of Girls in China Today." *Journal of Population Research*, 21 (1): 19–45.

Barnett, Ola, Cindy L. Miller-Perrin, and Robin D. Perrin. 2005. *Family Violence across the Lifespan: An Introduction*, 2nd ed. Thousand Oaks, CA: Sage Publications.

Barry, Kathleen. 1995. *The Prostitution of Sexuality*. New York: New York University Press.

Barstow, Anne Llewellyn, ed. 2000. *War's Dirty Secret: Rape, Prostitution, and Other Crimes against Women*. Cleveland, OH: Pilgrim Press.

Becker, Howard S., 1966. *Outsiders: Studies in the Sociology of Deviance*. New York: Free Press.

Becker, Jasper. 1997. *Hungry Ghosts: Mao's Secret Famine*. New York: Free Press.

Benson, Michael L. 2002. *Crime and the Life Course: An Introduction*. Los Angeles: Roxbury Publishing.

Bishop, Ryan, and Lillian S. Robinson. 1998. *Night Market: Sexual Cultures and the Thai Economic Miracle*. New York: Routledge.

Boswell, John. 1988. *The Kindness of Strangers: The Abandonment of Children in Western Europe from Late Antiquity to the Renaissance*. New York: Pantheon.

Brazil, David. 1998. *No Money, No Honey: A Candid Look at Sex-for-Sale in Singapore*, 4th ed. Singapore: Angsana Books.

Brightman, Hank J., and Lindsey W. Howard. 2009. *Today's White-Collar Crime: Legal, Investigative, and Theoretical Perspectives*. New York: Routledge.

Brown, Louise. 2000. *Sex Slaves: The Trafficking of Women in Asia*. London: Virago Press.

Brownmiller, Susan. 1993. *Against Our Will: Men, Women and Rape*. New York: Fawcett Columbine.

Buzawa, Eve S., and Carl G. Buzawa. 2002. *Domestic Violence: The Criminal Justice Response*, 3rd ed. Thousand Oaks, CA: Sage Publications.

Byron, John, and Robert Pack. 1992. *The Claws of the Dragon: Kang Sheng, The Evil Genius behind Mao and His Legacy of Terror in People's China*. New York: Simon & Schuster.

Cawthorne, Nigel. 2009. *Pirates of the 21st Century: How Modern-Day Buccaneers are Terrorizing the World's Oceans*. London: John Blake.

Chang, Iris. 1997. *The Rape of Nanking: The Forgotten Holocaust of World War II*. New York: Basic Books.

Chang, Maria Hsia. 1985. *The Chinese Blue Shirt Society: Fascism and Developmental Nationalism*. Berkeley: Institute of East Asian Studies, University of California.

_____. 2004. *Falun Gong: The End of Days*. New Haven, CT: Yale University Press.

Chapkis, Wendy. 1996. *Live Sex Acts: Women Performing Erotic Labor*. New York: Routledge.

Cheng, Nien. 1987. *Life and Death in Shanghai*. New York: Grove Press.

Cheng, Zoe. 2007. "The Biggest Leap: Being a 'New Taiwanese' Immigrant Is Not Easy." *Taiwan Review*, 57 (2): 4–11.

Chesney-Lind, Meda, and Lisa Pasko. 2003. *The Female Offender: Girls, Women, and Crime*. 2nd ed. Thousand Oaks, CA: Sage Publications.

Chin, Ko-lin.1999. *Smuggled Chinese: Clandestine Immigration to the United States*. Philadelphia: Temple University Press.

_____. 2001. "The Social Organization of Chinese Human Smuggling." In David Kyle and Rey Koslowski, editors, *Global Human Smuggling: Comparative Perspectives*, pp. 216–234. Baltimore, MD: Johns Hopkins University Press.

Chow, Tse-tsung. 1960. *The May Fourth Movement: Intellectual Revolution in Modern China*. Cambridge, MA: Harvard University Press.

Ciborski, Marion. 2000. "Guatemala: 'We Thought It Was Only the Men They Would Kill.'" In Anne Llewellyn Barstow, editor, *War's Dirty Secret: Rap, Prostitution, and Other Crimes against Women*, pp. 124–138. Cleveland, OH: Pilgrim Press.

Cling, B. J., ed. 2004. *Sexualized Violence against Women and Children*. New York: Guilford Press.

Clubb, O. Edmund. 1978. *20th Century China*, 3rd ed. New York: Columbia University Press.

Coale, Ansley J. 1991. "Excess Female Mortality and the Balance of the Sexes in the Population: An Estimate of the Number of 'Missing Females.'" *Population and Development Review*, 17 (3): 517–523.

Coale, Ansley J., and Judith Banister. 1994. "Five Decades of Missing Females in China." *Demography*, 31 (3): 459–479.

Copper, John F. 1996. *Taiwan: Nation-State or Province?* 2nd ed. Boulder, CO: Westview Press.

Courtois, Stéphane, Nicolas Werth, Jean-Louis Panné, Andrzej Paczkowski, Karel Bartošek, and Jean-Louis Margolin. 1999. *The Black Book of Communism: Crimes, Terror, Repression* Translated by Jonathan Murphy. Cambridge, MA: Harvard University Press.

Croll, Elisabeth. 2000. *Endangered Daughters: Discrimination and Development in Asia*. New York: Routledge.

Daniels, Roger. 1993. *Prisoners without Trial: Japanese Americans in World War II.* New York: Hill and Wang.

Das Gupta, Monica. 2005. "Explaining Asia's 'Missing Women': A New Look at the Data." *Population and Development Review,* 31 (3): 529–535.

Davidson, Julia O'Connell. 2005. *Children in the Global Sex Trade.* Malden, MA: Polity Press.

Daye, Douglas D. 1996. *A Law Enforcement Sourcebook of Asian Crime and Cultures: Tactics and Mindsets.* Boca Raton, FL: CRC Press.

DeBaggio, Thomas. 2003. *Losing My Mind: An Intimate Look at Life with Alzheimer's.* New York: Free Press.

della Porta, Donatella, and Mario Diani. 1998. *Social Movements: An Introduction.* Malden, MA: Blackwell Publishers.

Domenach, Jean-Luc. 1995. *The Origins of the Great Leap Forward: The Case of One Chinese Province* Translated by A. M. Berrett. Boulder, CO: Westview Press.

Douglas, John E., Ann W. Burgess, Allen G. Burgess, and Robert K. Ressler. 1997. *Crime Classification Manual: A Standard System for Investigating and Classifying Violent Crimes.* San Francisco: Jossey-Bass.

Dunham, Mikel. 2004. *Buddha's Warriors: The Story of the CIA-Backed Tibetan Freedom Fighters, the Chinese Invasion, and the Ultimate Fall of Tibet.* New York: Jeremy P. Tarcher/Penguin.

Durkheim, Emile. 1966. *Suicide: A Study in Sociology,* translated by John A. Spaulding and George Simpson. New York: Free Press.

Dutton, Michael. 2005. *Policing Chinese Politics: A History.* Durham, NC: Duke University Press.

Eastman, Lloyd E. 1984. *Seeds of Destruction: Nationalist China in War and Revolution, 1937–1949.* Stanford, CA: Stanford University Press.

_____. 1986. "Nationalist China during the Sino-Japanese War, 1937–1945." In John K. Fairbank and Albert Feuerwerker, editors, *The Cambridge History of China,* vol. 13, pp. 547–608. Taipei: Caves Books.

_____. 1990. *The Abortive Revolution: China under Nationalist Rule, 1927–1937.* Cambridge, MA: Harvard University Press.

_____, Jerome Chen, Suzanne Pepper, and Lyman P. Van Slyke. 1991. *The Nationalist Era in China, 1927–1949.* New York: Cambridge University Press.

Ebbe, Obi N. I. 2008. "Causes of Trafficking in Women and Children." In Obi N. I. Ebbe and Dilip K. Das, *Global Trafficking in Women and Children,* pp. 33–38. Boca Raton, FL: CRC Press.

Ebrey, Patricia Buckley. 1996. *The Cambridge Illustrated History of China.* New York: Cambridge University Press.

Edgerton, Robert B. 1998. *Warriors of the Rising Sun.* Boulder, CO: Westview.

Elias, James E., Vern L. Bullough , Veronica Elias, and Gwen Brewer, ed. 1998. *Prostitution: On Whores, Hustlers, and Johns.* Amherst, NY: Prometheus Books.

Esbenshade, Jill. 2004. *Monitoring Sweatshops: Workers, Consumers, and the Global Apparel Industry.* Philadelphia, PA: Temple University Press.

Fairbank, John King. 1992. *China: A New History.* Cambridge, MA: Belknap Press of Harvard University Press.

Fariello, Griffin. 1995. *Red Scare: Memories of the American Inquisition, an Oral History.* New York: Avon Books.

Farr, Kathryn. 2005. *Sex Trafficking: The Global Market in Women and Children.* New York: Worth.

Fay, Peter Ward. 1997. *The Opium War, 1840–1842: Barbarians in the Celestial Empire in the Early Part of the Nineteenth Century and the Way by Which They Forced Her Gates Ajar.* Chapel Hill: University of North Carolina Press.

Fei, John, C. H., Gustav Ranis, and Shirley W. Y. Kuo. 1979. *Growth with Equity: The Taiwan Case*. New York: Oxford University Press.

Felson, Marcus, and Rachel Boba. 2010. *Crime and Everyday Life*, 4th ed. Thousand Oaks, CA: Pine Forge Press.

Ferree, Myra Marx. 1992. "The Political Contexts of Rationality: Rational Choice Theory and Resource Mobilization." In Aldon D. Morris and Carol McClurg Mueller, *Frontiers in Social Movement Theory*, pp. 29–52. New Haven, CT: Yale University Press.

Ferrell, Jeff, and Clinton R. Sanders, eds. 1995. *Cultural Criminology*. Boston, MA: Northeastern University Press.

Flanagan, William G. 2010. *Urban Sociology: Images and Structure*, 5th ed. Boulder, CO: Rowman & Littlefield.

Flowers, R. Barri. 1998. *The Prostitution of Women and Girls*. Jefferson, NC: McFarland.

_____. 2001. *Runaway Kids and Teen Prostitution: America's Lost, Abandoned, and Sexually Exploited Children*. Westport, CT: Praeger.

Fox, Stephen. 1990. *The Unknown Internment: An Oral History of the Relocation of Italian Americans during World War II*. Boston, MA: Twayne Publishers.

Frank, Katherine. 2002. *G-Strings and Sympathy: Strip Club Regulars and Male Desire*. Durham, NC: Duke University Press.

Frantz, Janet E., and Hajime Sato. 2005. "The Fertile Soil for Policy Learning." *Policy Sciences* 38: 159–176.

Friedrich, Carl J., and Zbigniew K. Brzezinski. 1966. *Totalitarian Dictatorship & Autocracy*, 2nd ed. New York: Frederick A. Praeger.

Gaon, Igor Davor, and Nancy Forbord. 2005. *For Sale: Women and Children, Trafficking and Forced Prostitution in Southeast Europe*. Victoria, BC: Trafford Publishing.

Geberth, Vernon. J. 2003. *Sex-Related Homicide and Death Investigation: Practical and Clinical Perspectives*. Boca Raton, FL: CRC Press.

Gedi, Noa, and Yigal Elam. 1996. "Collective Memory: What Is It?" *History & Memory*, 8(1): 30–50.

"Gendercide." The Economist (2010, March 6), 11.

Giddens, Anthony. 1986. *The Constitution of Society: Outline of the Theory of Structuration*. Berkeley & Los Angeles: University of California Press.

Glatt, John. 2002. *Cries in the Desert: The Shocking True Story of a Sadistic Torturer*. New York: St. Martin's Press.

Glenny, Misha. 2008. *McMafia: Crime without Frontiers*. London: Bodley Head.

Godbeer, Richard. 2002. *Sexual Revolution in Early America*. Baltimore, MD: Johns Hopkins University Press.

Goffman, Erving. 1959. *The Presentation of Self in Everyday Life*. New York: Anchor Books.

_____. 1966. *Behavior in Public Places: Notes on the Social Organization of Gatherings*. New York: Free Press.

_____. [1967] 1982. *Interaction Ritual: Essays on Face-to-Face Behavior*. New York: Pantheon Books.

_____. 1986. *Stigma: Notes on the Management of Spoiled Identity*. New York: Touchstone Book.

Goodwin, Janet R. 2006. *Selling Songs and Smiles: The Sex Trade in Heian and Kamakura Japan*. Honolulu: University of Hawaii Press.

Gould, Tony. 2005. *A Disease Apart: Leprosy in the Modern World*. New York: St. Martin's Press.

Gu, Minkang. 2008. "Trafficking in Women and Children in China." In Obi N. I.

Ebbe and Dilip K. Das, *Global Trafficking in Women and Children*, pp. 55–66. Boca Raton, FL: CRC Press.

Hare, Robert D. 1998. *Without Conscience: The Disturbing World of the Psychopaths among Us*. New York: Guilford Press.

Harff, Barbara, and Ted Robert Gurr. 2003. *Ethnic Conflict in World Politics*, 2nd ed. Boulder, CO: Westview Press.

Hausfater, Glenn, and Sarah Blaffer Hrdy, ed. 2008. *Infanticide: Comparative and Evolutionary Perspectives*. New Brunswick, NJ: Aldine Transaction.

Hawkes, Gail. 2004. *Sex and Pleasure in Western Culture*. Malden, MA: Polity Press.

Hazelwood, Roy, and Stephen G. Michaud. 2001. *Dark Dream: Sexual Violence, Homicide, and the Criminal Mind*. New York: St. Martin's Press.

Hershatter, Gail. 1997. *Dangerous Pleasures: Prostitution and Modernity in Twentieth-Century Shanghai*. Berkeley & Los Angeles: University of California Press.

Hesse-Biber, Sharlene Nagy. 2007. *The Cult of Thinness*, 2nd ed. New York: Oxford University Press.

Hicks, George. 1995. *The Comfort Women: Japan's Brutal Regime of Enforced Prostitution in the Second World War*. New York: W.W. Norton.

Hines, Denise A., and Kathleen Malley-Morrison. 2005. *Family Violence in the United States: Defining, Understanding, and Combating Abuse*. Thousand Oaks, CA: Sage Publications.

Hinton, William. 1966. *Fanshen: A Documentary of Revolution in a Chinese Village*. New York: Vintage Books.

Hirschi, Travis. [1969] 2001. *Causes of Delinquency*. New Brunswick, NJ: Transaction Publishers.

Hodgson, James F. 1997. *Games Pimps Play: Pimps, Players and Wives-in-Law: A Quantitative Analysis of Street Prostitution*. Toronto, ON: Canadian Scholars' Press.

Hodgson, James F., and Debra S. Kelley, ed. 2004. *Sexual Violence: Policies, Practices, and Challenges in the United States and Canada*. New York: Criminal Justice Press.

Holland, Jack. 2006. *Misogyny: The World's Oldest Prejudice*. New York: Carroll & Graf.

Holmes, Ronald M., and Stephen T. Holmes, ed. 2002. *Current Perspectives on Sex Crimes*. Thousand Oaks, CA: Sage Publications.

_____. 2009a. *Profiling Violent Crimes: An Investigative Tool*, 4th ed. Thousand Oaks, CA: Sage Publications.

_____. 2010. *Fatal Violence: Case Studies and Analysis of Emerging Forms*. Boca Raton, FL: CRC Press.

Holmes, Stephen T., and Ronald M. Holmes. 2009b. *Sex Crimes: Patterns and Behavior*, 3rd ed. Thousand Oaks, CA: Sage Publications.

Hong Kong Alzheimer's Disease Association. "About Dementia." www.hkada.org.hk.

Hsu, Immanuel C. Y. 2000. *The Rise of Modern China*, 6th ed. New York: Oxford University Press.

Hudson, Valerie. M., and Andrea M. den Boer. 2004. *Bare Branches: The Security Implications of Asia's Surplus Male Population*. Cambridge, MA: MIT Press.

Huggins, Martha K. 1998. *Political Policing: The United States and Latin America*. Durham, NC: Duke University Press.

Huston, Peter. 1995. *Tongs, Gangs, and Triads: Chinese Crime Groups in North America*. Boulder, CO: Paladin Press.

Isaacs, Harold R. 1961. *The Tragedy of the Chinese Revolution*, 2nd ed. New York: Atheneum.

Jackson, Billy, ed. 2004. *We Sing a Song of Sadness: Tibetan Political Prisoners Speak Out*. Baltimore, MD: PublishAmerica.

Jansen, Marius B. 2000. *The Making of Modern Japan.* Cambridge, MA: Belknap Press of Harvard University Press.

Jaschok, Maria. 1988. *Concubines and Bondservants: A Social History of a Chinese Custom.* London: Zed Books.

Jenkins, Philip. 2001. *Beyond Tolerance: Child Pornography on the Internet.* New York: New York University.

Jiang, Quanbao, Marcus W. Feldman, and Xiaoyi Jin. 2005. "Estimation of the Number of Missing Females in China: 1900–2000." Paper for the XXV International Population Conference, Tours, France.

Johansson, Sten, and Ola Nygren. 1991. "The Missing Girls of China: A New Demographic Account." *Population and Development Review*, 17 (1): 35–51.

Johnson, Kay Ann. 2004. *Wanting a Daughter, Needing a Son: Abandonment, Adoption, and Orphanage Care in China.* St. Paul, MN: Yeong & Yeong Book.

Jordan, Brent Kenton. 2004. *Stripped: Twenty Years of Secrets from Inside the Strip Club*, 4th ed. Kearney, NE: Satsu Multimedia Press.

Jordan, David, K. 1972. *Gods, Ghosts, and Ancestors: The Folk Religion of a Taiwanese Village.* Berkeley & Los Angeles: University of California Press.

Kalberg, Stephen. 1994. *Max Weber's Comparative-Historical Sociology.* Chicago: University of Chicago Press.

Kaplan, David E. 1992. *Fires of the Dragon: Politics, Murder, and the Kuomintang.* New York: Atheneum

Kara, Siddharth. 2009. *Sex Trafficking: Inside the Business of Modern Slavery.* New York: Columbia University Press.

Kaufman, Sharon R. 2006. "Dementia-Near-Death and 'Life Itself.'" In Annette Leibing and Lawrence Cohen, editors. *Thinking About Dementia: Culture, Loss, and the Anthropology of Senility*, pp. 23–42. New Brunswick, NJ: Rutgers University Press.

Kim-Gibson, Dai Sil. 1999. *Silence Broken: Korean Comfort Women.* Parkersburg, IA: Mid-Prairie Books.

King, Gilbert. 2004. *Woman, Child for Sale: The New Slave Trade in the 21st Century.* New York: Chamberlain Bros.

Kipnis, Laura. 1999. *Bound and Gagged: Pornography and the Politics of Fantasy in America.* Durham, NC: Duke University Press.

Klandermans, Bert. 1992. "The Social Construction of Protest and Multiorganizational Fields." In Aldon D. Morris and Carol McClurg Mueller, *Frontiers in Social Movement Theory*, pp. 77–103. New Haven, CT: Yale University Press.

Klasen, Stephen. 1994. "'Missing Women' Reconsidered." *World Development*, 22 (7): 1061–1071.

Klasen, Stephen, and Claudia Wink. 2002. "A Turning Point in Gender Bias in Mortality? An Update on the Number of Missing Women." *Population and Development Review*, 28 (2): 285–312.

Knox, George W. 2000. *An Introduction to Gangs*, 5th ed. Peotone, IL: New Chicago School Press.

Krammer, Arnold. 1997. *Undue Process: The Untold Story of America's German Alien Internees.* Lanham, MD: Rowman & Littlefield Publishers.

Kristof, Nicholas D., and Sheryl WuDunn. 1994. *China Wakes: The Struggle for the Soul of a Rising Power.* New York: Times Books.

_____. 2000. *Thunder from the East: Portrait of a Rising Asia.* New York: Alfred A. Knopf.

Kurse-Swanger, Karel, and Jacqueline L. Petcosky. 2003. *Violence in the Home: Multidisciplinary Perspectives.* New York: Oxford University Press.

Kwong, Peter. 1997. *Forbidden Workers: Illegal Chinese Immigrants and American Labor.* New York: Free Press.

_____. 2001. "Impact of Chinese Human Smuggling on the American Labor Market." in David Kyle and Rey Koslowski, *Global Human Smuggling: Comparative Perspectives*, pp. 235–254. Baltimore, MD: Johns Hopkins University Press.

Lai, Tse-han, Ramon H. Myers, and Wei Wou. 1991. *A Tragic Beginning: The Taiwan Uprising of February 28, 1947.* Stanford, CA: Stanford University Press.

Lan, Pei-chia. 2006. *Global Cinderellas: Migrant Domestics and Newly Rich Employers in Taiwan.* Durham, NC: Duke University Press.

Langley, Erika. 1997. *The Lusty Lady.* Zurich: Scalo.

Laser, Julie Anne, and Nicole Nicotera. 2011. *Working with Adolescents: A Guide for Practitioners.* New York: Guilford Press.

Lee, Maggy and Louise Shelley. 2007. "Introduction: Understanding Human Trafficking." In Maggy Lee, editor, *Human Trafficking*, pp. 1–25. Portland, OR: Willan Publishing.

Lehmann, Arthur C., and James E. Myers. 2000. *Magic, Witchcraft, and Religion: An Anthropological Study of the Supernatural.* Mountain View, CA: Mayfield Publishing.

Leung, Angela Ki Che. 2009. *Leprosy in China: A History.* New York: Columbia University Press.

Lewis, Paul H. 2002. *Guerrillas and Generals: The "Dirty War" in Argentina.* Westport, CT: Praeger.

Li, Minghuan. 1999. "'To Get Rich Quickly in Europe!': Reflections on Migration Motivation in Wenzhou." In Frank N. Pieke and Hein Mallee *Internal and International Migration: Chinese Perspectives*, pp. 181–198. Surrey, UK: Curzon.

Li, Shuzhuo, Chuzhu Zhu, and Marcus W. Feldman. 2004. "Gender Differences in Child Survival in Rural China: A County Study." *Journal of Biosocial Science*, 36 (1): 83–109.

Liang, Zai, and Wenzhen Ye. 2001. "From Fujian to New York: Understanding the New Chinese Immigration." In David Kyle and Rey Koslowski, *Global Human Smuggling: Comparative Perspectives*, pp. 187–215. Baltimore, MD: Johns Hopkins University Press.

Lincoln, W. Bruce. 1989. *Red Victory: A History of the Russian Civil War.* New York: Touchstone.

Little, Daniel. 1991. *Varieties of Social Explanation: An Introduction to the Philosophy of Social Science.* Boulder, CO: Westview Press.

Lock, Margaret, Stephanie Lloyd, and Janalyn Prest. 2006. "Genetic Susceptibility and Alzheimer's Disease." In Annette Leibing and Lawrence Cohen, *Thinking About Dementia: Culture, Loss, and the Anthropology of Senility*, pp. 123–154. New Brunswick, NJ: Rutgers University Press.

Lombroso, Cesare, and Guglielmo Ferrero. 2004. *Criminal Women, the Prostitute, and the Normal Woman*, translated by Nicole Hahn Rafter and Mary Gibson. Durham, NC: Duke University Press.

Lowry, Thomas P. 1994. *The Story the Soldiers Wouldn't Tell: Sex in the Civil War.* Mechanicsburg, PA: Stackpole Books.

_____. 2006. *Sexual Misbehavior in the Civil War: A Compendium.* Philadelphia, PA: Xlibris Corporation.

Ma, L. Eve Armentrout. 1990. *Revolutionaries, Monarchists, and Chinatowns: Chinese Politics in the Americas and the 1911 Revolution.* Honolulu: University of Hawaii Press.

MacFarquhar, Roderick. 1974. *The Origins of the Cultural Revolution; 1: Contradictions among the People, 1956–1957.* New York: Columbia University Press.

_____. 1997. *The Origins of the Cultural Revolution; 3: The Coming of the Cataclysm, 1961–1966.* New York: Oxford University Press and Columbia University Press.

Malarek, Victor. 2004. *The Natashas: Inside the New Global Sex Trade.* New York: Arcade Publishing.

Malley-Morrison, Kathleen, and Denise A. Hines. 2004. *Family Violence in a Cultural Perspective: Defining, Understanding, and Combating Abuse.* Thousand Oaks, CA: Sage Publications.

Mark, Mary Ellen. [1981] 2005. *Falkland Road: Prostitutes of Bombay.* Göttingen, Germany: Steidl.

Martin, Brian G. 1996. *The Shanghai Green Gang: Politics and Organized Crime, 1919–1937.* Berkeley & Los Angeles: University of California Press.

Martin, Gus. 2009. *Understanding Terrorism: Challenges, Perspectives, and Issues,* 3rd ed. Thousand Oaks, CA: Sage Publications.

McCord, Edward A. 1993. *The Power of the Gun: The Emergence of Modern Chinese Warlordism.* Berkeley & Los Angeles: University of California Press.

McDaniel, Tim. 1991. *Autocracy, Modernization, and Revolution in Russia and Iran.* Princeton, NJ: Princeton University Press.

McGough, James. 1981. "Deviant Marriage Patterns in Chinese Society." In Arthur Kleinman and Tsung-Yi Lin, *Normal and Abnormal Behavior in Chinese Culture,* pp. 171–201. Boston, MA: Kluwer.

Meyer, Cheryl L., and Michelle Oberman. 2001. *Mothers Who Kill Their Children: Understanding the Acts of Moms from Susan Smith to the "Prom Mom."* New York: New York University Press.

Michaud, Stephen G., and Roy Hazelwood. 1999. *The Evil That Men Do: FBI Profiler Roy Hazelwood's Journey into the Minds of Sexual Predators.* New York: St. Martin's Press.

Miller, Geoffrey. 2000. *The Mating Mind: How Sexual Choice Shaped the Evolution of Human Nature.* London: Heinemann.

Moon, Katharine H. S. 1997. *Sex among Allies: Military Prostitution in U.S.-Korea Relations.* New York: Columbia University Press.

Morris, Desmond. 2005. *The Naked Woman: A Study of the Female Body.* New York: Thomas Dunne.

Mungello, D. E. 2008. *Drowning Girls in China: Female Infanticide since 1650.* Lanham, MD: Rowman & Littlefield.

Nagel, Joane. 2003. *Race, Ethnicity, and Sexuality: Intimate Intersections, Forbidden Frontiers.* New York: Oxford University Press.

Naquin, Susan, and Evelyn S. Rawski. 1987. *Chinese Society in the Eighteenth Century.* New Haven, CT: Yale University Press.

Oldenburg, Venna Talwar. 2002. *Dowry Murder: The Imperial Origins of a Cultural Crime.* New York: Oxford University Press.

Outshoorn, Joyce, ed. 2004. *The Politics of Prostitution: Women's Movements, Democratic States and the Globalization of Sex Commerce.* New York: Cambridge University Press.

Perry, Barbara. 2001. *In the Name of Hate: Understanding Hate Crimes.* New York: Routledge.

Pier, Maria W. 1978. *Infanticide: Past and Present.* New York: W.W. Norton.

Piquero, Alex, and Paul Mazerolle. 2000. *Life-Course Criminology: Contemporary and Classic Readings.* Belmont, CA: Wadsworth.

Pope-Hennessy, James. [1967] 2004. *Sins of the Fathers: The Atlantic Slave Trade, 1441–1807.* Edison, NJ: Castle Books.

Purcell, Catherine E., and Bruce A. Arrigo. 2006. *The Psychology of Lust Murder: Paraphilia, Sexual Killing, and Serial Homicide.* Burlington, MA: Academic Press.

Rabe, John. 1998. *The Goodman of Nanking: The Diaries of John Rabe.* New York: Alfred A. Knopf.

Rediker, Marcus. 2007. *The Slave Ship: A Human History.* New York: Viking.

Reid, Ken. 1999. *Truancy and Schools.* New York: Routledge.

Ressler, Robert K., Ann W. Burgess, and John E. Douglas. 1988. *Sexual Homicide: Patterns and Motives.* New York: Free Press.

Roth, Guenther, and Claus Wittich, ed. 1978. *Max Weber: Economy and Society — An Outline of Interpretive Sociology,* 2 vols. Berkeley & Los Angeles: University of California Press.

Rummel, R. J. 1994. *Death by Government.* New Brunswick, NJ: Transaction Publishers.

Sabat, Steven R. 2001. *The Experience of Alzheimer's Disease: Life through a Tangled Veil.* Malden, MA: Blackwell Publishers.

Sampson, Robert J., and John H. Laub. 1993. *Crime in the Making: Pathways and Turning Points through Life.* Cambridge, MA: Harvard University Press.

Schafer, Stephen. 1974. *The Political Criminal: The Problem of Morality and Crime.* New York: Free Press.

Schlesinger, Louis. B. 2003. *Sexual Murder: Catathymic and Compulsive Homicides.* Boca Raton, FL: CRC Press.

Schumacher, Frank. 2007. "The United States: Empire as a Way of Life?" In Robert Aldrich, editor, *The Age of Empires,* pp. 278–303. New York: Thames & Hudson.

Schwartz, Lita Linzer, and Natalie K. Isser. 2000. *Endangered Children: Neonaticide, Infanticide, and Filicide.* Boca Raton, FL: CRC Press.

Scully, Diana. 1990. *Understanding Sexual Violence: A Study of Convicted Rapists.* New York: Routledge.

Seabrook, Jeremy. 2001. *Travels in the Skin Trade: Tourism and the Sex Industry.* Sterling, VA: Pluto Press.

Selden, Mark. 1995. *China in Revolution: The Yenan Way Revisited.* Armonk, NY: M.E. Sharpe

Sen, Amartya. 1990. "More Than 100 Million Women Are Missing." *The New York Review of Books,* December 20: 61–66.

Sen, Mala. 2002. *Death by Fire: Sati, Dowry Death, and Female Infanticide in Modern India.* New Brunswick, NJ: Rutgers University Press.

Shelley, Louise. 2007. "Human Trafficking as a Form of Transnational Crime." Pp. 116–137 in *Human Trafficking,* edited by Maggy Lee. Portland, OR: Willan Publishing.

Shlain, Leonard. 2003. *Sex, Time, and Power: How Women's Sexuality Shaped Human Evolution.* New York: Viking.

Shoemaker, Donald J. 2009. *Juvenile Delinquency.* Lanham, MD: Rowman & Littlefield.

_____. 2010. *Theories of Delinquency: An Examination of Explanations of Delinquent Behavior.* New York: Oxford University Press.

Shreeve, Jimmy Lee. 2008. *Human Sacrifice: A Shocking Expose of Ritual Killing Worldwide.* Fort Lee, NJ: Barricade Books.

Skocpol, Theda. 1979. *States and Social Revolutions: A Comparative Analysis of France, Russia, and China.* New York: Cambridge University Press.

_____. 1994. *Social Revolutions in the Modern World.* New York: Cambridge University Press.

Skrobanek, Siriporn, Nataya Boonpakdee, and Chutima Jantateero. 1997. *The Traffic in Women: Human Realities of the International Sex Trade.* New York: Zed Books.

Smith, Paul J., ed. 1997. *Human Smuggling: Chinese Migrant Trafficking and the*

Challenge to America's Immigration Tradition. Washington, D.C.: Center for Strategic & International Studies.

Snow, Edgar. 1968. *Red Star over China,* enlarged ed. New York: Grove Press.

Snow, Lois Wheeler. 1983. *Edgar Snow's China: A Personal Account of the Chinese Revolution Compiled from the Writings of Edgar Snow.* New York: Vintage Books.

Snow, David A., and Robert D. Benford. 1992. "Master Frames and Cycles of Protest." In Aldon D. Morris and Carol McClurg Mueller, *Frontiers in Social Movement Theory,* pp. 133–155. New Haven, CT: Yale University Press.

Sofsky, Wolfgang. 1996. *The Order of Terror: The Concentration Camp,* translated by William Templer. Princeton, NJ: Princeton University Press.

Soh, C. Sarah. 2008. *The Comfort Women: Sexual Violence and Postcolonial Memory in Korea and Japan.* Chicago: University of Chicago Press.

St. Clair, William. 2007. *The Door of No Return: The History of Cape Coast Castle and the Atlantic Slave Trade.* New York: Blue Bridge.

Stein, Peter J. 1981. "Understanding Single Adulthood." In Peter J. Stein, *Single Life: Unmarried Adults in Social Context,* pp. 9–21. New York: St. Martin's Press.

Stiglmayer, Alexandra, ed. 1994. *Mass Rape: The War against Women in Bosnia-Herzegovina.* Lincoln: University of Nebraska Press.

Stinchcombe, Arthur L. [1968] 1987. *Constructing Social Theories.* Chicago: University of Chicago Press.

Strong, Marilee. 2008. *Erased: Missing Women, Murdered Wives.* San Francisco, CA: Jossey-Bass.

Sturdevant, Saundra Pollock, and Brenda Stoltzfus. 1993. *Let the Good Times Roll: Prostitution and the U.S. Military in Asia.* New York: New Press.

Sutherland, Edwin H., Donald R. Cressey, and David F. Luckenbill. 1992. *Principles of Criminology,* 11th ed. Dix Hills, NY: General Hall.

Sutton, Donald S. 1980. *Provincial Militarism and the Chinese Republic: The Yunnan Army, 1905–25.* Ann Arbor: University of Michigan Press.

Sykes, Gresham M., and David Matza. 1957. "Techniques of Neutralization: A Theory of Delinquency." *American Sociological Review,* 22: 664–670.

Tanaka, Yuki. 2001. *Japan's Comfort Women: Sexual Slavery and Prostitution during World War II and the U.S. Occupation.* New York: Routledge.

Tang, Isabel. 1999. *Pornography: The Secret History of Civilization.* London: Channel 4 Books.

Tao, Jie, Zheng Bijun, and Shirley L. Mow, ed. 2004. *Holding Up Half the Sky: Chinese Women — Past, Present, and Future.* New York: Feminist Press.

Tarrow, Sidney. 1994. *Power in Movement: Social Movements, Collective Action and Politics.* New York: Cambridge University Press.

Taylor, Andrew. 2008. *Empires That Shook the World.* New York: Metro Books.

Taylor, Jay. 2000. *The Generalissimo's Son: Chiang Ching-kuo and the Revolutions in China and Taiwan.* Cambridge, MA: Harvard University Press.

_____. 2009. *The Generalissimo: Chiang Kai-shek and the Struggle for Modern China.* Cambridge, MA: Belknap Press of Harvard University Press.

Taylor, Richard. 2006. *Alzheimer's from the Inside Out.* Baltimore, MD: Health Professions Press.

Teixeira, Bernardo. 1965. *The Fabric of Terror: Three Days in Angola.* New York: Devin-Adair.

Thapa, Govind Prasad, 2008. "Plight of Trafficked Women in Nepal." In Obi N. I. Ebbe and Dilip K. Das *Global Trafficking in Women and Children,* pp. 91–108. Boca Raton, FL: CRC Press.

Theoharis, Athan G. 1996. "Political Policing in the United States, The Evolution of the FBI, 1917–1956." In Mark Mazower, *The Policing of Politics in the Twentieth Century*, pp. 191–211. Providence, RI: Berghahn Books.

Teng, Shu-fen. 2010. "The Pitfalls of Home Care Assessment." *Taiwan Panorama*, Vol. 35, No. 11: 78–87.

Tien, Hung-mao. 1972. *Government and Politics in Kuomintang China, 1927–1937*. Stanford, CA: Stanford University Press.

_____. 1989. *The Great Transition: Political and Social Change in the Republic of China*. Stanford, CA: Hoover Institution Press.

Tittle, Charles R. 1995. *Control Balance: Toward a General Theory of Deviance*. Boulder, CO: Westview Press.

Tobias, Sheila. 1997. *Faces of Feminism: An Activist's Reflections on the Women's Movement*. Boulder, CO: Westview Press.

Tsai, Shih-shan Henry. 1996. *The Eunuchs in the Ming Dynasty*. Albany: State University of New York Press.

Tuljapurkar, Shripad, Nan Li, and Marcus W. Feldman. 1995. "High Sex Ratios in China's Future." *Science*, 267: 874–876.

Turk, Austin T. 1981. "Organizational Deviance and Political Policing." *Criminology*, 19 (2): 231–250.

Tyler, Christian. 2004. *Wild West China: The Taming of Xinjiang*. New Brunswick, NJ: Rutgers University Press.

Versluis, Arthur. 2008. *The Secret History of Western Sexual Mysticism: Sacred Practices and Spiritual Marriage*. Rochester, VT: Destiny Books.

Vukelich, Donna. 2000. "'Nicaragua: In My Country of Water and Fire....'" In Anne Llewellyn Barstow, *War's Dirty Secret: Rap, Prostitution, and Other Crimes against Women*, pp. 139–154. Cleveland, OH: Pilgrim Press.

Wakeman, Frederic, Jr. 1995. *Policing Shanghai, 1927–1937*. Berkeley & Los Angeles: University of California Press.

_____. 2003. *Spymaster: Dai Li and the Chinese Secret Service*. Berkeley & Los Angeles: University of California Press.

Wang, Hsiao-wen. 2005. "Leper Colony to Stage Dramatic Protest at WHO's HQ." *Taipei Times*, May 14, p. 4.

Wang, Hua-zhong. 2010. "Professor Jailed for Organizing Group Sex Parties." *China Daily USA*: May 21–23: acrosschina 3.

Warren, James. 2008. *Pirates, Prostitutes, and Pullers: Explorations in the Ethno- and Social History of Southeast Asia*. Crawley: University of Western Australia Press.

Wasserstrom, Jeffrey N. 1991. *Student Protests in Twentieth-Century China: The View from Shanghai*. Stanford, CA: Stanford University Press.

Weitz, Rose, ed. 2003. *The Politics of Women's Bodies: Sexuality, Appearances, & Behavior*, 2nd ed. New York: Oxford University Press.

Weller, Robert P. 1994. *Resistance, Chaos and Control in China: Taiping Rebels, Taiwanese Ghosts and Tiananmen*. Seattle, WA: University of Washington Press.

White, Tyrene. 2006. *China's Longest Campaign: Birth Planning in the People's Republic, 1949–2005*. Ithaca, NY: Cornell University Press.

Wickham-Crowley, Timothy P. 1991. *Guerrillas & Revolution in Latin America: A Comparative Study of Insurgents and Regimes Since 1956*. Princeton, NJ: Princeton University Press.

Woods, Shelton. 2004. *Japan: An Illustrated History*. New York: Hippocrene Books.

Wu, Harry, and George Vecsey. 1996. *Troublemaker: One Man's Crusade against China's Cruelty*. New York: Times Books.

Wu, Ning-kun. 1993. *A Single Tear: A Family's Persecution, Love, and Endurance in Communist China*. New York: Atlantic Monthly Press.

Yalom, Marilyn. 1997. *A History of the Breast*. New York: Alfred A. Knopf.
Yamamoto, Masahiro. 2000. *Nanking: Anatomy of an Atrocity*. Westport, CT: Praeger.
Yang, Mayfair Mei-hui. 1994. *Gifts, Favors, and Banquets: The Art of Social Relationships in China*. Ithaca, NY: Cornell University Press.
Yoshimi, Yoshiaki. 2000. *Comfort Women: Sexual Slavery in the Japanese Military during World War II*, translated by Suzanne O'Brien. New York: Columbia University Press.
Yu, Mao-chun. 1996. *OSS in China: Prelude to Cold War*. New Haven, CT: Yale University Press.
Zhang, Sheldon X. 2007. *Smuggling and Trafficking in Human Beings: All Roads Lead to America*. Westport, CT: Praeger.
Zheng, Tian-tian. 2009. *Red Lights: The Lives of Sex Workers in Postsocialist China*. Minneapolis: University of Minnesota Press.
Zuckerman, Larry. 2003. *The Rape of Belgium: The Untold Story of World War I*. New York: New York University Press.

Non–English Language References

CHINESE

Based on customary usage, certain places and names are spelled with the Wade-Giles system; aside from those cases, the pinyin system is used. Books published in China are written in simplified form; books published in Hong Kong and Taiwan are written in complicated/traditional form.

Bao, Zong-hao. 2006. *Hun Su Yu Zhong Guo Chuan Tong Wen Hua* (Marriage Customs and China's Traditional Culture). Guilin, China: Guangxi Normal University Press.
Cai, Wen, and Li Gen-zhi. 2006. *Ji Yi De Shang Hen* (A Trauma in Memory). Kunming, China: Chen Guang Publishers.
Chen, Jian-po. 1989. *Zhong Hua Min Guo Chun Qiu* (The Chronicle of the Republic of China), 4th ed. 2 vols. Taipei: San Min Bookstore.
Chen, Li-fei. 2006. *Ri Jun Wei An Fu Zhi Du Pi Pan* (A Critique of the Comfort Women System Created by the Japanese Military). Beijing: Zhong Hua Book.
_____. and Su Zhi-lian. 2005. *Zhui Suo—Chao Xian "Wei An Fu" Pu Yong Xin Han Ta De Jie Mei Men* (Seeking—Korean "Comfort Women" *Pu Yong Xin* and Her Companions). Guangzhou, China: Guangdong People's Publishers.
Chen, Rui-yun. 1988. *Xian Dai Zhong Guo Zheng Fu, 1919–1949* (Modern Chinese Government, 1919–1949). Chang Chun, China: Jilin Wen Shi Publishers.
Dai, Du-xing. 1998. *Bai Se Jiao Luo* (The White Corner). Taipei: Ren Jian Publishers.
Dai, Xuan-zhi. 1990. *Zhong Guo Mi Mi Zong Jiao Yu Mi Mi Hui She* (Chinese Underground Sects and Secret Societies), 2 vols. Taipei: Shang Wu Yin Shu Guan.
Feng, Wei. 2000. *Zhong Guo Ren Yu Ri Ben Ren* (The Chinese and the Japanese). Taipei: Lin Yu Publishers.
Fu, Ming. 1994. *Xiang Gang Hong Deng Qu* (Red-Light Districts of Hong Kong). Hong Kong: Takungpao Publishing.
He, Pin and Wang Zhao-jun. 1993. *Zhong Guo Ta Lu Hei She Hui* (The Criminal World of China). Taipei: Shi Bao Wen Hua Publishers.
Hsieh, Yung-kuang. 1995. *Ri Jun Wei An Fu Nei Mu* (Scandalous Stories Concerning Comfort Women Serving in Japanese Troops). Taipei: Lian Ya Publishers.
Huang, Ji-qing. 1949. "Zhong Guo Fa Xi Si Te Wu Wang Na Li Qu (Where Should the Chinese Fascist Secret Agents Go)?" Pp. 1–36 in *Zhong Guo Fa Xi Si Tu Wu Zhen*

Xiang (The True Stories about the Chinese Fascist Secret Agents, published by Xin Hua Bokstore (editor and publication location unknown).

Huang, Ping-ying. 2008. *Tai Wan Min Jian Xin Yang "Gu Nian" De Feng Si: Yi Ge She Hui Shi De Kao Cha* (The Worship of "Single Females" in the Folk Belief of Taiwan: An Examination of a Social History). Taipei: Dao Xiang Publishers.

Huang, Ren-ke. 1993. *Lu Jun Jian Yu* (The Army Prison). Beijing: Zhong Gong Zhong Young Dang Xiao Publishers.

Huang, Xiu-hua. 1995. *Wu Han Da Lu She* (Wu Han Grand Hotel). Taipei: Qian Wei Publishers.

Ishida, Yoneko, and Uchida Tomoyuki, ed. 2008 *Fa Sheng Zai Huang Tu Cun Zhuang Li De Ri Jun Xing Bao Li: Da Nian Men De Zhan Zheng Shang Wei Jie Shu* (Sexual Violence Committed by Japanese Troops in the Yu County, Shanxi Province: The War Is Not Ended for Victimized Elderly Women), translated by Zhao Jin-gui. Beijing: Social Sciences Academic Press.

Jiang, Hao. 1998. *Kua Guo Dan An: Zhong Guo Wei An Fu* (Transnational Archives: Chinese Comfort Women). Hong Kong: Cosmos Books.

Jiang, Shao-zhen. 1994. *Dai Li Han Jun Tong* (Dai Li and the Military Commission's Bureau of Investigation and Statistics). Zhengzhou, China: Henan People's Publishers.

Ju, Qing, ed. 2008. *Zhong Guo Liu Lang Er Tong Yan Jiu Bao Gao* (A Research Report on Street Children of China). Beijing: People's Publishers.

Lai, Graceia, Wu Hui-ling, and Yu Ju-fen. 2005. *Chen Mo De Shang Hen: Ri Jun Wei An Fu Li Shi Ying Xiang Shu* (Silent Scars: History of Sexual Slavery by the Japanese Military — A Pictorial Book), translated by Sheng-mei Ma. Taipei: Business Weekly.

Liberty Times. 2005. "Kuai Che Dao Jiu Ren, Hu Guo Ren Zhu Shi Zhi Lao Ren Hui Jia" (Rescuing People on Fast Traffic Lanes, Officer Hu Guo Ren Helps an Old Man with Dementia Return Home) www.libertytimes.com/2005/new/dec/9/today-north6.htm.

Lin, Hong-ping. 1991. "'Ji Zhong Ying' Han 'Lao Dong Ying'" ("'Concentration Camps' and 'Labor Camps'"). Pp. 123–132 in *Min Guo She Hui Da Guan* (The Magnificent Spectacle of Nationalist China), edited by Xin Ping, Hu Zheng-hao, and Li Xue-chang. Fuzhou, China: Fujian People's Publishers.

Lin, Shu-zhi. 1997. *Bai Se Kong Bu X Dang An* (The X Files of the White Terror). Taipei: Qian Wei Publishers.

Liu, Jie-lu, and Wu Ru-cheng. 1994. "Wo Men Suo Zhi Dao De Xu En-zeng (What We Knew about Xu En-zeng)." Pp. 81–94 in *Zhong Tong Tou Zi Xu En-zeng* (Boss of the Central Executive Committee's Bureau of Investigation and Statistics: Xu En-zeng), edited by Chai Fu. Taipei: Xin Rui Publishers.

Ma, Yu-shan. 1999. *Zhong Guo Gu Dai Ren Kou Mai Mai* (Human Trades in Ancient China). Taipei: Shang Wu Yin Shu Guan.

Meng, Li. 1996. *Guomindang Ji Zhong Ying Dang An* (Archives on the Nationalist Party's Concentration Camps). Chengdu, Sichuan: Sichuan Wen Yi Publishers.

Qiu, Ren-zong, ed. 2001. *Ta Men Zai Hei An Zhong: Zhong Guo Ta Lu Ruo Gan Cheng Shi Ai Zi Bing Yu Mai Yin Chu Bu Diao Cha* (They Live in Thick Darkness: A Preliminary Survey on AIDS and Prostitution in Some Cities of Mainland China). Beijing: Chinese Academy of Social Sciences Press.

Sa, Kong-liao. 1985. *Liang Nian, Zai Guomindang Ji Zhong Ying* (Being Incarcerated in a Nationalist Government's Concentration Camp for Two Years). Beijing: Zhong Guo Wen Shi Publishers.

Shen Zui. 1994. *Jun Tong Nei Mu* (The Secrets of the Military Commission's Bureau of Investigation and Statistics). Taipei: Xin Rui Publishers.

Shi, Yi, ed. 2002. *Zhong Guo "San Pei" Jie Mi* (Disclosing the Phenomenon of "San Pei" in China). Hong Kong: Limited Publishers.

Sun, Meng-cheng. 1985. "Tai Wan Wu Da Qing Zhi Xi Tong (The Great Five Secret Service Authorities in Taiwan)." Pp. 52–62 in *Tou Shi Qing Zhi Xi Tong* (Examining the Secret Service Authorities), edited by the Editing Committee of the Feng Yun Lun Tang Publishers. Taipei: Feng Yun Lun Tang Publishers.

Tai, Bao-lin. 1993. *Tai Wan She Hui Qi Wen Dan An* (Collected Cases of Awesome Events in Taiwan). Beijing: Hong Qi Publishing House.

Taipei Women's Rescue Foundation. 1999. *Tai Wan Wei An Fu Bao Gao* (A Report on Taiwan's Comfort Women). Taipei: Shang Wu Yin Shu Guan.

Taitung County Government. 2005. "Taitung Jin Fan Yu Zhi Gong Fa Hui Ta Ai, Xie Zhu Shi Zhi Lao Ren An Quan Fan Jia" (The Police Department of Taitung County and Volunteers Show Great Love, Helping an Old Woman with Dementia Return Home Safely). www.taitung.gov.tw/chinese/news/t_newview.php?n_id=2974.

Tang, Zhu-guo [Su Ming-de]. 1997. *Zui Gao Ji Mi* (The Topmost Secrecy). Taipei: Xin Xin Wen Publishers.

Wang, Bin. 2007. "Nan Zi Lian Sha Liu Ming Fu Nu, Mai Shi Pei Yin Hun, She Xian Wu Ru Shi Ti Zui" (A Male Serial Killer Murdered Six Women, Sold the Bodies for Spiritual Marriage, and Was Charged with the Crime of Offending the Bodies). http://b5.chinanews.sina.com/news/2007/0511/20281989010.html.

Wang, Cong-lin. 2010. *Ling Ren Zhan Li De Kong Bu Yin Luan Shi* (A Shocking and Horrendous History of Licentious Sexual Behaviors). Taipei: Ba Fun Publishing.

Wang, Jin-ling, ed. 2007. *Kua Di Yu Guai Mai Huo Guai Pian: Hua Dong Wu Sheng Liu Ru Di Ge An Yan Jiu* (Woman Trading/Trafficking across Provinces: A Case Study of Five Inflow Provinces of East China). Beijing: Social Sciences Academic Press.

Wang, Rong-zu, and Li Ao. 1995. *Jiang Jie-shi Ping Zhuan* (A Biographic Critique of Chiang Kai-shek). Taipei: Shang Zhou Wen Hua Publishers.

Wang, Shu-nu. 2006. *Chang Ji Shi* (A History of Prostitution). Taipei: Masterpiece.

Wu, Li-zi. 2009. *Nong Min De Jie Gou Xing Pin Kun: Ding Xian Zai Diao Cha De Pu Pian Xing Jie Lun* (Structural Poverty of the Peasant: A Final Conclusion Based on the Re-investigation of Ding County). Beijing: Social Sciences Academic Press.

Xie, Zhong-hou, ed. 2005. *Ri Ben Qin Lue Hua Bei Zui Xin Shi Gao* (Historical Documents about the War Crimes Committed by Japanese Troops in North China). Beijing: Social Sciences Academic Press.

Xin Tai Wan Yan Jiu Wen Jiao Ji Jin Hui (The New Taiwan Research Foundation), ed. 1999. *Bao Li Yu Shi Ge: Kao Hsiung Shi Jian Yu Mei Li Dao Da Shen* (Violence and Hymns: The Formosa Incident in Kaohsiung and Its Trial). Taipei: Shi Bao Wen Hua Publishers.

Yang, Zhe-sheng. 1994. *Te Gong Wang Dai Li* (Dai Li: The Lord of Secret Service). Taipei: Xin Rui Publishers.

Yao, Han-qiu. 1991. *Tai Wan Hun Su Gu Jin Tan* (An Introduction to Taiwan's Traditional and Modern Marriage Customs). Taipei: Tai Yuan Publishers.

_____. 1999. *Tai Wan Sang Zang Gu Jin Tan* (An Introduction to Taiwan's Traditional and Modern Funeral Customs). Taipei: Tai Yuan Publishers.

Yi, Zhao-feng. 2005. *Zhong Guo Hei Dao Bang Hui* (China's Criminal Associations and Organized Gangs), 2 vols. Beijing: Da Zhong Wen Yi Publishers.

You, Zhen-sheng. 2010. "Si Shi Liu Nian Hou … Kong Nan Nu Ru Meng, Yao Qiu Gong Shi Yi Fu" (After 46 Years … Woman Who Died in an Airplane Crash Entering Dream, Asking to Share a Husband). http://www.worldjournal.com (January 18, 2010).

Zhang, Ji-he. 1996. *Dan Xin Bi Xue: Jiu Zhong Guo Li Ci Xue Chao Shi Lu* (Absolute Loyalty and Supreme Courage: The Historical Records of Student Movements in Nationalist China). Baoding, China: Hebei University Press.

Zhang, Wei-han. 1992. "Dai Li Yu Pang Da De Jun Tong Ju Zu Zhi (Dai Li and the Gigantic Organization of Military Commission's Bureau of Investigation and Statistics)." Pp. 277–358 in *Xi Shuo Zhong Tong Jun Tong* (A Detailed Account of the Central Executive Committee's Bureau of Investigation and Statistics and the Military Commission's Bureau of Investigation and Statistics), edited by Zhuan Ji Wen Xue Za Zhi She. Taipei: Zhuan Ji Wen Xue Chu Ban She (Biographical Literature).

Zhang, Wen. 1988. "Zhong Tong Er Shi Nian (Serving in the Central Executive Committee's Bureau of Investigation and Statistics for Twenty Years)." Pp. 1–141 in *Te Gong Zong Bu: Zhong Tong* (The Headquarters of Secret Service: The Central Executive Committee's Bureau of Investigation and Statistics), edited by Zhong Yuan Publishers. Hong Kong, China: Zhong Yuan Publishers.

Zhang, Yan-fo. 1995. "Xi Bei: Mo Ying Chong Chong (Spooky Northwest China)." Pp. 116–141 in *Jun Tong Shi Lu* (The Historical Records on the Military Commission's Bureau of Investigation and Statistics), edited by Cao Ying. Beijing: Tuan Jie Publishers.

Zhang, Yan-xian, and Chen Feng-hua. 2000. *Han Cun De Ku Qi: Lu Ku Shi Jian* (The Crying of Chilly Villages: The Lu Ku Incident). Taipei: Taipei County Government.

Zhang, Yan-xian and Gao Shu-yuan. 1998. *Lu Ku Shi Jian Diao Cha Yan Jiu* (The Investigative Report of the *Lu Ku* Incident). Taipei: Taipei County Government.

Zhao, Yu-lin. 1988. "Zhong Tong Wo Jian Wo Wen (What I Saw and Heard about the Central Executive Committee's Bureau of Investigation and Statistics)." Pp. 189–221 in *Te Gong Zong Bu: Zhong Tong* (The Headquarters of Secret Service: The Central Executive Committee's Bureau of Investigation and Statistics), edited by Zhong Yuan Publishers. Hong Kong: Zhong Yuan Publishers.

_____. 1994. "Xu-En-zeng De Li Shi Han Huo Dong Pian Duan (The Personal Background and Activities of Xu-En-zeng)." Pp. 59–80 in *Zhong Tong Tou Zi Xu En-zeng* (Boss of the Central Executive Committee's Bureau of Investigation and Statistics: Xu En-zeng), edited by Chai Fu. Taipei: Xin Rui Publishers.

Zheng, Si-li. 1996. *Zhong Guo Xing Wen Hua: Yi Ge Qian Nian Bu Jie Zhi Jie* (Sexual Culture in China: A Gordian Knot). Taipei: Shu Lin Publishers.

Zi, Ping, ed. 1999. *Zhong Gong Gao Guan Se Qing Dang An* (Collected Cases of Sex Scandal among High-Ranking Chinese Communist Officials). Hong Kong: Xia Fei Er International Publishers.

JAPANESE

Hata, Ikuhiko. 1999. *Ianfu to Senjo no Sei* (Comfort Women and Sex on the Battlefield). Tokyo: Shinchosha.

Kim, Il-myon. [1976] 1992. *Tennou no Guntai to Chosenjin Ianfu* (Imperial Japanese Troops and Korean Comfort Women). Tokyo: Sanichi Shobo.

_____. 1997. *Yūjo, Karayuki, Ianfu no Keifu* (Traveling Girls, Japanese Prostitutes Who Go Overseas, the Genealogy of Comfort Women). Tokyo: Yuzankaku Shuppan.

Senda, Kako. [1978] 1992. *Jugun Ianfu* (Japanese Troop-Affiliated Comfort Women), 2 vols. Tokyo, Sanichi Shobo.

Suzuki, Yūko. 1992. *Jugun Ianfu: Naisen Kekkon* (Japanese Troop-Affiliated Comfort Women: Marriage between the Japanese and the Korean). Tokyo: Miraisha.

Index